# Restriction and Saturation

**Linguistic Inquiry Monographs**
Samuel Jay Keyser, general editor

1. *Word Formation in Generative Grammar*, Mark Aronoff
2. *X̄ Syntax: A Study of Phrase Structure*, Ray Jackendoff
3. *Recent Transformational Studies in European Languages*, ed. Samuel Jay Keyser
4. *Studies in Abstract Phonology*, Edmund Gussmann
5. *An Encyclopedia of AUX: A Study in Cross-Linguistic Equivalence*, Susan Steele
6. *Some Concepts and Consequences of the Theory of Government and Binding*, Noam Chomsky
10. *On the Nature of Grammatical Relations*, Alec Marantz
12. *Logical Form: Its Structure and Derivation*, Robert May
13. *Barriers*, Noam Chomsky
15. *Japanese Tone Structure*, Janet Pierrehumbert and Mary Beckman
16. *Relativized Minimality*, Luigi Rizzi
18. *Argument Structure*, Jane Grimshaw
19. *Locality: A Theory and Some of Its Empirical Consequences*, Maria Rita Manzini
20. *Indefinites*, Molly Diesing
21. *Syntax of Scope*, Joseph Aoun and Yen-hui Audrey Li
22. *Morphology by Itself: Stems and Inflectional Classes*, Mark Aronoff
23. *Thematic Structure in Syntax*, Edwin Williams
24. *Indices and Identity*, Robert Fiengo and Robert May
25. *The Antisymmetry of Syntax*, Richard S. Kayne
26. *Unaccusativity: At the Syntax–Lexical Semantics Interface*, Beth Levin and Malka Rappaport Hovav
27. *Lexico-Logical Form: A Radically Minimalist Theory*, Michael Brody
28. *The Architecture of the Language Faculty*, Ray Jackendoff
29. *Local Economy*, Chris Collins
30. *Surface Structure and Interpretation*, Mark Steedman
31. *Elementary Operations and Optimal Derivations*, Hisatsugu Kitahara
32. *The Syntax of Nonfinite Complementation: An Economy Approach*, Željko Bošković
33. *Prosody, Focus, and Word Order*, Maria Luisa Zubizarreta
34. *The Dependencies of Objects*, Esther Torrego
35. *Economy and Semantic Interpretation*, Danny Fox
36. *What Counts: Focus and Quantification*, Elena Herburger
37. *Phrasal Movement and Its Kin*, David Pesetsky
38. *Dynamic Antisymmetry*, Andrea Moro
39. *Prolegomenon to a Theory of Argument Structure*, Ken Hale and Samuel Jay Keyser
40. *Essays on the Representational and Derivational Nature of Grammar: The Diversity of* Wh-*Constructions*, Joseph Aoun and Yen-hui Audrey Li
41. *Japanese Morphophonemics: Markedness and Word Structure*, Junko Ito and Armin Mester
42. *Restriction and Saturation*, Sandra Chung and William A. Ladusaw

Restriction and Saturation    Sandra Chung and
                              William A. Ladusaw

The MIT Press
Cambridge, Massachusetts
London, England

© 2004 Massachusetts Institute of Technology

All rights reserved. No part of this book may be reproduced in any form by any electronic or mechanical means (including photocopying, recording, or information storage and retrieval) without permission in writing from the publisher.

This book was set in Times New Roman on 3B2 by Asco Typesetters, Hong Kong.
Printed and bound in the United States of America.

Library of Congress Cataloging-in-Publication Data

Chung, Sandra.
  Restriction and saturation / Sandra Chung and William A. Ladusaw.
    p.  cm. — (Linguistic inquiry monographs ; 42)
  Includes bibliographical references (p. ) and index.
  ISBN 0-262-03313-5 (hc. : alk. paper) — ISBN 0-262-53254-9 (pbk. : alk. paper)
  1. Semantics. 2. Grammar, Comparative and general—Syntax. I. Ladusaw, William A., 1952– II. Title. III. Series.
P325.C386 2004
401′43—dc21                                                 2003051379

10 9 8 7 6 5 4 3 2 1

To Jim and Ken

# Contents

Preface xi

**Chapter 1**
**Modes of Composition** 1

1.1 The Calculus of Saturation 2

1.2 Predicate Restriction 4

1.3 Syntactic versus Semantic Saturation 6

1.4 Saturation at the Event Level 11

1.5 Scope Constraints 13

1.6 The Property Theory of Indefinites 14

1.7 Summary 18

**Chapter 2**
**Indefinites in Maori** 21

2.1 A Dash of Maori Grammar 23

2.2 The Syntax of *He* and *Tētahi* 26

2.3 The Semantic Similarity of *He* and *Tētahi* 30

|  |  |
|---|---|
| | 2.4 Some Semantic Contrasts 40 |
| | 2.5 Our Account 45 |
| | 2.6 Two Further Semantic Contrasts 55 |
| | 2.7 A Dash of Pragmatics 65 |
| | 2.8 Conclusion 69 |
| **Chapter 3** **Object Incorporation in Chamorro** 75 | 3.1 A Dash of Chamorro Grammar 77 |
| | 3.2 Incorporation 81 |
| | 3.3 The Incorporated Object Is Semantically Incomplete 85 |
| | 3.4 The Extra Object 88 |
| | 3.5 The Extra Object Is a Semantic Argument 94 |
| | 3.6 Our Account 107 |
| | 3.7 Restriction without Saturation 118 |
| | 3.8 Conclusion 125 |
| **Appendix A** **The Syntax of Chamorro Incorporation** 131 | A.1 Previous Approaches 131 |
| | A.2 Some Preliminary Results 134 |
| | A.3 Some More Conclusive Results 141 |

Contents ix

　　　　　　　　　　　　　A.4　The Attachment Site of the Extra Object　146

**Appendix B**
**Maori and Chamorro**　149

Notes　153

References　163

Index　171

# Preface

Our joint interest in the issues addressed here probably goes back to three seminars at the University of California, Santa Cruz, on the syntax and semantics of indefinites, which we co-taught with our colleague Jim McCloskey in 1990. But the beginning of our investigation of restriction and saturation was a conversation about Maori *he* on a ferry in New Zealand in 1994. That conversation achieves a degree of closure in this monograph, which we hope will contribute both to the growing literature on the formal semantic analysis of non-Indo-European languages and to the theoretical understanding of semantic compositionality.

Chapters 2 and 3 of this monograph draw on Chung's research on Austronesian languages. But our ultimate focus is not on Maori or Chamorro grammar, but on the ways in which they can illuminate the alternatives for semantic interpretation and their interaction with syntactic structure. In particular, we are concerned with the varieties of indefiniteness, understood in the sense that has become generally referred to as the Kamp-Heim theory of indefinites. This theory, it is said, takes indefinites to be interpreted as "restricted free variables."

A meditation on this slogan is useful background for understanding how we came to focus on restriction and saturation as fundamental semantic operations. It attributes three properties to indefinites: that they are variables, that those variables are free, and that those free variables are restricted.

To say that the free variables are *restricted* is to acknowledge that the visible semantic content of an indefinite provides (at least) a property of individuals. But using such a property as a restriction on a variable introduces a degree of freedom between the syntactic position of the indefinite and its semantic effect. If a variable is restricted to a proper subdomain of individuals, then the effect of the restriction can be seen wherever the variable occurs. Lurking behind the discussion that follows is the suspicion that the talk of "restricted variables" undermines claims about where in the syntactic structure the restriction of a variable happens. Indeed, we see choice function analyses of indefinites as a way of explicitly detaching the question of scope from the semantic operation of restriction. Given this suspicion, we have taken restriction as a basic semantic operation that can be exploited at the lowest level possible: the connection between predicates and their arguments.

To say that indefinites are *free* is to raise the possibility that they can be bound, distinguishing them from referential and quantificational terms based on evidence that they can be targeted for binding by other operators. But the complement of that ability is the requirement that they are elsewhere subject to existential closure. Asking what motivates existential closure led us back to Frege's notion of semantic completeness. Free variables offend this completeness in a way that must be remedied by binding. But binding determines a scope only for the binder, not for the bound element. From this perspective, a choice function analysis of indefinites separates semantic restriction from the fixing of scope (and from the remediation of semantic incompleteness). But it is striking that indefinites as a class show such contrary scope behavior: some indefinites seem oblivious to all structural constraints on operator scoping; other indefinites have no ability at all to escape their structurally determined fate.

Finally, the appeal to *variables* seems to be a strategy for eating one's cake and having it too. A variable saturates a predicate in one sense, but not in another. As variable-free analyses make clear, a predicate with a free variable argument is not distinct in semantic completeness from the predicate itself. What does the association of (all) indefinites with (entity) variables contribute to an understanding of the variation among them? When we began to think about these questions, our expectation was that an indefinite's scope properties, its discourse dynamism, and its morphosyntactic complexity were generally aligned. On one side were independent Determiner Phrases (DPs), which supported discourse anaphora and scoped freely; on the other were Noun Phrases (NPs), in argument position or morphologically incorporated into predicates, which were not dynamic in discourse and always took narrow scope. When we looked first at Maori, and later at object incorporation in Chamorro, these expectations were not borne out.

During the time that we have worked on these issues, a good deal of research has appeared (in print or in manuscript) illustrating the rich behavior of indefinites. We have not attempted to survey all of that work here. Some of it has found its way into the analyses below; all of it has increased our appreciation of the theoretical issues. We hope that the two case studies offered here, and our larger focus on modes of composition, will contribute to the goal of a more explanatory account of the interaction among form, position, and semantic interpretation.

As mentioned earlier, the journey chronicled here began in 1994, with Maori *he*. For judgments on the Maori examples, we are indebted to T. S. Karetu, Te Haumihiata Mason, J. W. Milroy, Tamati Reedy, and the late Bruce Biggs. Our thanks to Ray Harlow for helping us to secure some crucial judgments, to Winifred Bauer for her incisive comments, and to Tamahou Temara for answering some queries by e-mail. We are grateful to all these people as well as to Laurie Bauer, Terry Crowley, and Elizabeth Pearce for their hospitality.

For judgments on the Chamorro examples, we are indebted to many speakers in Saipan and California, especially Priscilla Anderson, Antonio Atalig, Manuel F. Borja, Teresina Garrido, Ray P. Lujan, William I. Macaranas, Maria T. Quinata, Maria P. Mafnas, Anicia Q. Tomokane, and Francisco Tomokane. Our thanks also to William I. Macaranas, Henry I. Sablan, and Carmen S. Taimanao for their assistance.

This work has benefited from the comments and suggestions of many friends at various stages in the process. Among those we especially want to acknowledge are Emmon Bach, Chris Barker, Winifred Bauer, Donka Farkas, Veerle van Geenhoven, Randall Hendrick, Pauline Jacobson, Edward L. Keenan, Jim McCloskey, Louise McNally, Barbara Hall Partee, Elizabeth Pearce, Tanya Reinhart, and a reviewer.

Portions of this work were delivered by one or both of us at the Twelfth Amsterdam Colloquium; the fifth meeting of the Austronesian Formal Linguistics Association (AFLA); the Conference on Explanation at the University of California, San Diego; the 1999 Colloque de Syntaxe et de Sémantique à Paris (CSSP); the first meeting of Semantics of Underrepresented Languages of the Americas (SULA); and the 2002 Western Conference on Linguistics (WECOL). It was also presented at colloquia at MIT; Stanford University; the University of California, Los Angeles; the University of California, Santa Cruz; the University of North Carolina at Chapel Hill; the University of Southern California; the University of Texas at Austin; and the Max-Planck Institute for Evolutionary Anthropology. Thanks to the audiences for their comments and reactions.

Chung's research was supported by a 1994 Fulbright Scholarship for teaching and research from the NZ-US Educational Foundation; by the National Science Foundation through Project BCS-0131767; and by faculty research funds granted by the University of California, Santa Cruz, through the Committee on Research and the Institute for Humanities Research.

We thank Ken Christopher for his assistance with the manuscript, and Anne Mark for her impressive copyediting.

# Chapter 1
## Modes of Composition

Strawson's (1959) discussion of "subject and predicate" examines the received view of the basis for distinguishing between the semantics of predicates and terms with reference to Frege's (1997[1862]) distinction between objects and concepts.

Frege characterizes the distinction between A4s [terms] and B4s [predicates] by means of a metaphor. Objects, he says, are *complete*, concepts *incomplete* or *unsaturated*. "Not all parts of a thought can be complete; at least one must be 'unsaturated' or predicative; otherwise they would not hold together." Of B2s [predicates] he says that it is only because their sense is unsaturated that they are capable of serving as a link. (1959, 152–153)

The idea that semantic predicates are unsaturated (to various degrees) and that this semantic incompleteness is made complete by composing them with semantically complete terms (of appropriate types) is fundamental to formal semantic analyses of natural language. It is the basis of Montague's (1973) application of type theory in his classic analysis of English, where all predicative expressions are assigned functional types and the fundamental composition operation is function application.

Strawson's discussion portrays the opposition between complete objects and incomplete concepts as a unifying theme that can be played out at the level of linguistic acts, linguistic categories, and propositional roles. He considers various approaches to the basis for this metaphor, noting that

[t]he main thing which I wish to carry away from consideration of Frege and Geach is the fact that both writers make an absolute distinction between two mutually exclusive classes of expressions, members of each of which can be combined with suitable members of the other to yield an assertion. Members of the two classes of expressions alike introduce terms; but members of one class introduce them assertively, and members of the other class do not. The List IV

distinction of non-linguistic terms merely mirrors, in a confused way, this discussion in the style of introduction. Essentially the distinction we have arrived at is a distinction between *styles of introduction of terms* [emphasis added]. It says nothing of any distinction between *types* or *categories* of terms, between *kinds* of object. (1959, 153)

This monograph is an investigation of different "styles of introduction" or what we will term *modes of composition* in the syntax and semantics of indefinites, and their application in two Austronesian languages, Maori and Chamorro. We start from the assumption that underlying the semantic composition of predicates with their arguments is a calculus of saturation. However, we question the assumption that what may appear syntactically to be a predicate-argument relation is uniformly interpreted by a mode of composition that saturates the predicate. We conclude that introducing a nonsaturating mode of composition, *(predicate) restriction*, will allow consideration of analyses that illuminate constructions in many languages.

In this chapter, we discuss the calculus of saturation and introduce predicate restriction. We relate these notions to other semantic proposals about the property theory of indefinites, existential closure, and so-called semantic incorporation. We introduce a general principle that forces saturation of predicates within a designated domain. The resulting system permits several options for the semantic composition of indefinites with their predicates. We show that the calculus of saturation allows for the possibility that an argument position of a predicate may be targeted by both modes of composition in one construction.

## 1.1 The Calculus of Saturation

What we are calling the calculus of saturation is illustrated by the standard type assignments assumed in the simple example (1).

(1) John fed Fido.

(2) $\lambda y \lambda x \, [\text{feed}'(y)(x)] \, (f) \, (j)$

The logical translation in (2) shows the semantic composition. The verb is given a function (of type $\langle e, \langle e, t \rangle \rangle$) that represents it as semantically incomplete in two respects, corresponding to argument roles assigned by the predicate. In the underlying type theory, semantic completeness is represented by the two types e (for entities) and t (for truth-values, standing in for a proposition). The type of the expression in (2) is t, showing that this composition achieves semantic completeness by resolving the two degrees of incompleteness in the predicate by combining the two semantically complete objects $f$ and $j$ with the predicate's semantic content, a function equivalent to a two-place relation between entities.

An important part of (2) is the mode of composition that achieves this semantic completeness by saturating the predicate. This is the operation of function application. This is rendered more explicit by (3), which represents that operation explicitly as FA, an operation that takes two arguments, the first of which is a function of domain type $\sigma$ and the second of which is an expression of semantic type $\sigma$. The value of the operation is an object of type $\tau$, the range type of the function.

(3) FA (**FA ($\lambda y \lambda x$ [feed'(y)(x)], f )**, j)

The boldface portion of (3) represents the first function application, whose value is a function of type $\langle e, t \rangle$.

Underlying the talk of saturation is the Fregean metaphor of unsaturation. The saturation of the predicate removes an incompleteness, yielding a complete thought (a proposition). From this underlying metaphor derives the fundamental effect of saturation.

(4) A saturated argument position is no longer available to semantic composition.

(4) states the obvious fact that the first instance of function application in (3) renders the $y$ position unavailable for further composition. The next instance of function application must target the only remaining source of incompleteness: the $x$ argument position.

Function application represents one mode of composition that saturates, but it is not the only one. Let us consider the semantic operation of existential closure. The functional incompleteness of the verb above can likewise be remedied by an operation that simply removes the incompleteness in favor of an existential quantification over the argument, as illustrated in (5), with *EC* representing the (unary) composition operation generally represented by $\exists v$.

(5) EC (**EC ($\lambda y \lambda x$ [feed'(y)(x)])**)

If we track the type changes in the expression in (5), we see that they parallel those in (3). The boldface portion represents a reduction from $\langle e, \langle e, t \rangle \rangle$ to $\langle e, t \rangle$, and the whole expression is of the complete type t.

The principle in (4) shows that existential closure likewise saturates the predicate, removing semantic incompleteness. The expression in (6), an attempt to provide individuals for composition after closure, does not cohere into a well-formed logical expression.

(6) FA (EC (**EC (λyλx [feed'(y)(x)]**)), f )

It consists of a proposition (truth-value) and an entity. In Frege's terms, they "do not hold together."[1]

Both of the saturating modes of composition are illustrated when we consider a Davidsonian version of (2).

(7) λyλxλe [feed'(y)(x)(e)] (f) (j)

Two instances of function application yield the reduced lambda expression in (8).

(8) λe [feed'(f)(j)(e)]

However, this expression is not semantically complete. Assuming that events are a sort of entity, then this is an expression of type ⟨e,t⟩. This is why Davidsonian analyses always invoke existential closure to complete the composition.

(9) ∃e [feed'(f)(j)(e)]

While it remains to be explained why it must be existential closure rather than function application that does the saturation of the event argument, that the derivation must achieve saturation follows from the deep Fregean assumption that semantic completeness is the goal of composition.

## 1.2 Predicate Restriction

We now consider another class of compositions to introduce another, nonsaturating mode of composition. Assume that the task is to interpret (10), where the noun *dog* is interpreted by a property, taken here as having type ⟨e,t⟩.

(10) John fed dog.

Given the type assumptions above, this is another composition that does not cohere, not because of a lack of semantic incompleteness but because there is a type mismatch between the incompleteness of the predicate in the first argument (type e) and the type of the expression provided for composition (type ⟨e,t⟩). For this composition to succeed, a mode of composition other than function application is needed.

There are two candidates. One is the type-shifting approach, which assimilates the potential argument to the appropriate type. One example of this is a unary operation that represents a choice function, a function that maps a property onto an entity that has the property (see, e.g., Reinhart 1997; Winter 1997; Kratzer 1998). Representing a choice function as *CF*, a coherent composition can be achieved as in (11).

(11) FA (**FA ($\lambda y \lambda x$ [feed'(y)(x)], CF (dog'))**, j)

The value of the choice function is an entity. After the choice function applies to the property, the derivation of (11) proceeds exactly as in (3). The choice function makes it possible to saturate an argument position with an argument interpretation of type $\langle e,t \rangle$.[2]

Let us now consider a different mode of composition, which we will call *predicate restriction*. In this mode, the property argument is interpreted as a restrictive modifier of the predicate. We define a binary operation that composes a predicate directly with a property to yield a predicate without changing the degree of unsaturation. Assuming that the predicate is interpreted as a function $f$, the result of restricting the predicate with property $p$ is the original function with its domain restricted to the subdomain of its original domain to elements that have the property $p$.[3] We call this mode of composition *Restrict* and illustrate it in (12).

(12) Restrict ($\lambda y \lambda x$ [feed'(y)(x)], dog')
    = $\lambda y \lambda x$ [feed'(y)(x) $\wedge$ dog'(y)]

The most important fact about Restrict is that it does not saturate the predicate. It does not therefore remove the possibility, or indeed the necessity, that the argument position it targets can be saturated by either of the saturating composition operations that we have considered. From the point in (12), we can proceed by existential closure and then saturate the remaining argument as in (13).

(13) FA (EC (Restrict ($\lambda y \lambda x$ [feed'(y)(x)], dog')), j)
    = $\exists y$ [feed'(y)(j) $\wedge$ dog'(y)]

This composition yields the proposition that John fed a dog, though no interpreted constituent corresponds to an existential quantifier over dogs. The truth conditions are created as a combination of predicate restriction and existential closure.

Note that (13) is logically equivalent to (11). (11) is true just in case some choice function applied to *dog* (and hence yielding an entity that is a dog) will yield a true value for the predicate. (We do not at this point represent the anchoring or existential closure of the choice function explicitly.) The difference is not one of content; the proposition expressed in the two cases is the same. But the semantic composition that leads to the proposition is different in the two cases. In (11), a particular dog is specified, though no conditions are placed on which dog it is. As a result, the predicate is saturated by that entity. In (13), however, no dog is specified; no entity saturates the predicate.

A consequence of the nonsaturating nature of Restrict is that the derivation (14) is possible.

(14) FA (FA (Restrict ($\lambda y \lambda x$ [feed$'$(y)(x)], dog$'$), f), j)
   = [feed$'$(f)(j) $\wedge$ dog$'$(f)]

(14) entails (3), that John fed Fido. The effect of Restrict is to explicitly incorporate the information suggested in (3) only by background knowledge about naming conventions, that Fido is a dog. The composition in (14) shares with (3) and (11) the fact that the predicate is fully saturated by function application to particular entities.

(14) provides a way of interpreting an expression like (15) or, suggesting one of the applications of Restrict that we will explore, (16).

(15) John fed (a) dog Fido.

(16) John dog-fed Fido.

Of course, neither of these is well formed in English. But under the assumptions we have made here, this is not a semantically interesting property of English. That is, it does not follow from the theory of semantic composition that these are impossible. This is in contrast to (17), where two entities are provided for composition with the same first argument of the predicate.

(17) John fed Fido Spot.

That (17) cannot be coherently interpreted follows from (4), the fact that once *Fido* saturates the predicate argument, the argument is no longer available for composition. This difference, the fact that saturation is possible after restriction but double saturation is not, will be important to the analysis developed in chapter 3.

## 1.3 Syntactic versus Semantic Saturation

We concentrate here on the compositional possibilities for combining a predicate with an argument phrase whose semantic content is a property. This poses a type conflict that we have shown can be resolved in one of two ways, by type-shifting the argument into the appropriate type or by treating the argument phrase as a predicate modifier. We have presented these two options as distinct *modes of composition*, treating them as alternatives available to a language for semantic composition.

We intend this to contrast with the traditional view of type-shifting, which likewise assumes that operations like the choice function type-shift are readily available for use in composition. Partee (1987) discusses type-shifting operations in a framework that assumes that linguistic categories or subcategories should have uniform semantic types. By defining partial mappings between the denotational types of generalized quantifiers, individuals, and predicates, semantically natural classes of noun phrases can be defined that ameliorate the need for systematic ambiguities of linguistic expressions. Type-shifting operations have become standard semantic tools, but they have generally been invoked as "last resort" operations to save derivations with type mismatches. De Swart (1999) surveys these operations within the assumption that function application is the prime mode of composition. Here we take the alternative approach, noted by de Swart (1999, 282), of developing a richer inventory of basic modes of composition.

We do this because we wish to view choice functions and predicate restriction as options that may be conventionally encoded by a language. This possibility is less salient when they are deployed within a theory that assumes a tight relationship between the interpretation of syntactic arguments and saturation by function application. We think that this assumption is not always a useful one when faced with the crosslinguistic variation in the interpretation of indefinite noun phrases.

To make this point, let us return to considering the composition in (14) and the ill-formedness of (15) in English.

The domain of semantic composition for a language is the set of expressions that the syntax of the language admits as well formed. On our view, the fact that (15) is a semantically interpretable but impossible expression of English is a syntactic fact. For concreteness, let us assume that it follows from Case theory (see, e.g., Chomsky 1981): the syntax of English does not license two DP expressions that can target the same argument of the predicate in semantic interpretation. When we make the notion "targeting an argument of the predicate" less obscure, we reveal a calculus of syntactic saturation that largely parallels the semantic one. This is the assumption that there is an isomorphism between syntactic saturation and semantic saturation.

This parallel is made explicit in Montague's classic analysis of English. In Montague 1973, the syntactic categories are defined in terms of Categorial Grammar as functions. The categories of English are systematically related to semantic types, so that function application can be the main mode of composition. At each step in semantic composition, the function that interprets the predicate is applied to the interpretation of the argument expression. After function application, the predicate's argument is satisfied and the composition must move on to target the next argument for composition. The homomorphism between the syntactic categories and semantic types ensures that each argument position will be targeted once in the composition and requires that saturation will be achieved at each point.

When this homomorphism is relaxed, the theory of modes of composition must be enriched. Partee's (1987) flexible type analysis attempts to maintain the assumption that all noun phrases are assigned to the generalized quantifier type ($\langle\langle e,t\rangle,t\rangle$) while still allowing for the occurrence of some of those noun phrases as predicates. The type-shifting operations feed derivations for predicate noun phrases. If we allow the syntactic category to be heterogeneous with regard to semantic type, (some) indefinite DPs being assigned a predicate type ($\langle e,t\rangle$) as their basic type, then type-shifting functions will assimilate those to quantifier or entity type to allow function application to remain the prime mode of semantic composition. For example, consider (18) under the assumption that the phrase *a dog* has only the property of being a dog as its semantic content.

(18) A dog barked: *FA ($\lambda x$ [bark$'$(x)], $\lambda y$ [dog$'$(y)])

If we assume a generally available type-shifting operation $A$ that maps the property content expression *a dog* into the type of generalized quantifiers, yielding an existential quantifier, the composition can continue (with the expected reversal of function-argument relation in generalized quantifiers).

(19) FA (A ($\lambda y$ [dog$'$(y)]), $\lambda x$ [bark$'$(x)])
 = FA ($\lambda P \exists y$ [dog$'$(y) $\wedge$ P(y)], $\lambda x$ [bark$'$(x)])

The important point is that even though the category-type isomorphism is relaxed here, the isomorphism between syntactic saturation and semantic saturation is not. Each step in the semantic composition achieves saturation of the predicate's argument at the point of composition.

This is the sense in which we referred above to our use of the choice function in (11) as a type-shifting option. The choice function maps an expression of type $\langle e,t \rangle$ into one of type e, ensuring that the composition of the property with the predicate will achieve saturation. In contrast to (19), applying the choice function type-shift yields the composition in (20).

(20) FA ($\lambda$x [bark$'$(x)], CF ($\lambda$y [dog$'$(y)]))
 = $\exists$**f** [bark$'$(**f**(dog$'$))]

It is a property of compositions that preserve this parallel between syntactic and semantic saturation that one argument position is saturated before another argument is composed. All of the compositions considered above, including those that include Restrict as a mode of composition, show this property. In the derivation in (14), for example, Restrict is followed immediately by function application targeting the same argument position. This is also illustrated in the derivation in (13), repeated here as (21).

(21) FA (**EC** (**Restrict** ($\lambda$y$\lambda$x **[feed$'$(y)(x)]**, **dog$'$**)), j)
 = $\exists$y [feed$'$(y)(j) $\wedge$ dog$'$(y)]

In this composition, the argument position targeted by Restrict is immediately saturated by existential closure.

Let us consider another possible composition, however.

(22) EC (FA (**Restrict** ($\lambda$y$\lambda$x **[feed$'$(y)(x)]**, **dog$'$**), j))
 = $\exists$y [feed$'$(j)(y) $\wedge$ dog$'$(j)]

In this composition, we do existential closure after function application. This is a well-formed composition, which yields a different proposition from the one in (21). It makes John the dog and the existential closure saturates the second argument. The traditional notation that we are using here implicitly incorporates the assumption that arguments must be saturated at the point at which they are targeted in composition. That is an assumption we will not maintain here in its strongest form. We need a notation that will not require semantic saturation to parallel syntactic saturation. To provide this, we will henceforth adopt the Davidsonian logical representation, which we think perspicuously represents the issue at hand.[4]

Let us return to the derivation in (13) in a Davidsonian form.

(23) Restrict ($\lambda$y$\lambda$x$\lambda$e [feed$'$(y)(x)(e)], dog$'$)

The result of this composition is still a function that is unsaturated in two entity arguments in addition to the event argument. The valence of this function should remain the same. However, on our view, the lambda prefix of this predicate is doing two jobs, a semantic one and a syntactic one. Semantically, it is tracking the degree of unsaturation of the predicate. Syntactically, however, it determines the order under which the arguments are targeted for composition. The syntactic function of the lambda prefix has been discharged in this derivation by composition using Restrict, even though the semantic function has not been eliminated.

Let us therefore adopt the notational assumption that when an argument is targeted by a composition operation, it is possible to demote it from the top of the lambda prefix to a position just above the event argument. By this convention, (23) will yield (24).

(24) Restrict ($\lambda y \lambda x \lambda e$ [feed$'$(y)(x)(e)], dog$'$)
  = $\lambda x \lambda y \lambda e$ [feed$'$(y)(x)(e) $\wedge$ dog$'$(y)]

This notation now has the right degree of unsaturation, but allows the next argument to be targeted for composition without the saturation of the $y$ argument.

For the composition in (22), this convention yields a different result.

(25) FA (**Restrict ($\lambda y \lambda x \lambda e$ [feed$'$(y)(x)(e)], dog$'$)**, j)
  = FA ($\lambda x \lambda y \lambda e$ [feed$'$(y)(x)(e) $\wedge$ dog$'$(y)], j)
  = $\lambda y \lambda e$ [feed$'$(y)(j)(e) $\wedge$ dog$'$(y)]

Now function application saturates the $x$ argument rather than the $y$ argument, making John the feeder. The result of this composition is still a predicate, unsaturated now in two places: the event argument and the restricted $y$ argument.

At this point, iterations of existential closure (or a polyvalent, exhaustive closure, such as unselective binding) suffice to remove the remaining semantic incompleteness by saturation, yielding the appropriate proposition.

(26) EC (EC ($\lambda y \lambda e$ [feed$'$(y)(j)(e) $\wedge$ dog$'$(y)]))
  = $\exists e \exists y$ [feed$'$(y)(j)(e) $\wedge$ dog$'$(y)]

What forces existential closure is the principle that semantic completeness is necessary. Here the closure of the restricted argument is forced at the end, just before the closure of the event argument.

## 1.4 Saturation at the Event Level

The view that semantic incompleteness of predicates must be eliminated in composition raises the issue of exactly when in the compositional process their incompleteness must be resolved. Is there some intermediate stage in the process of composition at which the predicate must achieve completeness, in the sense that every one of its arguments must be saturated? We believe there is such a stage, and it occurs when the composition reaches the event argument associated with the predicate. At that stage, which we refer to as the *event level*, every one of the predicate's (participant) arguments has already been targeted for composition and has therefore had a chance to become complete. We claim that at the event level, the predicate must achieve completeness: every one of its arguments, except the event argument, must be saturated. We assume the following principle to enforce this:

(27) Predicates must have their participant arguments (semantically) saturated at the event level.

Previous approaches to formal semantics have not felt any need for a saturation requirement of the sort we are proposing. This strikes us as unsurprising. Where syntactic saturation and semantic saturation are assumed to be isomorphic, (27) is not needed. In such systems, semantic composition is accomplished via function application and is therefore saturating. The predicate will automatically become complete when composition has targeted all of its participant arguments.

The situation is different in our system, because Restrict does not saturate when it targets an argument. Given this larger architecture, the rationale for the saturation requirement becomes clear: predicates must achieve semantic completeness. This is no longer guaranteed by the mere process of composition. Once this is acknowledged, it must then be determined at exactly what stage of the process unsaturation must be resolved and semantic completeness achieved. We have two reasons for believing that the relevant stage is the event level.

Our first reason concerns the special character of the event argument. In the version of Davidsonian event semantics that we assume here (see Davidson 1967; Parsons 1990), every semantic predicate has an event argument as its highest argument. (Alternatively, one could adopt Kratzer's (1995) view that only stage-level predicates have an event argument as their highest argument, but for simplicity's sake we do not pursue this route.) The event argument differs from the typical argument in two ways: it designates an event as opposed to a participant, and it is ineligible for saturation by the usual means—it cannot be completed by composition with the meaning of an expression. In this special sense, the event argument must remain semantically incomplete. One way to draw the relevant distinction between the event argument and all other arguments is to assume that the predicate must achieve completeness at the stage when the event argument is about to be integrated into the composition. The result will be that the event argument will escape saturation via composition, but all other arguments of the predicate must be saturated. This, in essence, is our proposal.

Our second reason has to do with the workings of existential closure. There is by now a substantial body of research that holds that there is a semantic domain smaller than the proposition (or its syntactic analogue, the clause) that is existentially closed. Heim (1982, 138) originally proposed that existential closure affects the nuclear scope of a tripartite quantificational structure. Building on this insight, Diesing (1992) develops an algorithm for mapping syntactic structure into logical form in which "material from VP is mapped into the nuclear scope" of a quantificational structure (Diesing 1992, 10; see also Kratzer 1995). Diesing further assumes that all arguments of the predicate, except the event argument, originate internal to VP. The result is that in her system, every participant argument of the predicate is, in principle, within the domain of existential closure, because it originates internal to VP and is therefore mapped into the nuclear scope, which is existentially closed. (We pass over Diesing's treatment of stage-level and individual-level predicates, as it is not strictly relevant for our purposes.)

We see Diesing's mapping hypothesis, and her view of existential closure in particular, as fully consistent with the idea that the saturation requirement is imposed at the event level, which is designated syntactically to be the point where a VP becomes the complement to an inflectional head. In our system, existential closure provides one route by which a predicate's argument can become saturated. The significance of Diesing's system for us is that it makes existential closure available to all participant arguments of the predicate—just what would be expected if these arguments must be saturated, and their predicate semantically complete, at the event level.

In sum, we assume that the general ban on semantic incompleteness is given a linguistically significant location—at what we referred to as the

Modes of Composition

event level. What is important for our system is that closure be forced at that level if it has not already occurred. We do not argue here against the idea that closure may happen sooner. However, given that we are not assuming that every composition operation that targets a predicate's argument will result in closure, and hence, for us, (27) is not a theorem of a tacit assumption about semantic composition, we make this requirement explicit by adopting (27).[5]

## 1.5 Scope Constraints

Given the reasoning above, it follows from our system that compositions invoking only Restrict on an argument position will eventually saturate that position at the event level by existential closure. Since Restrict does not saturate the argument position, that position will be existentially closed at the event level if no further composition saturates it (as it would in the case of a derivation like (14)).

Under the standard assumption that negation is interpreted above the event level, it follows from this that any argument that is interpreted by Restrict rather than a saturating operation must be an existentially closed argument with necessarily narrow scope with respect to negation. Consider again the composition in (26). If this were negated, the existential closures would fall in the scope of negation. The effect of (27) is to ensure that the (nuclear) scope of negation will be saturated by existential closure, as stipulated for operators in general in Heim's (1982) system.

When we consider the question with regard to other (generalized) quantifiers, whether nominal or adverbial, we get a similar result. To show this, however, we must make our assumptions about the interpretation of quantifiers explicit. A fundamental property of all analyses that assume something analogous to quantifier raising (QR; see May 1985) is that generalized quantifiers are interpreted higher than what we have called the event level. Consider the interpretation of (28). Under the assumption that generalized quantifiers do not combine directly with first-order relations to saturate argument positions, the interpretation of (28) will result from the composition of the two meanings in (29).

(28) John fed every dog.

(29) $\lambda P \forall x [dog'(x) \rightarrow P(x)], \lambda y [\exists e [feed'(y)(j)(e)]]$

Though the same result can be achieved without making clear the relation between the quantifier and its nuclear scope in syntactic representation, we will, for concreteness, assume that semantic composition is done on structures that result from a syntactic rule of construal like QR. In this way, the existential closure of the nuclear scope of the quantifier assumed in Heim's (1982) system, as well as the interpretation of the quantification over events as having narrow scope with respect to negation,[6] follows from (27).

This example calls attention to an important point about the interpretation of variables, however. The variable $y$ in (29) is free in the expression below the event quantifier, but that free variable does not represent semantic incompleteness in the predicate for the purposes of (27). Hence, it does not trigger existential closure at the event level. The function of variables in logical representations is to saturate predicates (in both the syntactic and the semantic senses) while allowing the specification of the value of the argument to be dependent upon context of interpretation. This seems to us to be the standard understanding of variables and is not unique to the assumptions made here. However, this understanding is crucial to the discussion below of how the property theory of indefinites is related to the inventory of composition operations that we defend.

## 1.6 The Property Theory of Indefinites

Since the work of Kamp (1981) and Heim (1982) in Discourse Representation Theory, it has become standard to assume that some or all indefinite DPs have semantic interpretations equivalent to properties, that is, of type $\langle e,t \rangle$. In building on this tradition, we are interested in whether indefinites necessarily saturate the predicates with which they combine. We believe that they need not, and that indefinites are the natural domain for the composition operation that we call Restrict.

Under the classic Kamp-Heim analysis, indefinites are treated as "restricted free variables." (Definites are treated similarly, but this is irrelevant to us here.) The property that represents their semantic content serves as the restriction on the variable, but their interpretation as variables ensures that they will saturate the predicates they combine with. That is, the "restricted free variable" avoids the type mismatch that we have assumed for property-content arguments. It can, in a sense, be viewed as a kind of type-shifting, analogous to the use of choice functions. We leave for further research the question of what the substantive difference is between the variable approach and the choice function approach assumed here. Both resolve the type mismatch by saturating and shifting scope resolution into the theory of variable closure and binding. If choice function variables are subject only to existential closure, then the difference will be found in contexts where the individual variables associated with indefinites are themselves targeted for binding by operators other than existential closure (as in, e.g., the treatment of donkey anaphora).

In this section, we discuss how our proposals are related to some recent work on the interpretation of indefinites. What unites this work is the idea that some indefinites must be interpreted in ways that ensure that they will necessarily have narrow scope with respect to other elements in the sentence. We believe that the cases discussed here can fruitfully be analyzed in terms of Restrict and that the proposals are clarified when issues of semantic saturation are addressed explicitly.

The fundamental problem posed for composition when a noun phrase that has only a property as its semantic content is presented by the syntax as an argument to a predicate is a type mismatch. The property, of type $\langle e,t \rangle$, cannot combine directly with the predicate, which is looking for a type e argument.[7] Under the assumption, which we do not make here, that semantic saturation must occur at the point where the predicate is syntactically saturated, there are only two options: immediate type-shifting to type e via a choice function or existential closure.[8] The result allows saturation via function application. The former is illustrated in (20), repeated here in Davidsonian form as (30).

(30) FA ($\lambda x \lambda e$ [bark$'$(x)(e)], CF ([dog$'$(y)]))
 = $\exists f \exists e$ [bark$'$(f(dog$'$))(e)]

The combination of applying a choice function followed by function application can be viewed as a compound mode of composition that we will call *Specify*, to contrast it with the nonsaturating Restrict.

Because we are focusing on the saturation of predicates, we see Specify as saturating, even though it reveals a kind of semantic incompleteness in that CF is generally thought of as a variable over choice functions— hence the need for existential closure of the choice function at some point. That is, (30) entails that a particular dog barked, but doesn't give any information about which dog barked. This choice function variable differs from the standard use of individual variables in that it cannot become the target of binding by any operator other than existential closure. There is considerable variation in proposals about the possibilities for closure of choice function variables.

The competing proposals are surveyed effectively by Matthewson (1999, 86). Reinhart (1997) and Winter (1997) assume that all choice function variables may be existentially closed at any point in composition. In contrast, Kratzer (1998) and Matthewson (1999) assume that the semantic incompleteness represented by a choice function variable is addressed only at the end of composition, the "widest scope" level. (Kratzer assumes that choice function variables are never existentially closed, but treated as free variables anchored in context; Matthewson assumes existential closure, but only at the top level.) In both cases, indefinites interpreted with choice functions will have possibilities for wide scope over other operators. Anticipating the analysis of chapter 2, we will assume with Reinhart and Winter that the choice function variables introduced by Specify may be existentially closed at any level. Hence, the scope possibilities of indefinites interpreted by Specify are a superset of those interpreted by Restrict.

The assumption that Specify leads to predicate saturation in the sense of (27) is crucial. Whatever the nature of the incompleteness represented by the choice function variable, it need not be resolved at the event level. Hence, there are no necessary limitations on the scope possibilities of indefinite noun phrases interpreted in this way. An indefinite composed by Specify should be able to have either narrow or wide scope with respect to other operators. However, (27) entails that indefinites interpreted by Restrict must be closed by the event level.

The core of our proposal is that property-content indefinites may in principle be directly composed with predicates. They may be composed either by Restrict or by Specify. We embed this proposal in a theory that allows for syntactic saturation to occur without semantic saturation, while still ensuring semantic saturation at the event level. We hope that by pointing out the independence of these two assumptions, we make clear their relevance to similar proposals for the interpretation of indefinites.

Farkas (1997) discusses the semantic typology of indefinites and points out several cases of indefinites that are usefully analyzed as predicate restrictions; among them are preverbal nominal predicate modifiers in Hungarian. She proposes a semantic interpretation of such indefinites that parallels our operation Restrict, allowing them to have only properties as their contents. Her proposal is embedded in Discourse Representation Theory, and she further assumes that predicate modifiers do not introduce discourse referents (and hence are not available to anchor discourse anaphora). We do not assume here that the dynamic property of introducing a discourse referent is systematically correlated with mode of composition. In the analysis of Maori in chapter 2, we will propose that certain indefinite DPs are interpreted by Restrict but are fully dynamic in supporting discourse and donkey anaphora. In addition, Farkas assumes (1997, 11) that predicate modifiers saturate the predicate despite their semantic type.

The operation that we call Restrict also resembles the account of "predicative" indefinites in van Geenhoven 1998. Van Geenhoven proposes a distinction between predicative indefinites, which have only a property as their content, and "free variable" indefinites, which are given existential force through accommodation. She claims that predicative indefinites are combined with their predicates in an operation that she terms *semantic incorporation*, which entails that such indefinites have necessarily narrow scope. There is a clear parallel between our proposed operation Restrict and van Geenhoven's semantic incorporation. However, she implements her operation in a way that renders it saturating. She defines semantic incorporation of a property $P$ into a verb's meaning as follows (1998, 132):

(31) $\lambda P \lambda w \lambda x \exists y [\text{Verb}_w(x,y) \wedge P_w(y)]$

On our view, (31) represents a kind of type-shifting of the predicate to resolve the type mismatch between the semantically incomplete argument and the predicate. It creates a predicate with a second-order incompleteness, allowing the predicate to compose directly with the property. On this view, the property semantically saturates the predicate. In addition, the existential closure of the entity variable is stipulated as part of the predicate interpretation, thus ensuring that this entity argument is saturated before composition. By contrast, Restrict is designed precisely to leave the predicate unsaturated. It is the saturating character of semantic incorporation that entails the need for van Geenhoven's "recomposition" strategy (1998, 148) to allow for further composition of material that targets this incorporated argument. By viewing Restrict as not saturating, we believe that we avoid this consequence while still capturing the essential prediction of narrow scope for "semantically incorporated" indefinites.

It is an attractive idea that indefinite noun phrases, both NPs and DPs, may have mere properties as their semantic content, and the idea that some occurrences of indefinite DPs are treated in this way is relatively uncontroversial.[9] The assumption accounts straightforwardly for their use as predicates in their own right, at least from the point of view of semantics.

The theory we have presented here builds on this insight, but distinguishes the fundamental assumption of property content from the various means by which these noun phrases are enabled to serve as arguments to predicates. As we have shown, there are several ways of resolving the inherent type conflict. We think it is useful to view particular analyses of indefinites as a combination of this fundamental assumption about content type and assumptions about what we have termed modes of composition. Every analysis of indefinites makes assumptions about the type of their semantic content and how that is related to their combinatoric possibilities in composition. We believe it is important to recognize the fundamental heterogeneity of mode of composition and to exploit that heterogeneity in linguistic analysis.

## 1.7 Summary

We have concentrated here on two modes of composition for indefinites. Specify assimilates properties to entities to allow semantic saturation to be simultaneous with syntactic saturation. Restrict represents an alternate route to semantic completeness, one that separates semantic saturation from syntactic saturation.

From these assumptions, two important properties of compositions follow that are important to the remainder of this monograph.

The first property is that Restrict entails narrow scope. The scope of a property-content indefinite is fixed by the constraints governing existential closure of the argument. The scope of an indefinite composed with Restrict is fixed not by Restrict but by the (necessary) existential closure. The assumption here is that this closure must occur by the point at which the composition reaches the event level. As a result, all indefinites interpreted by Restrict must have narrow scope with respect to elements interpreted above that level. This includes all operators that bind the event variable and those that take scope over that level: negation, adverbial quantification, and nominal quantification. Hence, the fundamental diagnostic of an indefinite interpreted by predicate restriction is its necessarily narrow scope.

By contrast, the scope of indefinites interpreted by Specify is fixed by assumptions about the treatment of choice function variables. Here we assume that choice function variables may be existentially closed at any point. Therefore, indefinites interpreted by Specify will have no constraints on their scope interactions with other operators.

The second important property is that between Restrict and existential closure, saturation may occur. The semantic incompleteness of an argument that remains after Restrict must be eliminated by the event level. When it is eliminated by existential closure, the composition yields an interpretation that is equivalent to one that involved Specify and existential closure (of the choice function) at the same point. However, the logical possibility exists that the argument may be rendered complete by a saturating operation before the level where existential closure would be forced. In a structure interpreted in this way, the argument would appear to be doubled: it would be associated with the indefinite that was interpreted by Restrict and also with the saturating term.

In the remainder of this monograph, we develop analyses of structures involving semantically incomplete noun phrases in two Austronesian languages.

In chapter 2, we focus on the analysis of two indefinite determiners in Maori. Maori has two indefinite articles that are indistinguishable truth-conditionally but differ in scope possibilities and other aspects of their distribution. We argue that the lexical contrast between the two determiners directly represents the difference in mode of composition for these indefinites, one being systematically interpreted by Restrict and the other by Specify.

In chapter 3, we examine an incorporation structure in Chamorro. The Chamorro verbs 'have' and 'not have' necessarily incorporate a semantically incomplete noun phrase as their internal argument. However, the internal argument can also be associated with an independent DP. We argue that such cases illustrate the possibility of saturation following predicate restriction.

# Chapter 2
## Indefinites in Maori

In chapter 1, we advanced the idea that an indefinite noun phrase can be semantically combined as an argument to a predicate by two different modes of composition: Restrict and Specify. Restrict composes the property supplied by the indefinite with the predicate, limiting the semantic domain of the predicate but leaving it unsaturated. Specify shifts the property to an individual, which then saturates the predicate's argument, rendering the predicate (more) semantically complete. Although these operations often lead to results that are truth-conditionally equivalent, we believe that the difference in composition is linguistically significant.

In particular, our theory of restriction and saturation makes an empirical prediction that we explore in this chapter. If indefinites and other semantically incomplete noun phrases can indeed be composed via different operations, then one might expect that the morphosyntax could explicitly reflect which composition operation is employed. A language could, for instance, use distinctive determiners or distinctive inflectional morphology to flag whether a given indefinite should be composed via Restrict or via Specify.

We show here that this prediction is borne out in remarkable detail in Maori, a Polynesian language of New Zealand. Maori has two articles, *he* and *tētahi* (plural *ētahi*), that are widely recognized to be indefinite in some sense.[1] These articles contrast, but not truth-conditionally, in sentences like the following (see appendix B for a list of abbreviations used in the Maori examples):

(1) a. Kua tae   mai   he manuhiri ki taku kāinga.
       T   arrive to.here a guest     to my house
       'Some visitors came to my home.' (Orbell 1992, 49)
    b. Ka tae   mai   tētahi taraka tino nui.
       T   arrive to.here a     truck very big
       'A huge truck came.' (Waititi 1974, 43)

(2) a. Homai    he wai    mo-ku.
       give.Pass a water T.of-me
       'Give me some water.' (H. W. Williams 1971[1844], 43)
   b. Kawe-a    atu    tetahi wai    mo-ku.
       bring-Pass away a        water T.of-me
       'Fetch me some water.' (H. W. Williams 1971[1844], 111)

(1)–(2) illustrate that there are contexts of use in which *he* and *tētahi* seem interchangeable. But there are also contexts in which only one of the two can occur, as we will show later. Significantly, the range of uses of these articles does not lend itself to an account in terms of received semantic contrasts, such as referential versus quantificational (see, e.g., Fodor and Sag 1982) or specific versus nonspecific (see, e.g., Enç 1991).

The literature on Maori grammar offers numerous attempts to come to grips with the semantic similarity of these articles and their distributional overlap. Biggs (1969, 20, 113), for instance, has this to say:

The indefinite article *he* is preposed to bases which are being used nominally and indefinitely.... The specifying definitive *tētahi* and its regular plural form *ētahi* may be translated '(a) certain'.... Note that the indefinite article *he* may not follow any of the locative prepositions *ki, i, hei, kei*. In this position *he* is replaced by *tētahi*.

Like Biggs, Chung (1978, 73) describes the distribution of *he* in purely morphosyntactic terms.

The nonspecific article *he* ... qualifies nouns only when they are subjects of intransitive clauses.

On the other hand, Bauer (1993, 357) characterizes the contrast between *he* and *tētahi* primarily in semantic terms. In her very careful commentary on definiteness in Maori, she says,

Perhaps more importantly, it seems to me that the use of the labels 'definite' and 'indefinite' obscures the crucial factor in determining the choice between *he* and *tētahi* in those places where choice can occur: *he* is used when the type of object is crucial, and *tētahi* is used when the number of individuals present is significant.

(See Bauer 1997, 165–169, for further development of this proposal.) Behind these observations and suggestions lie some deeper questions. Why would a language have two indefinite articles in the first place? Why do *he* and *tētahi* seem semantically so similar but intuitively different? What is the semantic difference between the two, and why is it so elusive?

We claim that the explanation is to be found in the theory of restriction and saturation. In our view, the two indefinite articles of Maori signal different modes of composition: *he* signals that the indefinite is composed via Restrict, whereas *tētahi* signals that it is composed via Specify. In this chapter, we support our proposal with evidence from the distribution and meaning of these two types of indefinites. Our aim is to show how the composition operations interact with other aspects of grammar, including some quite parochial aspects of Maori, to give a principled account of *he*, *tētahi*, and their partial overlap.

If our account is correct, it offers striking evidence for our claim that semantically incomplete noun phrases can be composed via different operations. It simultaneously offers a challenge to approaches that employ type-shifting mechanisms, either freely or as a last resort, to reconcile the intuition that indefinite noun phrases are property-denoting with the observation that they often correspond to arguments (see, e.g., Partee 1987; de Swart 2001).

Section 2.1 offers a bit of background on Maori grammar. Section 2.2 describes the syntactic similarities between *he* and *tētahi*; section 2.3 describes their semantic similarities. Section 2.4 documents two striking contrasts. In section 2.5, we present our account and argue that it is superior to an approach in which function application, mediated by type-shifting, is the only composition operation. Section 2.6 discusses two further distributional contrasts between *he* and *tētahi*, while section 2.7 sketches some pragmatic contrasts between them. We suggest that all these contrasts are consistent with our account, once other aspects of Maori grammar are factored in. Finally, section 2.8 concludes.

## 2.1 A Dash of Maori Grammar

Like other Polynesian languages, Maori is a head-initial language whose syntax is relatively unencumbered by inflectional morphology. Clauses are projected from a category, T(ense), that occurs at the far left and typically indicates tense-aspect-mood. This category is followed by the predicate, which can be of any major category type, and then by the predicate's arguments. The grammatical relations of the arguments are indicated by prepositions. Consider the following sentences, in which the predicate is a verb (3a), an adjective (3b), or a prepositional phrase (3c):

(3) a. Ka noho a    Pāoa i  te  whare ra.
       T  sit  Pers Pāoa at the house that
       'Pāoa remained inside.' (Jones and Biggs 1995, 167 [22.11])

b. Ka tino koa a  Tamahae i te puta-nga   mai  o tēnei
   T very glad Pers Tamahae at the emerge-Nmlz to.here of this
   whakaatu.
   news
   'Tamahae was really happy when this news reached him.' (Waititi 1974, 164)
c. Kei te  taha moana ngā   kōtiro.
   T.at the side sea    the.pl girl
   'The girls are at the seaside.' (Biggs 1969, 40)

When the predicate is a noun phrase, T indicates whether it is predicational (glossed *Pred*) or identificational (*Ident*). We return to this later.

(4) a. He     wahine tino whakapono a    Te Puea.
       Pred.a woman very believing   Pers Te Puea
       'Te Puea was a very religious woman.' (Karetu 1974, 98)
    b. Ko    Ngahue tana hoa.
       Ident Ngahue his  friend
       'His friend was Ngahue.' (Waititi 1974, 81)

Three other characteristics of the syntax of clauses should be mentioned at this point. First, Maori is a VSO language—more accurately, an XSO language. The unmarked word order of clauses is Predicate-Subject-Other Arguments, though as Bauer (1993, 89) observes, "a variety of other orders is also possible." We can afford to remain agnostic on the issue of how XSO and the other word orders are derived (but for some proposals, see Bauer 1993, 89–91, 241–246, and 1997, 54–64; Chung 1998, 164–173). Second, Maori is a null argument language. Virtually every kind of argument can be realized by a null pronoun whose content is not recoverable from agreement—because Maori has no morphological agreement—but must be inferred from context. In (5), the parts of the English translation that correspond to Maori null arguments appear in brackets.

(5) Ka tō-ia      anō  ki uta, ka waru-hia ano, kātahi ka pai.
    T  drag-Pass again to shore T thin-Pass again then   T  good
    '[The canoe] was dragged ashore and thinned down again, and then [all] was well (lit. [it] was good).' (Jones and Biggs 1995, 29 [3.24])

Third, Maori exhibits a clear preference for the passive over the active (see Bauer 1993, 398–401, and the references cited there). This preference is strong enough that many Maori passive sentences are most naturally translated into English as active sentences—a practice we follow in citing the examples.

(6) Ka patu-a e Raka', tanu-mia iho ki roto i nga
    T kill-Pass by Raka' bury-Pass down at inside DO the.pl
    maramara o te waka.
    shaving of the canoe
    'Raka' killed [him] and buried [him] among the shavings from the canoe.' (Jones and Biggs 1995, 21 [3.11])

The syntax of noun phrases will be important here and later, in chapter 3. Following Abney (1987), we assume that the Maori category we informally call the noun phrase is a DP, headed by the category D(eterminer), which occurs at the left. To the right of D are the noun, its complements, and modifiers, all of which we take to form the phrase identified by Abney as the NP complement of D. The examples in (7) illustrate some typical Maori determiners: the definite article *te* (plural *ngā*) and the demonstratives. (In (7b) and all other examples cited from H. M. Ngata 1994, italics are used to indicate the dictionary entry cited.)

(7) a. te mea tuatahi ki te whakatū komiti
       the person first Infin establish committee
       'the first one to set up a committee' (Karetu 1974, 106)
    b. te tūnga-ā-iwi tino teitei o tēnei whenua
       the public.office very high of this land
       'the highest public *office* in this land' (H. M. Ngata 1994, 306)
    c. ngā anga o aua kai
       the.pl shell of the.pl.aforem food
       'the shells of that food' (Karetu 1974, 48)

The determiners include *he* and *tētahi*, as we show in a moment, but few if any true quantifiers. In Maori, the clearest candidate for a determiner quantifier is *ia* 'each' (see Bauer 1997, 155–156), which also functions as a demonstrative meaning 'that, the said' (H. W. Williams 1971[1844], 74). The slimness of the inventory of determiner quantifiers is consistent with what is reported by Bach et al. (1995) for some other languages.

Possessors in Maori occur as prepositional phrases headed by the preposition *a*, which indicates "dominant" possession, or the preposition *o*, "subordinate" possession. The choice between *a* and *o* is semantically and pragmatically determined (see, e.g., Biggs 1969, 43–45; Bauer 1993, 197–

216, and 1997, 390–407). Like other prepositional phrases, possessors can serve as predicates of clauses.

(8) No te iwi katoa ngā whenua.
    T.of the tribe all the.pl land
    'The lands belong to the whole tribe (lit. The lands are of the whole tribe).' (Biggs 1969, 57)

Within the noun phrase, possessors occur to the right of the noun or else can combine with the definite article to form a complex determiner.

(9) a. te ātaahua o tēnei whenua
      the beauty of this land
      'the beauty of this land' (Waititi 1974, 81)
   b. tōu whare
      your house
      'your house'
   c. tō Hone whare
      the.of John house
      'John's house' (Bauer 1993, 201)

Like the surface word order of arguments within the clause, the word order of possessors within the noun phrase is irrelevant here. What matters is that, like Abney, we assume that possessors within the noun phrase occupy the specifier of D at some point. The analysis commits us to the view that D and the possessor are subconstituents of DP but not of D's NP complement—a point to which we will return.

## 2.2 The Syntax of *He* and *Tētahi*

With the stage set to this extent, we now introduce the indefinite articles, *he* and *tētahi* (plural *ētahi*).

We claimed above that *he* and *tētahi* are realizations of D and in this sense syntactically alike. The claim is, in one sense, uncontroversial. *He* and *tētahi* occur within the noun phrase in exactly the same position as other determiners: at the left edge, followed by the noun, its complements, modifiers, and the possessor. In the examples in (10), the relevant noun phrases are bracketed.

(10) a. Kua riro [he pukapuka a Mere].
      T be.taken a book of Mere
      'A book of Mere's was taken.'

b. Kua riro     [tētahi pukapuka a  Mere].
T   be.taken  a        book     of Mere
'A book of Mere's was taken.'

c. Ka tae-a     e   koe te whakahiato [he tāngata ruarua nei
T  arrive-Pass by you the assemble    a   people few     this
hai   āwhina i    a      tātau]?
so.as help     DO Pers us
'Can you *assemble* a few people to give us a hand?' (H. M. Ngata 1994, 20)

d. I tiro-hia      e  mātau [tētahi tikanga hou hai    whawhao
T look.into-Pass by us      a      method new so.as pack
hua].
fruit
'We *experimented* with a new way to pack the fruit.' (H. M. Ngata 1994, 140)

There is another sense in which some caution might be called for. Students of Maori might find the syntactic similarity of *he* and *tētahi* obscured by two curious morphological differences. Although these differences are well documented in the literature on Maori grammar, there is no consensus on their analytic significance. Here we detour briefly to discuss them, in order to make the point that they are ultimately irrelevant: neither stands in the way of our identifying *he* and *tētahi* as indefinite determiners.

The first difference is that *he* is morphologically unanalyzable, but *tētahi* appears to be morphologically complex. It evidently consists of the definite article *te* plus the numeral 'one', whose counting and ordinal form is *tahi* (see Biggs 1969, 48; Bauer 1993, 110, and 1997, 151). As far as we can tell, it is etymologically correct to decompose *tētahi* into *te* plus *tahi*, and the decomposition is probably still more or less salient morphologically. Nonetheless, we believe that the analysis is no longer syntactically or semantically viable in Maori. Here are our reasons for thinking so.

If *tētahi* were semantically analyzable as 'the' plus 'one' in Modern Maori, then the noun phrases projected from it ought to be semantically definite. Now, definites are insensitive to the scope of sentential operators like negation, an insensitivity sometimes characterized by saying that they have maximally wide scope. If the noun phrases headed by *tētahi* were definite, then they too should display insensitivity to scope. But the facts are not consistent with this prediction. Examples like (11) show that noun phrases headed by *tētahi* can have narrow scope with respect to negation.

(11) Kaore anō tētahi tangata kia taha i   te   ara.
    T.not yet a         person   T pass on the path
    'No one had yet passed along the track.' (H. M. Ngata 1994, 304; *observation*)

We will return to this point later.

Further, if *tētahi* were syntactically analyzable as 'the' plus 'one' in Modern Maori, then *tahi* ought to have the syntactic distribution of cardinal numerals generally and of the numeral 'one' in particular. But the cardinal numeral 'one' that occurs everywhere else in Maori—within noun phrases and as the predicate of clauses—is not *tahi* but *kotahi* (see Biggs 1969, 111; Bauer 1993, 495–497, and 1997, 276–279).[2]

(12) a. Kāore [he take    kotahi].
      T.not a reason one
      'There's no reason at all (lit. There is not one reason).'
   b. Kāore i mau      [tētahi tuna kotahi] i     a     Tamahae.
      T.not T be.caught a      eel   one  Cause Pers Tamahae
      'Tamahae didn't catch one eel.' (Waititi 1974, 7)
   c. E kotahi tonu [he uri           mō-na    a tērā o ana    wāhine].
      T one still    a descendant T.of-him of that of his.pl wives
      'He had only one offspring from that one of his wives (lit. A descendant for him of that one . . . was only one).' (Jones and Biggs 1995, 119 [15.15])

The conclusion seems clear that *tētahi* should not be decomposed into 'the' plus 'one' for semantic or syntactic purposes. Whatever its internal morphological structure, it is—for these other purposes—simply an indefinite determiner.

The second difference is that *he* has a more limited distribution than *tētahi*. Whereas *tētahi* can occur within any noun phrase at all, *he* cannot immediately follow a preposition. This restriction has been very widely noticed for Standard Maori, where its consequences are dramatic (see, e.g., W. L. Williams 1923[1862], 18; A. T. Ngata 1926, 9, 18; Hohepa 1967, 104; Biggs 1969, 113; Bauer 1993, 356, and 1997, 147). In Standard Maori, prepositions are used to signal every grammatical relation but the subject. Given that *he* cannot immediately follow a preposition, what this means for the standard language is that noun phrases headed by *he* must be subjects. They cannot bear any other grammatical relation.

Such a restricted distribution might seem inconsistent with the idea that *he* is a determiner. However, closer inspection reveals that there are circumstances under which noun phrases headed by *he* can serve as direct objects or adjuncts. These exceptional cases strongly suggest that *he* is a determiner after all, but one whose occurrence is constrained very narrowly by morphology.

(a) In the Ngāti Porou dialect of Maori, spoken on the East Coast of the North Island, it is possible for noun phrases headed by *he* to serve as direct objects or adjuncts of location, means, and so forth. These grammatical relations are ordinarily signaled by the Maori preposition *i*, which has a very wide range of uses. What is special about the Ngāti Porou dialect is that it permits the preposition *i* to have a *he* indefinite as its object. Interestingly, when that happens, the preposition itself is not pronounced. Consider the *he* indefinites in (13), which include a direct object (13a) and adjuncts denoting path (13b), means of conveyance (13c), and location (13d).

(13) a. I te whakaahua rātau [he pakipūmeka mo Tokomaru].
     T film       they  a documentary T.of Tokomaru
     'They have been *filming* a documentary on Tokomaru Bay.'
     (H. M. Ngata 1994, 152)
  b. Me haere tātou [he huarahi kē].
     T  go    we    a  way     different
     'Let us take (lit. go by) another way.' (A. T. Ngata 1926, 64)
  c. Me eke     tātou [he kareti   kē].
     T embark we     a  carriage different
     'We must change carriage (lit. set out in a different carriage).'
     (A. T. Ngata 1926, 85)
  d. I tīmata tonu te oriori        [he mihi  ki te tamaiti].
     T begin  still the lullaby.chant a praise to the child
     'The beginning of a lullaby *chant* is always couched in terms of praise (lit. the lullaby always begins in praise) for the child.'
     (H. M. Ngata 1994, 53)

We see the pattern in (13) as a different strategy for dealing with the restriction that prevents *he* from occurring immediately after a preposition. Whereas Standard Maori reacts to the restriction by barring *he* indefinites from every grammatical relation except the subject, the Ngāti Porou dialect reacts—in at least some instances—by deleting the preposition when it would occur before *he* (see Cook 1999, 54–57, 61–63, for a

Hawaiian parallel). On this view, the relevant restriction is fundamentally not syntactic (contra Chung 1978). Rather, it is a morphological ban on the combination of overt preposition plus *he*—a ban that poses no threat to our claim that *he* is a determiner.

(b) Polinsky (1992, 236–237) and Bauer (1993, 309, 356) have observed that a *he* indefinite can serve as object of the preposition *me* 'like, as'. This appears to be possible in Standard Maori (see (14a)) as well as the Ngāti Porou dialect (14b).

(14) a. Ka tū    ki uta    o te wai,  me he Kōtuku.
       T  stand to shore of the water like a  white.heron
       'She stepped out of the water, like a white heron.' (Bauer 1993, 309)
   b. Me    he kuini tonu tana tū.
      T.like a queen still her bearing
      'She has the *bearing* of a queen.' (H. M. Ngata 1994, 30)

For Polinsky, the ability of *he* indefinites to serve as objects of *me* provides evidence that *he* is associated with predication as opposed to identification. We will come back to her analysis, which is close to ours in certain ways, in section 2.8.

To sum up, despite their morphological eccentricities, both *he* and *tētahi* are syntactic determiners.

## 2.3 The Semantic Similarity of *He* and *Tētahi*

Far more mysterious than the syntactic similarity of *he* and *tētahi* is their semantic similarity. We noted at the outset that there is a range of uses in which these articles seem interchangeable. These uses, which we now investigate, help to make precise the senses in which *he* and *tētahi* are semantically indefinite.

We begin with a wide scope use of indefinites (in section 2.3.1) and then proceed to some narrow scope uses (in section 2.3.2).

### 2.3.1 Wide Scope in Episodic Sentences

One classic use of indefinites is to introduce a referential argument in episodic sentences. As should come as no surprise by now, both *he* and *tētahi* can be used this way. Consider the sentences in (15)–(17), which describe single past events. Each sentence contains a noun phrase headed by *he* or *tētahi* (enclosed in brackets) that introduces a referential argument. In (15), the relevant noun phrases are surface subjects of passive verbs.

(15) a. Ka hopu-kia  e  ia  [he poaka], ka whiu-a    ki runga ki te
       T  catch-Pass by him  a  pig     T throw-Pass to top    to the
       ahi.
       fire
       'Then he caught a pig and threw it onto the fire.' (Orbell 1992, 20)
   b. Ka whakapā-ngia    atu   e  Rewi [tētahi rākau] ki te  waewae
       T  make.touch-Pass away by Rewi  a       branch to the leg
       o Tamahae.
       of Tamahae
       'Rewi touched a branch to Tamahae's leg.' (Waititi 1974, 6)

In (16), they are subjects of (identical) unaccusative verbs. Notice that *tētehi* (plural *ētehi*) in (16b) is a dialectal form of *tētahi* from the Waikato-Maniapoto area (Biggs 1969, 113).

(16) a. Kua puta    [he rū       nui] ki Pōneke.
       T   come.out  a  earthquake big  at Wellington
       'A severe earthquake occurred in Wellington.' (A. T. Ngata 1926, 60)
   b. Ka puta      mai    [tētehi tangata rangatira].
       T  come.out to.here  a      person  chiefly
       'A man of high rank appeared.' (Orbell 1992, 67)

In (17a), from the Ngāti Porou dialect, and in (17b), the relevant noun phrases are direct objects.

(17) a. I takatū   mātau [he hākari] mo   to rātau hokinga mai.
       T prepare  we     a  feast   T.of their    coming to.here
       'We prepared a feast for their *homecoming*.' (H. M. Ngata 1994, 207)
   b. I moe   ia  i   [tētahi Pākehā nō    Ingarangi].
       T marry she DO  a      Pakeha T.of  England
       'She married a Pakeha (European) from England.' (Waititi 1974, 40)

In Discourse Representation Theory, the use of indefinites illustrated in (15)–(17) would be taken to indicate that both *he* and *tētahi* can introduce a new discourse referent. Consistent with this, noun phrases headed by these articles can serve as antecedents for discourse anaphora, whether the anaphors are pronouns or definite noun phrases. This can be seen from the examples in (18), each of which begins a stretch of narrative. The indefinites in these examples occur as subjects of the nonverbal predicate *tērā* 'over there'. In (18a), *he tangata* 'a man' antecedes the possessive pronoun *tana* 'his', which occurs several clauses later. In (18b), *tētehi wahine puhi* 'a virgin' antecedes the noun phrase *taua wahine* 'the (aforementioned) woman', which occurs exactly as many clauses later.

(18) a. Tērā    [he tangata], ko    Rua-rangi te    ingoa, ko
over.there a person    Ident Rua-rangi the name Ident
Tawhaitū te    ingoa o    tana hoa.
Tawhaitū the name of his    friend
'Once there was a man called Rua-rangi; Tawhaitū was the name of his wife.' (Orbell 1992, 20)
b. Na, tērā    [tētehi wahine puhi], ko    Pare te    ingoa, he
now over.there a    woman virgin Ident Pare the name Pred.a
tino rangatira taua    wahine.
very chiefly    the.aforem woman
'Now once there was a woman, called Pare, who was a puhi (virgin). This woman was of very high birth.' (Orbell 1992, 67)

Further, as our characterization suggests, and as is expected of indefinites generally, the discourse referents contributed by *he* and *tētahi* must be new. This amounts to saying that the noun phrases headed by these articles must obey Heim's (1982) Novelty Condition. We can see the Novelty Condition at work in stretches of Maori narrative in which there are two noun phrases with the same descriptive content. If the second noun phrase is headed by *he* or *tētahi*, it must have a reference distinct from that of the first noun phrase, because the discourse referent that it contributes cannot have already been introduced. Sentence (19a), for instance, literally means 'Some$_i$ slept and some$_j$ woke to do their work'. This sentence cannot mean 'Some$_i$ slept, and (then) they$_i$ woke to do their work', though there would be nothing incoherent about such an interpretation. The reason is that each instance of *ētehi*, not just the first, must contribute a novel discourse referent.[3] Similarly, (19c) means 'They appeared at that part$_i$ of the fort, then rushed and appeared at another part$_j$ of the fort'. It cannot mean 'They appeared at that part$_i$ of the fort and then rushed and appeared at that part$_i$ of the fort again'. The second meaning is impossible because *he wāhi* 'a part' must introduce a discourse referent different from the discourse referent of *tēnā wāhi* 'that part'.

(19) a. Ka moe [ētehi], ka ara    ko   [ētehi] ki ta rātou mahi.
       T  sleep a.pl  T  awake Ident a.pl to their   work
       'While some slept, others stayed awake to keep up the work.'
       (Jones and Biggs 1995, 191 [26.4])
    b. Ko   ngā   rangatira i [tētahi pito], ko   ngā   tūtūā      [he
       Ident the.pl chief    at a     end   Ident the.pl commoner  a
       pito kē]   anō.
       end different again
       'The chiefs were at one end, the common people at another end.'
       (Orbell 1992, 162)
    c. Ta rāua mahi he         whakaputa ake i [tēnā wāhi o te  pā], ka
       their.du work Pred.a appear       up at that place of the fort T
       rere, ā,   ka whakaputa ake [he wāhi] anō.
       rush and T  appear     up   a  place  again
       'They appeared at [that] part of the fort, then rushed to another
       part.' (Jones and Biggs 1995, 191 [26.4])

In Heim's theory, the Novelty Condition is the principal constraint imposed on the wide scope uses of indefinites. The fact that this condition exercises its power on noun phrases headed by *he* as well as noun phrases headed by *tētahi* argues that both articles are semantically indefinite.

### 2.3.2 Narrow Scope in Quantificational Constructions

Another classic property of indefinites—one that plays a major role in current semantic theory—is their ability to have narrow scope with respect to logical operators such as negation and quantification. In this use too, *he* and *tētahi* seem interchangeable. Because the availability of narrow scope has not been widely noticed for *tētahi*, we will document the evidence with some care. Various quantificational constructions are examined below: conditional sentences, sentences expressing universal quantification or negation, modal sentences, questions, and generic sentences. We begin our discussion of each construction with some brief remarks about syntax. This is where most of the idiosyncrasies reside, since—as will become evident—the scope facts are fully general.

Conditional sentences we take to be constructions that express quantification over cases, in the sense of Barker (1991). In Maori, sometimes the antecedent clause is explicitly marked as subordinate by means of a complementizer such as *ki te* or *me(hemea)* 'if'. Other times the antecedent clause appears to be coordinated with the consequent clause; the two are simply juxtaposed, with the antecedent preceding the consequent and no intervening conjunction or complementizer (see (20b) and (20d)). What is relevant is that indefinites in the antecedent clause can routinely have narrow scope with respect to the quantification expressed by the conditional. Further, narrow scope is available whether the indefinite is headed by *he* or *tētahi*.

The conditional sentences in (20) are typical. The most natural interpretation of these sentences is one in which the indefinite has narrow scope. In (20b), which contains the indefinite *he tangata* 'a person', the choice of person is dependent on the choice of case; in (20c), which contains the indefinite *tētahi hara* 'a crime', the choice of crime is dependent on the choice of case. In (20d), which contains two indefinites, *he tohora* 'a whale' and *tētahi kaititiro* 'a lookout', the choice of whale and the choice of lookout are both dependent on the choice of case. More generally, the indefinites in all these examples have narrow scope.

(20) a. Ki te tae    mai   [he ope]          ki tō   kāinga, ā,  kāore
        if  arrive to.here a   visiting.party at your house  and T.not
        i te nui    ō      kai,  hei  aha   atu.
        T  abundant your.pl food T.for what? away
        'If a visitor arrives at your house, and you don't have much
        food, don't let it worry you.' (Karetu 1974, 59)

   b. Ka tata       [he tangata] ka neke  haere aua            rākau ki
      T  approach  a  person    T  move  go    the.aforem.pl tree  to
      tawhiti.
      distance
      'If anyone approached, [those trees] receded to a distance.'
      (Jones and Biggs 1995, 223 [32.4])

   c. Ki te mahi te   tangata i  [tētahi hara], ka hopu-kina e  te
      if  do   the person   DO a   crime    T  arrest-Pass by the
      ture.
      law
      'A person who commits a crime will be *arrested* (lit. If the
      person commits a crime, he is arrested by the law).' (H. M.
      Ngata 1994, 19)

   d. Ka kite-a    [he tohora] e  [tētahi kaititiro], ka whakatū-ria te
      T  see-Pass a   whale   by a   lookout       T  raise-Pass  the
      haki o tōna kāinga.
      flag of his house
      'If a lookout spotted a whale, he would raise the flag of his
      house.' (Waititi 1974, 132)

e. Ki te whakawhiti [he Māori] ki tāwāhi ki te kimi i  [tētahi
   if  cross.over  a Maori  to overseas Infin seek DO  a
   mātauranga] mō-na, ... ko   Hoani tonu te mea   tuatahi
   educaton     T.of-him Ident Hoani still the person first
   ki te whakatū komiti.
   Infin set.up    committee
   'If a Maori went abroad to seek an education for himself, Hoani
   was always the first person to set up a committee.' (Karetu
   1974, 94)

Notice especially (20d–e), in which both types of indefinites co-occur in the antecedent clause. Examples like these serve to emphasize that narrow scope is just as much an option for *tētahi* as for *he*.

A similar picture emerges from sentences expressing universal quantification. We have already mentioned that aside from *ia* 'each', Maori has few if any determiner quantifiers. Universal quantification is more usually expressed outside the determiner system: by *katoa* 'all' or the post-head adverbial *tonu* 'still, always', by reduplication of the noun phrase that expresses the restriction, and so on. Whatever the formal means of expression, indefinites in the same clause as a universal quantifier can routinely have narrow scope with respect to the universal quantification. Once again, narrow scope is possible whether the indefinite is headed by *he* or *tētahi*.

The observation is nicely illustrated by the sentences in (21), which are practically a minimal pair. Each sentence begins with the prepositional phrase *i ia tau* 'in each year', followed by an indefinite subject: *he kaiwhakahaere hou* 'a new chairperson' in (21a) and *tētahi tangata* 'a person' in (21b). The obvious interpretation of (21a) is that a (potentially) different new chairperson is elected each year. The most natural interpretation of (21b) is that a (potentially) different person is lost in the bush each year. In other words, both types of indefinites have narrow scope.

(21) a. I   ia   tau  ka pōti-tia    [he kaiwhakahaere hou].
       in each year T elect-Pass  a chairperson     new
       'Each year a new *chairperson* is elected.' (H. M. Ngata 1994, 52)
    b. I   ia   tau, e ngaro    ana [tētahi tangata] i te ngahere.
       in each year T be.forgotten   a   person    in the bush
       'Every year, someone gets lost in the *bush*.' (H. M. Ngata 1994, 44)

Two more examples of indefinites that have narrow scope with respect to universal quantification are given in (22).

(22) a. I tito-a        [he waiata] ia    tau, ia    tau.
      T compose-Pass    a    song      each year each year
      'Each year, songs were composed.'
    b. I ia    purei hoiho ka pēke ahau i    [tētahi mōwaho].
      at each play   horse   T   back I    DO    a       outsider
      'I (usually) back one *outsider* at every race meeting.' (H. M. Ngata 1994, 316)

Sentences expressing negation conform to this pattern as well. Maori has a fairly elaborate syntax of negation. To begin with, negative sentences are syntactically complex: the sentential negatives are main verbs that take the negated clause as complement (see, e.g., Hohepa 1969; Chung 1978; Bauer 1993, 139–146, and 1997, 459–476). Negative sentences are also hosts to raising, the movement operation that turns the subject of an embedded clause (here, the negated clause) into the subject of a higher verb (here, the negative verb). Among other things, raising alters the surface word order so that the subject precedes the predicate that originally selected it; this can be seen in (23a–d). For our purposes, what is noteworthy about these aspects of the syntax of negation is that they do not affect the semantics of scope. Specifically, they have no impact on the ability of an indefinite in a negative sentence to take narrow scope with respect to negation. Narrow scope is possible whether the indefinite is a subject or a nonsubject and whether it has undergone raising or not. Moreover, narrow scope is possible whether the indefinite is headed by *he* or *tētahi*. This is what we are interested in.

(23) a. Kāore [he tangata] i    āta-kite.
      T.not    a    person    T clearly-see
      'No one actually saw it.' (Jones and Biggs 1995, 85 [8.10])
    b. Kaore a      au e   pīrangi kia kite [he tangata].
      T.not Pers I   T want    T    see    a    person
      'I do not want to see *anyone*.' (H. M. Ngata 1994, 15)
    c. Kaore [tētahi tangata] e mahi mā-na.
      T.not    a       person    T work T.of-him
      'No one would work for him.' (H. M. Ngata 1994, 325; *particular*)

d. Kāore anō te nuinga o ngā tamariki nei kia kite i
   T.not yet the majority of the.pl children this T see DO
   [tētahi tereina].
   a train
   'Most of the children had never seen a train before.' (Waititi 1974, 98)
e. Kīhai i ora [tētahi].
   T.not T alive a
   'Not one was left alive.' (Orbell 1992, 127)
f. Kaore anō kia kite-a e [tētahi tangata] [he rongoā mo
   T.not yet T discover-Pass by a person a cure T.of
   te mate parekore].
   the AIDS
   'No one has yet *discovered* a cure for AIDS.' (H. M. Ngata 1994, 101)

The examples in (23) show *he* indefinites and *tētahi* indefinites bearing various grammatical relations in negative sentences: as subjects that have undergone raising (in (23a) and (23c)), as subjects that have not been raised ((23e) and the *he* indefinite in (23f)), as direct objects ((23b) and (23d)), and as prepositional objects (the *tētahi* indefinite in (23f)). In every case, it is clear—from the narrative context (in (23d)), from real-world knowledge ('a cure for AIDS' in (23f)), or from the English translation supplied in the original text—that the indefinite has narrow scope with respect to the negation. Notice especially (23f), in which both types of indefinites co-occur. As before, examples like this serve to emphasize that the narrow scope reading is just as available for *tētahi* as for *he*.

We take it to be established, then, that the option of narrow scope extends indifferently to both types of indefinites in Maori. If the generalization is real, of course, it ought to hold for logical operators besides those just described. To make this idea plausible, we now round out the picture with a representative sample of other quantificational constructions in Maori: modal sentences, questions, and generic sentences. It will become clear immediately that the two types of indefinites are just as eligible for narrow scope here as elsewhere.

Modality in Maori is usually expressed as a verb or else realized in Tense. Consider the sentences in (24), which are headed by *me* 'must, should', a tense-aspect-mood particle that expresses "a wide range of degrees of obligation" (Bauer 1993, 460; see also Bauer 1997, 136–137).

The most natural interpretation of these sentences is that the indefinites have narrow scope with respect to the modal operator. In (24a–c), the translation supplied by the text makes it clear that the choice of warning (24a), food (24b), or thing that gives (24c) is relativized to the choice of possible world. In (24d), the narrative context reveals that it is completely unimportant who will go to show the way. Crucially for our purposes, narrow scope is equally available for both types of indefinites: the indefinites in (24a–b) are headed by *he*, while those in (24c–d) are headed by *tētahi*.

(24) a. He    tikanga no   ērā   rā   me puta    anō   [he kupu
Pred.a custom T.of those time T  come.out again  a  word
whakatūpato].
warning
'Giving warnings (lit. that warnings should be given) was a custom of those times.' (Jones and Biggs 1995, 283 [45.11])

b. Me kohi anō   tātau [he kai] mo te  mutunga wiki.
T  get.in again we     a  food T.of the end     week
'We'll have to *get in* more food for the weekend.' (H. M. Ngata 1994, 177)

c. Me whakangāwari [tētahi mea].
T  give         a     thing
'Something has got to *give*.' (H. M. Ngata 1994, 178)

d. Me haere atu   anō   [tētehi tangata] o konei hei   ārahi atu
T  go  away again a       person  of here so.as direct away
i   a   koe.
DO Pers you
'Someone from here must go as well, to show you the way.' (Orbell 1992, 49)

We turn next to questions. In Maori, the syntactically most straightforward questions are polar (yes-no) questions, which have the same syntax as declarative sentences. Now in questions generally, it is the question operator that has widest scope, so we would expect indefinites within questions to have narrow scope. This expectation is borne out for indefinites in Maori whether they are headed by *tētahi* or *he*. In (25a), for instance, whether *he tangata* 'a person' has a referent depends on how the question is answered. The same holds true for *tētahi mea rerekē* 'a strange thing' in (25d).

(25) a. I mate anō   [he tangata]?
       T die indeed  a  person
       'Did anyone die?'
   b. Kua rongo anō    koe [he kōrero mo te  aituā]?
       T   hear  indeed you a  talk   T.of the accident
       'Have you heard anything *concerning* the accident?' (H. M. Ngata 1994, 64)
   c. E pai   rānei koe ki te homai i    [tētahi hereni]?
       T good Q    you Infin give  DO a       shilling
       'Will you lend me a shilling?' (A. T. Ngata 1926, 40)
   d. I kite anō    koe i   [tētahi mea rerekē] i to     haerenga mai?
       T see indeed you DO a      thing strange at your going to.here
       'Did you *observe* anything strange when you came?' (H. M. Ngata 1994, 304)

Finally, consider generic sentences. In Maori, generic sentences—like polar questions—do not have a distinctive morphosyntax. Context makes clear when a sentence is intended to be interpreted generically. What is relevant for our purposes is that indefinites in generic sentences can have narrow scope with respect to the generic operator. In (26a), for instance, *he koroua* 'old men' does not refer to any particular group of old men, but to whatever old men attend the typical meeting; in (26b), *tētahi tikanga* 'a plan' does not refer to any particular plan, but to whatever plan emerges from the typical situation of lacking money. Consistent with the evidence we have already given, narrow scope is just as much an option for *tētahi* as for *he*.

(26) a. Ka tino kōrero [he koroua] i  ngā     hui.
       T very speak   a  old.man  at the.pl meeting
       'Old men talk a lot at meetings.'
   b. Ko    te pai   o te iwi      Māori, ahakoa      kāore he moni,
       Ident the good of the people Maori  although    T.not a money
       ka kimi-hia [tētahi tikanga] e kite-a       ai  he moni.
       T seek-Pass a      plan     T find-Pass Pro a   money
       'The good thing about the Maori people is, when there's no money, they look for a way to get money.' (Waititi 1974, 85)

We conclude that for the purposes of expressing narrow scope in quantificational constructions, *he* and *tētahi* are essentially interchangeable.

## 2.4 Some Semantic Contrasts

Even though *he* and *tētahi* seem equivalent for many purposes, there are also contexts of use in which only one of the two can occur. This section is devoted to two contrasts between them that seem fundamentally semantic. One involves a wide scope use of indefinites (section 2.4.1) and the other, a narrow scope use (section 2.4.2).

### 2.4.1 Wide Scope in Quantificational Constructions

As was first noticed by Polinsky (1992), the two types of indefinites differ in their ability to have wide scope with respect to logical operators in quantificational constructions. Indefinites headed by *tētahi* can take wide scope with respect to the operator; indefinites headed by *he* cannot.

We illustrate the general point with negation, an operator whose meaning leads to a wide scope reading for the indefinite that does not entail its narrow scope reading. Consider the following sentences, all of which contain noun phrases headed by *tētahi*. In (27a), what is asserted is the existence of a person who has the property of not singing; in (27b), the existence of certain kinds of trees that have the property of not growing here; and in (27c), the existence of a hoe that has the property of his not having seen it. In every case, the *tētahi* indefinite has wide scope with respect to the negation.

(27) a. Kāore tētahi tangata i waiata mai.
      T.not a     person T sing  to.here
     'A (particular) person didn't sing (= There was a person who didn't sing).'
b. Kaore ētahi momo rākau e tipu i konei.
   not  a.pl kind  tree  T grow at here
  '*Certain* trees will not grow here.' (H. M. Ngata 1994, 52)
c. Kāore ia i kite i   tētahi hō e takoto ana i  roto  i  ngā
   not   he T see DO a     hoe T lie      at inside at the.pl
  karaehe.
  grass
  'He didn't see a hoe (= there was a hoe that he didn't see) lying in the grass.' (Waititi 1974, 59)

In contrast, indefinites headed by *he* cannot have wide scope with respect to negation (Polinsky 1992, 237). To see this, consider (28). Quite different from the examples in (27), the ones in (28) cannot be interpreted as asserting the existence of some individual or individuals—a person in (28a) or men in (28b). They can only be understood to assert *non*existence. The only reading possible for the *he* indefinite, in other words, is one in which it has narrow scope with respect to the negation.

(28) a. Kāore he tangata i waiata mai.
    T.not a person T sing to.here
    'No one at all sang.' (But: '*A (particular) person didn't sing.')
   b. Kāhore he tāngata i te mahi.
    T.not a people T work
    'Nobody is at work.' (But: '*Some men are not at work.')
   (Polinsky 1992, 237)

Unfortunately, the contrast illustrated in (27)–(28) does not emerge as clearly from our data on the other quantificational constructions of section 2.3.2. In our only examples of these constructions in which the indefinite has wide scope, the indefinite's wide scope reading entails its narrow scope reading, so the reading of interest here is effectively impossible to pick out. Further research is obviously needed. Meanwhile, it does not seem unreasonable to suppose that these other constructions conform to the pattern just documented. We therefore state our generalization in its broadest form: indefinites headed by *tētahi* can have wide scope with respect to logical operators in quantificational constructions, but indefinites headed by *he* cannot.

### 2.4.2 The Existential Construction

The two types of indefinites also differ in their ability to serve as pivots of existential sentences. Indefinites headed by *he* can serve as pivots; indefinites headed by *tētahi* cannot. As far as we know, this contrast has not been observed before, so we discuss it in some depth.

The syntax of the existential construction in Maori may seem intricate at first glance. On the surface, there are three sentence types to consider: affirmative existentials, their archaic counterparts, and negative existentials. Significantly, all of these sentence types exhibit the contrast we are interested in.[4]

In Modern Maori, affirmative existential sentences look as though they consist simply of an indefinite noun phrase. These sentences have no overt verb or other predicate, as (29) shows.

(29) a. Āe, he taniwha.
      yes a   taniwha
      'Yes, there are taniwhas.' (Bauer 1993, 78)
   b. He aituā    i  runga i  te huarahi i  te ata       nei.
      a  accident at top     at the road    in the morning this
      'There was an *accident* on the road this morning.' (H. M. Ngata 1994, 3)
   c. He tuna no   roto  i    nga    awa, ā,   he manu no   runga
      a   eel  T.of inside DO the.pl river and a  bird  T.of top
      i    nga    maunga.
      DO the.pl mountain
      'There were eels in the rivers and birds in the ranges.' (Jones and Biggs 1995, 195 [27.3])

The lone indefinite noun phrase in this sentence type is a DP, since it can have a possessor in its specifier. In such cases, the construction expresses existential 'have' (see, e.g., Keenan 1987).

(30) a. He mana tipua     o  Māui.
      a   power abnormal of Maui
      'Maui possessed *abnormal* powers.' (H. M. Ngata 1994, 1)
   b. He tūtohutanga       a  te rīpoata mo nga     mahi kai te
      a   recommendation of the report  T.of the.pl deed    T
      heke     mai.
      go.down to.here
      'The report makes (= has) *recommendations* for future action.'
      (H. M. Ngata 1994, 381)

We think that existentials of this type are most plausibly analyzed as clauses with a null existential verb that takes the lone indefinite noun phrase as its argument. But for our purposes, it does not much matter what analysis is adopted. What is important is that the lone indefinite must be an indefinite headed by *he* (see, e.g., Bauer 1993, 78, and 1997, 34–35). More generally, affirmative existentials can be formed only with *he*, not with *tētahi* or—for that matter—any other determiner.[5]

Although affirmative existentials do not display an overt existential verb in Modern Maori, an overt verb was evidently present at an earlier stage of the language. The nineteenth-century scholars H. W. Williams (1971[1844]) and W. L. Williams (1923[1862]) cite examples in which affirmative existential sentences are formed with the verb *ai* '(there) is', which is now viewed as archaic.[6] This verb, revealingly, is homophonous with the oblique pronoun *ai*, some of whose functions resemble functions of English *there* (see, e.g., Chapin 1974). The examples in (31) are cited by W. L. Williams. Notice that in (31b), a tensed form of the possessor PP also occurs and the construction expresses existential 'have'.

(31) a. ki te ai    he toki
      if   exist a   axe
      'if there should be an axe' (W. L. Williams 1923[1862], 40)
   b. Ka ai    he toki mā-na.
      T exist a   axe T.of-him
      'There is an axe for him (= He has an axe).' (W. L. Williams 1923[1862], 40)

The relevant point is that in both of these examples, *ai*'s argument is an indefinite headed by *he*. Interestingly, there are hints in the literature that this indefinite had to be headed by *he* as opposed to any other determiner. In his discussion of the Maori constructions commonly used to express 'have', W. L. Williams (1923[1862], 41) describes one such construction as consisting of "the verb *ai* ... followed by the preposition *ma* or *mo*; but this use is permissible only when the noun is preceded by the definitive *he*." The statement suggests that in its existential use, *ai* may well have accepted only *he* indefinites as pivots, just as is the case for the Modern Maori counterparts of this construction (29)–(30).

What about negative existential sentences? These consist of a negative verb—most usually, *kāhore* or its variant *kāore*—that selects an indefinite noun phrase as argument.[7] Consider:

(32) a. Kāhore he taniwha.
      T.not    a   taniwha
      'There are no taniwhas.' (Bauer 1993, 78)
   b. ānō kāore he kino i waenganui i     a       rātou
      as.if T.not a bad at between    DO Pers them
      'as if there were no quarrel between them' (Jones and Biggs 1995, 285 [45.12])
   c. Kāore he take    kotahi.
      T.not   a    reason one
      'There's no reason at all.'
   d. Kāore he take    i tua      atu i       tēnā?
      T.not   a    reason at behind away DO that
      'Is there no reason beyond that?' (Karetu 1974, 165)

As might be expected by this point, the indefinite noun phrase can have a possessor as its specifier, in which case the construction expresses the negation of existential 'have'.

(33) a. Kāore kē    he tamariki ake a Te Puea.
       T.not instead a children own of Te Puea
       'Te Puea had no children of her own.' (Karetu 1974, 97)
   b. Kaore he hua o te manei   o te utu i nga tikanga
       T.not a fruit of the fluctuate of the price at the.pl arrangement
       whakatakoto kaupapa moni.
       make.lie      plan      money
       '*Fluctuating* prices do not help (= have no benefit in) budgeting.'
       (H. M. Ngata 1994, 159)
   c. Na te aha i kore ai   he moko o tana kauae me ana ngutu.
       why?       T not Pro a tattoo of his chin with his.pl lip
       'Why he was not tattooed (= had no tattoos) on the chin and lips.' (Jones and Biggs 1995, 289 [46.6])

Once again, the key question is what sorts of indefinites can be the argument of *kāhore* in its existential use. The answer offered by native speakers and supported by textual sources is that *he* indefinites can serve this function, but *tētahi* indefinites cannot.[8]

(34) a.    *Kāhore ētahi taniwha.
         T.not a.pl taniwha
         ('There are no taniwhas.')
   b.    *Kāore tētahi take kotahi.
         T.not a      reason one
         ('There's no reason at all.')
   c.    *Kāore tētahi take i tua atu i tēnā?
         T.not a     reason at behind away DO that
         ('Isn't there any reason beyond that?')
   d.    ?*/*Kāore kē      ētahi tamariki ake a Te Puea.
         T.not instead a.pl children own of Te Puea
         ('Te Puea had no children of her own.')

The overall contrast seems clear: indefinites headed by *he* can serve as pivots of existential sentences, but indefinites headed by *tētahi* cannot.

## 2.5 Our Account

Why does Maori have two indefinite articles? The most interesting answer, it seems to us, is that the choice of *he* versus *tētahi* is correlated with some single semantic contrast among indefinites. Such a hypothesis is intuitively appealing. It would explain why there are contexts of use in which these articles are not interchangeable. The puzzle is what the relevant contrast could be.

Since Karttunen 1976, three semantic contrasts have figured prominently in the literature on indefinites: "specific" versus "nonspecific," "referential" versus "quantificational," and "wide scope" versus "narrow scope." (In the following, we set aside the complicated issue of whether indefinites also permit intermediate scope, since the relevant Maori facts are not available to us. For general discussion, see among others Abbott 1976, Farkas 1981, Fodor and Sag 1982, Abusch 1993–4, Reinhart 1997, Winter 1997, and Kratzer 1998.) A moment's reflection is enough to reveal that none of these contrasts offers a transparent solution to the distributional puzzle that Maori presents us with.

Take the contrast "referential" versus "quantificational" as an example. These terms characterize the two interpretations that Fodor and Sag (1982) claim are available to indefinites. Referential indefinites are interpreted as referring expressions—individual constants—whereas quantificational indefinites are interpreted as existentially quantified. The difference correlates with a difference in scope-taking behavior. Because quantificational indefinites have scope but referential indefinites are scope-insensitive, only quantificational indefinites can have narrow scope with respect to another operator.

This difference is enough to make it clear that the choice of *tētahi* versus *he* is not transparently correlated with whether the indefinite has a referential or a quantificational interpretation. In Maori, both *he* and *tētahi* can introduce a quantificational indefinite—an indefinite that has narrow scope with respect to an(other) operator. But if that is so, then it seems unlikely that these articles transparently encode the contrast "referential" versus "quantificational."

For essentially the same reason, the choice of *tētahi* versus *he* is not transparently correlated with whether the indefinite has wide or narrow scope. Nor, evidently, is the choice correlated with specificity. Matters here are complicated by the different understandings of the terms *specific* and *nonspecific*, which we will not attempt to choose among (see, e.g., Farkas 1995 for an overview). But if we assume that narrow scope indefinites are nonspecific, then we are led again to the same conclusion. Because both *he* and *tētahi* are nonspecific in some contexts, it seems unlikely that they encode the contrast "specific" versus "nonspecific."

More generally, what prevents these familiar contrasts from being useful to us in their pure form is the high degree of overlap between *tētahi* and *he*. (For similar observations, see Bauer 1997, 151–152 and 165–166.) This overlap includes referential, specific, wide scope uses (see section 2.3.1) as well as quantificational, nonspecific, narrow scope uses (see section 2.3.2). The nature of the overlap is such that none of the familiar contrasts have much to contribute to an understanding of why one article is used as opposed to the other. If the choice of *he* versus *tētahi* is indeed correlated with some general semantic contrast among types of indefinites, then the contrast must be one that has not been investigated before.

### 2.5.1 Restrict versus Specify

We claim that the choice of *he* versus *tētahi* signals which composition operation is used to enter the meaning of the indefinite into semantic composition. *He* signals that the indefinite is composed via the nonsaturating mode Restrict; *tētahi* signals that the indefinite is composed via the type-shifting mode Specify. In other words, these two articles serve as morphological flags for the modes of composition available to semantically incomplete DPs. Such a proposal offers a novel solution to the puzzle we have just posed. Because Restrict and Specify often lead to truth-conditionally equivalent results, an account in which each is flagged by a different article will have no trouble dealing with the fact that in many contexts, the articles seem interchangeable.

We now present the specifics of our account. We deal first with the semantic similarity of *he* and *tētahi* and then with the contrasts between them.

Section 2.3 documented two respects in which *he* and *tētahi* are semantically similar: both can introduce a referential argument in episodic sentences, and both can have narrow scope with respect to logical operators. And in fact, Restrict and Specify lead to equivalent results as far as these uses of indefinites are concerned.

Consider first the calculation of the meaning of wide scope indefinites in episodic sentences. If an indefinite is headed by *he*, as in the constructed

# Indefinites in Maori 47

example (35) (compare (15a)), then the property that it supplies must be composed via the nonsaturating mode Restrict.

(35) Ka hopu-kia   e   Rewi [he poaka].
     T  catch-Pass by Rewi a   pig
     'Rewi caught a pig.'

Let us assume for simplicity's sake that passive verbs like *hopu-kia* 'be caught' are two-place predicates (of type $\langle e, \langle e, t \rangle \rangle$), differing from their active counterparts only in the order in which their arguments are targeted for composition. In the construction of the meaning of (35), therefore, the hunter argument of *hopu-kia* 'be caught' will be targeted for composition first, and the prey argument will be targeted second. What interests us is the step of the compositional process when the prey argument is targeted and composed with the indefinite *he poaka* 'a pig'. As *he* demands, Restrict simply adds the property supplied by *poaka* as a restriction on the argument, leaving the argument unsaturated. See (36). (Here and throughout, our semantic translations are Davidsonian; but for clarity, we give semantic types that represent only the participant arguments, not the event argument.)

(36)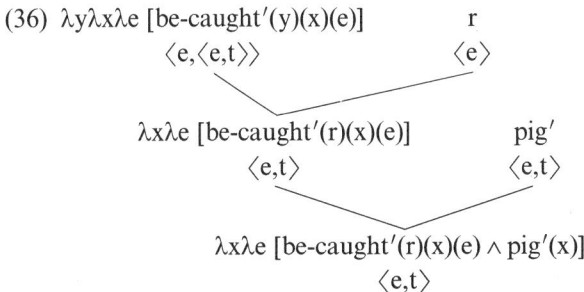

On the other hand, if an indefinite is headed by *tētahi*, as in (37)—a constructed example minimally different from (35)—then the property that it supplies must be composed via the type-shifting mode Specify.

(37) Ka hopu-kia   e   Rewi [tētahi poaka].
     T  catch-Pass by Rewi a      pig
     'Rewi caught a pig.'

Once again, let us move immediately to the relevant step of the compositional process. As *tētahi* demands, Specify targets the prey argument and type-shifts the property supplied by *poaka* to an individual—more precisely, to a "free function variable that assigns an individual to the restriction predicate" (Winter 1997, 409), where the variable in question ranges over choice functions (see Reinhart 1997; Winter 1997). In this case, the free function variable assigns a pig individual to the property supplied by *poaka*. Function application then composes the individual with the argument, saturating the argument. The degree of unsaturation of the predicate *hopu-kia* 'be caught' is correspondingly reduced by one. This combination of choice function followed by function application is the mode of composition that we call Specify. All this is shown in (38). (In the examples below, we use *f* to represent a variable over choice functions.)

(38)

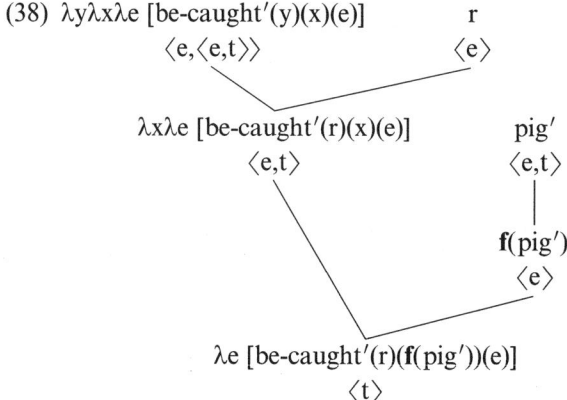

A glance at the derivations in (36) and (38) makes two things clear. First, Restrict and Specify do indeed differ in their immediate impact on the composition: Specify saturates the targeted argument, but Restrict does not. Second, even though all the predicate's participant arguments are saturated in (38), both derivations are still incomplete. (36) is incomplete because the argument targeted by Restrict remains unsaturated; (38) is incomplete because the function variable is free.

Our theory claims that both sorts of incompleteness are resolved by the same mechanism: existential closure. In (36), existential closure of a type e argument steps in to amnesty the unsaturation of the argument, with the result that the predicate is now fully saturated: all of its participant arguments have achieved semantic completeness. The result, following existential closure of the event argument, is a proposition that is true in the model M if and only if there is an eventuality of the catching type involving Rewi and a pig individual in M.

(39) ∃e∃x [be-caught′(r)(x)(e) ∧ pig′(x)]
⟨t⟩

In (38), the predicate is already fully saturated as far as its participant arguments are concerned. Existential closure steps in to bind the free function variable. Once the event argument is closed as well, the result is a well-formed proposition. This proposition too is true in the model M if and only if there is an eventuality of the catching type involving Rewi and a pig individual (supplied by some choice function) in M. (Here we illustrate the option where the choice function variable is closed at the highest level.)

(40) ∃f∃e [be-caught′(r)(f(pig′))(e)]
⟨t⟩

In these cases, in other words, Restrict and Specify lead to completely equivalent results.

Consider next the calculation of the meaning of narrow scope indefinites in quantificational constructions.

In Discourse Representation Theory, quantifiers relate a domain (the restriction) to a claim about the domain (the nuclear scope). Quantification constructions therefore have a tripartite logical structure. Following Kamp (1981), Heim (1982), and many others, we take the varying quantificational force of indefinites in these constructions, first observed by Lewis (1975), to follow from two assumptions. First, indefinites have no inherent quantificational force, as is suggested by their treatment as restricted free variables. Second, indefinites in quantificational constructions can inherit their quantificational force by relating to the operator in a predictable way. Indefinites in the restriction can act as if bound by the operator, either because the operator binds unselectively (as in Heim 1982) or because the restriction is existentially closed (see Kratzer 1995, 158). Indefinites in the nuclear scope can be existentially closed within that scope. The result, in both cases, is the narrow scope reading of indefinites.

This thumbnail sketch is enough to reveal why narrow scope is possible for indefinites in quantificational constructions whether they are composed via Restrict or via Specify. As we have noted, each composition operation gives rise to some semantic incompleteness—each leaves some relevant variable unbound. When existential closure intervenes within the tripartite structure to remedy this incompleteness, the narrow scope reading of the indefinite emerges.

For instance, in the constructed conditional in (41) (compare (20d)), the quantification is over cases and both types of indefinites occur in the restriction.

(41) Ka kite-a [he tohora] e [tētahi kaititiro], ka karanga atu rātou.
T see-Pass a whale by a lookout T call away they
'If a lookout spotted a whale, they would call out.'

Let us focus for the moment on the semantic composition of the restriction. First, Specify targets the perceiver argument, type-shifts the property supplied by *kaititiro* 'lookout' to an individual, and composes that with the argument. The perceiver argument is now saturated, by a function variable that happens to be free. Next, Restrict targets the object-of-perception argument and composes it with the property supplied by *tohora* 'whale', leaving the argument unsaturated. The compositional process has now reached the event level, so existential closure must apply. Closure binds the free function variable and saturates the object-of-perception argument, as shown in (42).

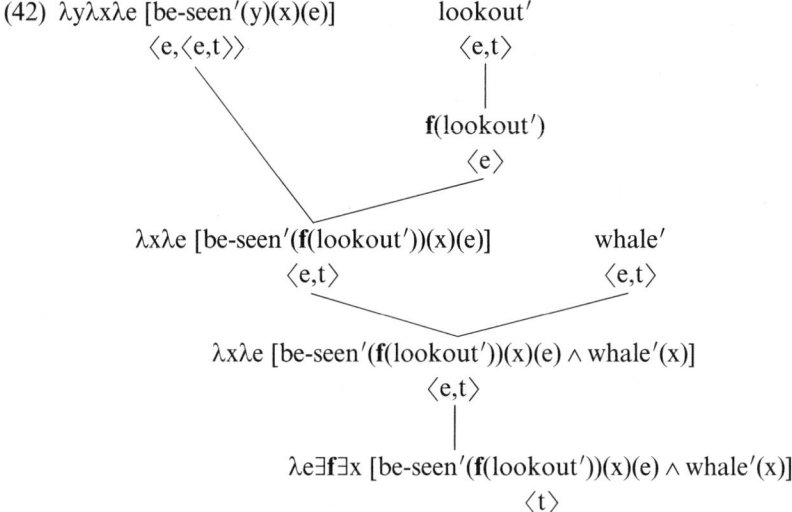

(42)

The ultimate result will be that both indefinites have narrow scope with respect to the quantification over cases. (Unselective binding within the restriction would produce comparable results.) The proposition corresponding to (41) is true in the model M if and only if every case of the seeing sort involving a lookout and a whale in M is also a case of the calling sort in M.

The compositional process works similarly for indefinites in the nuclear scope (see (21)–(23)), though we do not show this here. The generalization should be clear by now: existential closure within the tripartite structure of quantification leads to narrow scope for an indefinite, whether the indefinite has been composed via Restrict or via Specify.

We are now ready to proceed to the two contrasts documented in section 2.4: *tētahi* but not *he* can have wide scope with respect to operators in quantificational constructions, and *he* but not *tētahi* can introduce the pivot of an existential sentence. Crucially, Restrict and Specify are *not* equivalent as far as these uses of indefinites are concerned. Only Specify can lead to wide scope for an indefinite, and only Restrict can be used in the existential construction.

To see why, consider first the issue of wide scope in quantificational constructions. We have just finished discussing the role of existential closure in producing narrow scope indefinites in these constructions. From that discussion, it should be evident what must happen in order for an indefinite to have wide scope with respect to the operator: it must be able to evade closure within the tripartite structure of quantification. The next question is under what circumstances closure can be evaded.

In our theory, semantic composition cannot proceed past the event level unless every argument of the predicate is saturated (see sections 1.4 and 1.5). That is how we capture the intuition that an event must have all its required participants in order to count as semantically complete. Notice that it does not matter whether the predicate's arguments are saturated via composition with an expression or via existential closure. What is important is that one way or another, every argument of the predicate must achieve saturation at the event level.

Now, arguments targeted by Specify automatically satisfy this requirement: they are saturated. But arguments targeted by Restrict can meet the demand only by submitting to existential closure at the event level. The practical consequence is that indefinites composed via Restrict never have an opportunity to take scope outside the tripartite structure of quantification, because the arguments with which they have been composed are required to be saturated, and therefore must be existentially closed, at an earlier stage of composition.

What about the free function variable introduced by Specify? Both the Reinhart-Winter view and the Kratzer-Matthewson view of such choice function variables allows for them to be grounded at the highest level. We assume, with Reinhart (1997) and Winter (1997), that the choice function can be existentially closed at any point. This assumption is crucial in allowing *tētahi* to have narrow scope with respect to other operators. (Hence, our analysis is inconsistent with the restrictions imposed by Kratzer (1998) and Matthewson (1999).) The closure of these function variables follows from a well-formedness condition on the output of semantic composition, not a requirement imposed at any specific intermediate stage of the compositional process. When this view is combined with the assumption that existential closure is optional (i.e., nonexhaustive), the result is that the full range of scope possibilities is open to indefinites composed via Specify. The reason is that the free function variable introduced by Specify can be closed at any point where closure is made available.

As an illustration, consider the constructed example in (43), in which the *tētahi* indefinite can have wide or narrow scope with respect to negation (compare (23c) and (27a)).

(43) Kāore tētahi tangata i mahi.
　　 T.not  a     person  T work
　　 'No one worked./A particular person didn't work.'

Suppose the indefinite is composed via Specify, as *tētahi* demands. Then existential closure can step in to bind the free function variable either at the event level or after the negation has been composed. The first option leads to (44a); the second, to (44b).

(44) a. $\neg \exists f \exists e \, [\text{work}'(f(\text{person}'))(e)]$
　　 b. $\exists f \, \neg \exists e \, [\text{work}'(f(\text{person}'))(e)]$

On the other hand, if the indefinite in (43) were replaced by a *he* indefinite (see (28b)), then the only possible composition would be (45). After this indefinite was composed via Restrict, the requirement that all the predicate's arguments must be saturated at the event level would force the targeted argument to be existentially closed at that level.

(45) $\neg \exists e \exists x \, [\text{work}'(x)(e) \wedge \text{person}'(x)]$

Finally, let us turn to the second contrast between *he* and *tētahi*: *he* indefinites can be pivots of existential sentences, but *tētahi* indefinites cannot.

Since the work of McNally (1992), there has been a growing consensus among semanticists that the definiteness effect exhibited by the pivot of the existential construction is best accounted for by assuming that the pivot must have a property as its content (see, e.g., Farkas 1997; van

Geenhoven 1998; de Swart 2001). McNally encodes this requirement directly in the type structure of the existential verb (for similar proposals, see Musan 1996; Dobrovie-Sorin 1997). We likewise assume that the definiteness effect is due to a requirement that the pivot must be a property. However, for reasons that will become clear in chapter 3, we do not enforce this in the type assignment to the existential predicate. We propose instead that the only composition operation that can target the internal argument of the existential verb is Restrict.

Once this proposal is in place, it follows immediately that other composition operations cannot target this argument. In particular, Specify cannot. We illustrate the point with the compositions of (32a) and (34a), which are repeated here.

(32) a. Kāhore he taniwha.
    T.not  a  taniwha
    'There are no taniwhas.' (Bauer 1993, 78)

(34) a. *Kāhore ētahi taniwha.
    T.not  a.pl  taniwha
    ('There are no taniwhas.')

Suppose we assume that *kāhore* means 'not exist', where the negation in question is sentential negation (see chapter 3). Then the composition of (32a), omitting types, is (46).

(46) λx [exist′(x)]          monster′(x)

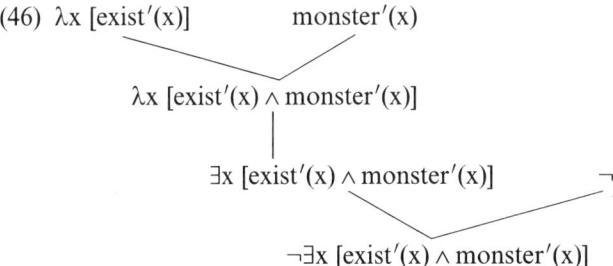

As shown in (47), the composition of (34a) does not proceed past the initial step, because the existential verb's demand that its argument must be composed via Restrict is not satisfied.

(47) λx [exist′(x)]          monster′(x)

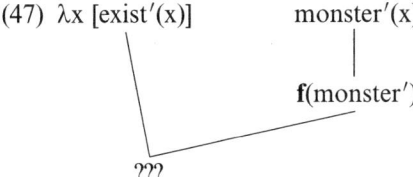

Summing up, the theory of restriction and saturation accounts straightforwardly for the semantic similarities and differences between *he* and *tētahi*. It does so by identifying each article with a different mode of composition available to indefinites.

### 2.5.2 Some Approaches Not Taken
At this juncture, it seems appropriate to ask whether the distribution of *he* and *tētahi* could also be accounted for *without* appealing to a difference in composition operations. We observed earlier that the choice between these two articles is not transparently correlated with any of the familiar semantic contrasts "referential" versus "quantificational," "wide scope" versus "narrow scope," or "specific" versus "nonspecific." But could *he* and *tētahi* be paired with these familiar notions in some other, more successful way?

We think the answer is no. The problem we see is this: any appeal to familiar notions that is flexible enough to allow *he* and *tētahi* to overlap will be unable to account for the differences between them. As illustrations of the point, here are two plausible alternatives to our account. Both alternatives assume that there is just one composition operation: function application. Our claim is that in the end, both prove to be unsatisfactory.

Our first alternative is that *he*—like English bare plurals—must have narrow scope, but *tētahi*—like English *a*—has no scope restrictions.

Such an alternative could account for the distribution of *he*, if we assume that the requirement of narrow scope is vacuously satisfied when no quantification is involved. Then the "wide" scope uses of *he* in episodic sentences would pose no difficulty; they would simply be reconfigured as (vacuously) narrow scope uses. The narrow scope uses of *he* in quantificational constructions would follow automatically. So would *he*'s ability to introduce pivots of existential sentences, which necessarily have narrow scope (see Heim 1987), and its inability to have wide scope with respect to operators such as negation.

Where this alternative would fail is in accounting for the distribution of *tētahi*—specifically, its inability to introduce pivots of existential sentences. If *tētahi* had no scope restrictions at all, then it should be compatible with the pivot, just like English *a*. But *tētahi* is excluded from the pivot, as we showed in section 2.4.2.

Our second alternative involves type-shifting, either as a free option or as a last resort. It goes like this: Indefinites headed by *he* denote properties ($\langle e,t \rangle$), whereas indefinites headed by *tētahi* denote generalized quantifiers ($\langle \langle e,t \rangle, t \rangle$). Any type mismatches encountered in the semantic composition of these indefinites can be remedied by the type-shifting operations proposed by Partee (1987).

Such an alternative could account for all the uses of indefinites for which *he* and *tētahi* seem interchangeable. The reason is obvious: whenever an indefinite might seem to be of the wrong type to be composed via function application, the mismatch would be remedied by type-shifting. For instance, even though *he* indefinites would denote properties, they could be composed with the arguments of typical predicates (e.g., *read*) once they had been type-shifted to generalized quantifiers by Partee's operation A, which takes properties to generalized quantifiers.

The difficulty with such an account is that it would be too successful. Type-shifting might well enable *he* to take wide scope with respect to operators in quantificational constructions, even though wide scope is, in fact, not an option. Type-shifting would certainly enable *tētahi* to introduce the pivot of an existential sentence, even if we assume, with McNally (1992), that the internal argument of the existential verb must have a property as its content. The type mismatch would simply be remedied by Partee's BE, which takes generalized quantifiers to properties.

More generally, Maori seems to us to pose a dilemma for approaches to semantic composition in which there is just one composition operation—function application—and mismatches are remedied by type-shifting, either freely or as a last resort. The dilemma is that there are uses of indefinites in this language for which the repair strategy of type-shifting must be turned off.

The theory of restriction and saturation avoids this dilemma, because it recognizes multiple composition operations and thereby allows for the possibility that the morphosyntax might signal which composition operation to employ. In our account of Maori, the claim that *he* indefinites must be composed by Restrict entails that no other composition operation can be substituted. The same is true for *tētahi* indefinites and Specify. In our view, the success of this account provides some compelling empirical motivation for our theory.

## 2.6 Two Further Semantic Contrasts

If our account of *he* and *tētahi* is correct, it should generalize to all contrasts between the two, even when other factors are also at play. To suggest that this is so, we now survey the other contrasts that we are aware of, and argue that they either follow from our account or are compatible with it.

This section deals with two syntactic-semantic contrasts between *he* and *tētahi* that are well known from the literature on Maori. The first involves the ability of indefinites to serve as subjects; the second, their ability to serve as predicates. The next section deals with two pragmatic contrasts.

**2.6.1 A Constraint on Subjects**

Now is the time to acknowledge that the two types of Maori indefinites are not equally free to serve as subjects of clauses. Setting aside existential sentences and other impersonal constructions, every Maori predicate can have a subject headed by *tētahi*, but not every predicate can have a subject headed by *he*. This pattern has been the focus of some attention since it was first observed by Kenneth Hale and Patrick W. Hohepa in MIT class lectures in 1969 (see, e.g., Chung 1978, 73–74; Hooper 1984, 44; Polinsky 1992; Bauer 1993, 356; Biggs 1997, 2–4; Bauer 1997, 149–150). Our presentation of the facts basically follows Chung, Mason, and Milroy 1995, 437–441 (henceforth CMM), although we take some shortcuts.

The basic descriptive generalization is that in episodic sentences, no subject that is an external argument can be introduced by *he*. This constraint has a direct impact on the three types of Maori predicates whose subject is an external argument: transitive verbs, unergative verbs, and individual-level predicates.

(a) In Maori, the subject of an (active) transitive verb is always an external argument. Hale and Hohepa originally noticed that when the subject of these verbs is indefinite, the indefinite can be headed by *tētahi* but not *he*. Compare (48) and (49).

(48) a. I whiu tētahi wahine i tāna mōkai ki te moana.
T throw a woman DO her pet into the ocean
'A woman threw her youngest child into the ocean.' (CMM 1995, 431)

b. Ka mutu te tōhi ki te Kuini, ka whai ake ētahi atu tōhi.
T ended the toast to the Queen T follow up a.pl away toast
'When the toast to the Queen was over, other toasts followed it.'
(Waititi 1974, 74)

c. Ka kī tētehi, nā-na    te tāne.
   T  say a       T.of-her the man
   'One said he (lit. the man) was hers.' (Jones and Biggs 1995, 117 [15.13])

(49) *I whiu he wahine i   tāna mōkai ki   te moana.
     T throw a  woman DO her  pet      into the ocean
     ('A woman threw her youngest child into the ocean.') (CMM 1995, 437)

(b) In Maori, the unergative verbs include intransitive verbs that denote speaking or communication, intentional activity, or manner of motion.[9] CMM observe that for these verbs too, the subject cannot be an indefinite headed by *he*. Compare the grammatical sentences in (50), in which the subjects are *tētahi* indefinites, with the ungrammatical sentences in (51).

(50) a. E kōrero ana tētahi wahine.
        T speak       a      woman
        'A woman was speaking.'
     b. E mahi ana tētahi tangata.
        T work     a       person
        'A man is working.' (CMM 1995, 431)
     c. Ka katakata ētahi, ka umere   ētahi, ka kohete ētahi.
        T  laugh    a.pl   T applaud a.pl   T scold    a.pl
        'Some laughed, some applauded, some scolded.' (Waititi 1974, 86)

(51) a. ?*E kōrero ana he wahine.
        T speak       a  woman
        ('A woman was speaking.') (CMM 1995, 439)
     b. ?*E mahi ana he tangata.
        T work     a  person
        ('A man is working.') (CMM 1995, 431)

(c) Finally, consider the individual-level predicates of Maori. These, we assume, include all noun phrase predicates, the prepositional phrase predicates headed by the tensed forms of the possessor prepositions, most adjectives, and a very few verbs (e.g., *mōhio* 'know'; see CMM).[10] The observation that the subjects of these predicates cannot be indefinites headed by *he* goes back to Hohepa (1969, 15), who cast it in somewhat different terms. Notice, once again, that indefinites headed by *tētahi* are allowed.

(52) a. Ko   Kawiti tētahi o ngā    tino rangatira o Ngā Puhi.
       Ident Kawiti a      of the.pl very chief      of Ngā Puhi
       'One of the true leaders of Ngā Puhi was Kawiti.' (*Ngā Tāngata Taumata Rau* 1990, 32)
    b. He    wai   Māori   hoki tētahi mea  i mau-ria.
       Pred.a water ordinary also a       thing T take-Pass
       'Another thing that was taken was fresh water.' (Waititi 1974, 117)
    c. Nā-na     tētehi tamāhine pai      rawa.
       T.of-him a      daughter excellent indeed
       'He had a most beautiful daughter.' (Orbell 1992, 147)
    d. He     porohita ētahi pōro.
       Pred.a round    a.pl  football
       'Some *footballs* are round.' (H. M. Ngata 1994, 161)
    e. Ka mōhio-tia  e  Pita tētahi mahi     toi.
       T  know-Pass by Pita a      practice art
       'Pita will understand a skill.'

(53) a. *Ko    Kawiti he tino rangatira o  Ngā Puhi.
        Ident Kawiti a  very chief      of Ngā Puhi
        ('A true leader of Ngā Puhi was Kawiti.')
     b. *Nō      Te Arawa he rangatira.
        T.of Te Arawa a  chief
        ('The Te Arawa tribe had a leader.')
     c. *I  makariri he kōhatu.
        T cold       a  stone
        ('A stone was cold.') (CMM 1995, 447)
     d. *Ka mōhio-tia  e  Pita he mahi     toi.
        T  know-Pass by Pita a  practice art
        ('Pita will understand a skill.') (cf. CMM 1995, 447)

Importantly, whatever constraint is responsible for the ungrammaticality of (49), (51), and (53) does not extend to subjects that are internal arguments. That is why, when we discussed wide scope indefinites in episodic sentences in section 2.3.1, all the standard Maori examples that we cited involved subjects that are internal arguments: subjects of passive verbs, unaccusative predicates, or prepositional phrase predicates of location. A few more examples are given in (54) and (55).[11]

(54) a. Ka karakia-tia    e   ia    i   reira ētehi rākau kahikatea e ono.
       T   enchant-Pass by him at there a.pl  tree   kahikatea T six
       'He bewitched (some) six kahikatea trees there.' (Jones and
       Biggs 1995, 223 [32.4])
   b. Ka whati mai     tētahi ngaru tino nui.
      T  break to.here a     wave  very big
      'An enormous wave broke.' (Waititi 1974, 121)
   c. Kei roto  ētahi o ngā    hipi   i    ngā   awaawa.
      T.at inside a.pl of the.pl sheep DO the.pl valley
      'Some of the sheep were in the valleys.' (Waititi 1974, 16)

(55) a. I  konei ka whakatō-kia e   Hoturoa he pōhutukawa.
       at here  T  plant-Pass  by Hoturoa a  pohutukawa
       'Here Hoturoa planted a pohutukawa.' (Jones and Biggs 1995,
       49 [3.69])
   b. Tuhera ana mai    he ara   mō-na     i  te  wai.
      open       to.here a  road T.of-him at the water
      'A path opened up for him through the water.' (Orbell 1992, 42)
   c. I   roto  i   te kirimini   he tikanga    kia kauā e
      T.at inside DO the agreement a  arrangement T  not  T
      neke-hia  te whare.
      move-Pass the house
      'Contained in the *agreement* was a condition not to move the
      house.' (H. M. Ngata 1994, 9)

What is the account of this pattern? We think that the most promising approach is to attribute the ungrammaticality of (49), (51), and (53) to a language-particular specificity constraint. It is well known that there are languages of the world that demand that subjects must be specific in some sense (see, e.g., Reuland 1987 and Diesing 1992, 80–84, on Dutch). What is less commonly recognized is that there are also languages that impose this requirement only on certain subtypes of subjects. For instance, Chamorro has a specificity constraint that affects only subjects that are external arguments—the subjects that could be viewed as prototypical (see Chung 1998, 111–117). What is striking about the Chamorro constraint is that the types of predicates affected are essentially the same as the Maori predicates whose subjects cannot be introduced by *he*.

Our hypothesis, then, is that Maori demands that the external argument must be specific. This constraint permits the external argument to be composed with indefinites headed by *tētahi*, since these indefinites are plausibly viewed as specific in our account: they are composed as individuals. But the constraint forbids the external argument to be composed with indefinites headed by *he*, because these indefinites are not specific: they are composed as properties.

For this hypothesis to be convincing, the specificity constraint must draw the right distributional distinctions not just for indefinites but for all other types of noun phrases as well. We think it does this, and for an interesting reason: there are no other types of Maori noun phrases that are plausibly characterized as nonspecific. The language has no negative noun phrases or noun phrases headed by weak quantifiers such as 'many' and 'few', because those operators are expressed as higher predicates, not noun phrase internally (see Bauer 1997, 290–300). We mentioned earlier that Maori does have universally quantified noun phrases. These are plausibly viewed as specific, because their domain of quantification is contextually determined (see Enç 1991, 10–11). Consistent with this, universally quantified noun phrases can occur as external arguments, as (56) shows.

(56) a. I whiwhi [ia    tama] ki ngā    takoha.
       T receive  each boy   to the.pl present
       'Each boy received presents.' (Bauer 1997, 300)
    b. Ka pakipaki [ngā    tāngata katoa].
       T  clap       the.pl people  all
       'Everyone clapped.' (Bauer 1997, 299)

In short, the only Maori noun phrases plausibly characterized as nonspecific are just those that cannot occur as external arguments: namely, indefinites headed by *he*.

There are further intricacies to the specificity constraint, but it would not be productive for us to pursue them here.[12] We therefore simply conclude that in Maori, the external argument must be specific in some sense, and that this demand can be satisfied by indefinites headed by *tētahi* but not *he*. Within our theory, the contrast follows from the fact that indefinites headed by *tētahi* are composed as individuals, but indefinites headed by *he* are not.

### 2.6.2 Two Types of Predicates

Both types of Maori indefinites can serve as predicates of clauses, but there is a difference. In predicate position, indefinites headed by *he* are always predicational (see Polinsky 1992); indefinites headed by *tētahi* are

Indefinites in Maori

always identificational. The semantic generalization glosses over some syntactic complexity that we will not be able to resolve. Nonetheless, it should be clear even at the outset that the semantic generalization is compatible with our account.

We asserted in section 2.1 that clauses in Maori are projected from T, which—among other things—indicates whether a noun phrase predicate is predicational or identificational. Here, in essence, is how the distinction is drawn: noun phrases that are predicational are introduced by *he*, whereas noun phrases that are identificational are introduced by *ko*.

We illustrate the generalization first with identificational predicates, since their syntax is quite straightforward. Clauses with identificational predicates begin with *ko*, which we take to occupy T. *Ko* is followed by the predicate, which is transparently DP, and then by the subject. As mentioned in section 2.1, certain dependents of the predicate XP can occur either within XP or to the right of the subject. We simply ignore this in what follows. Some examples of clauses with identificational predicates are shown in (57). Note that the DP predicate is bracketed.[13]

(57) a. Ko  [koe] anake te  koretake!
       Ident you alone the useless
       'The useless one is you!' (Waititi 1974, 7)
   b. Ko  [Kura] tana ingoa.
       Ident Kura  her  name
       'Her name was Kura.' (Waititi 1974, 40)
   c. Ko  [te wā tuarua] tēnei i tatau hē-tia      ai e koe
       Ident the time second this  T count wrong-Pass Pro by you
       taku utu.
       my   pay
       'This is the second time you have *miscalculated* my pay.' (H. M. Ngata 1994, 280)
   d. Ko  [nga kāinga i  nga  tahatika o Waikato] nga wāhi i
       Ident the.pl village at the.pl bank     of Waikato the.pl place T
       noho ai a    Mahuta.
       live Pro Pers Mahuta
       'The home of Mahuta ... was the villages on the banks of the Waikato River.' (Jones and Biggs 1995, 163 [22.3])

The phrase structure of clauses with identificational predicates seems unproblematic. We assume that it looks like this:

(58)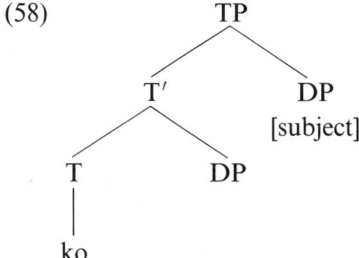

The point of interest is that indefinites headed by *tētahi* can serve as identificational predicates in clauses introduced by *ko*.[14]

(59) a. Ko [tētehi pakanga kaha] tēnā.
  Ident a   battle   strong that
  'It was a fierce battle.' (Jones and Biggs 1995, 369 [64.7])
 b. Ko tōna kāinga ko [tētahi ana i Kaipara].
  Ident its home Ident a   cave at Kaipara
  'As for its home, it was a cave at Kaipara.' (Karetu 1974, 41)

But indefinites headed by *he* cannot. Traditional Maori grammars are quite explicit about the fact that a *he* indefinite cannot occur immediately after *ko* (see, e.g., W. L. Williams 1923[1862], 25; A. T. Ngata 1926, 24). In other words, sentences such as *Ko he pakanga kaha tēnā* (cf. (59a)) are ungrammatical.

The explanation traditionally given for the fact that a *he* indefinite cannot occur immediately after *ko* is that *he* cannot immediately follow a preposition, and *ko* is a preposition (see, e.g., Biggs 1969, 54–56; Bauer 1997, 28, 147). However, the evidence for treating identificational *ko* as a preposition is slight.[15] Just as good an account can be given, we believe, by appealing to the semantics of *ko* as opposed to its syntactic category. Suppose that *ko* has a meaning like the English identificational copula: it expresses a two-place relation between individuals, as shown in (60).

(60) $I(x, y) \leftrightarrow x = y$

Then the ability of *tētahi* indefinites to serve as identificational predicates follows immediately from the fact that they are composed as individuals, via Specify. Similarly, the inability of *he* indefinites to serve as identificational predicates seems natural, given that they are composed as properties, via Restrict.

We turn next to predicational noun phrases, whose syntax is more complicated. Clauses with predicational noun phrase predicates begin

Indefinites in Maori 63

with *he*, whose syntactic category and function here are precisely what is at issue. This *he* is followed by a phrase that is evidently NP as opposed to DP, and then by the subject (see, e.g., Reedy 1979, 31; Polinsky 1992, 233–234; Bauer 1997, 28–29, 147). In the examples in (61), we have arbitrarily chosen to bracket the predicate NP.

(61) a. He    [kōrero ātaahua] tēnā.
Pred.a speech beautiful that
'That's a beautiful saying.' (Karetu 1974, 61)
b. I whakaaro-hia [he    [tohu no    te    mate] te    ngārara].
T think-Pass    Pred.a sign T.of the death the lizard
'*Lizards* were often regarded as (lit. it was thought that lizards were) omens of death.' (H. M. Ngata 1994, 259)
c. He    [whanaunga] a    Mōtai-tangata-kotahi ki a
Pred.a relation    Pers Mōtai-tangata-kotahi to Pers
Tū-parahaki.
Tū-parahaki
'Mōtai was related (lit. a relative) to Tū-parahaki.' (Jones and Biggs 1995, 151 [20.3])
d. He    [tohunga]    ia e mōhio ana ki nga    mahi mākutu.
Pred.a skilled.person he T know    to the.pl work bewitch
'He was a priest skilled in black magic.' (Jones and Biggs 1995, 221 [32.2])

Now because *he* occurs first in the clause and is followed by an NP constituent, two syntactic analyses are possible in principle: *he* might occupy T, just as *ko* does, or it might be the head of a DP predicate, just like *tētahi* in clauses of type (59). The complication is that each analysis has some evidence supporting it.

The clearest evidence that *he* occupies T in clauses such as those in (61) is that *he* can also introduce predicates that are verbs or adjectives (see, e.g., Reedy 1979, 43–47; Waite 1994; Bauer 1997, 77, 498). This is one standard way to form clauses when the verb or adjective is individual-level, or when it has a generic or habitual interpretation. Consider:

(62) a. Engari ra    koe, he    mōhio ki te    wai    o konei.
but    that you Pred.a know    to the water of here
'But you are knowledgeable about the water here.' (Orbell 1992, 43)
b. He    tika    te kōrero ā    tō    koroua.
Pred.a correct the speech of your grandfather
'What your grandfather said is correct.' (Karetu 1974, 59)

c. He    mate te  taina     o  Hata.
   Pred.a die   the yo.sibling of Hata
   'Hata's younger sister is sickly/*dead.'
d. He    mate tonu ngā   kai o Whakatāne i     te  waipuke.
   Pred.a die   still  the.pl food of Whakatane Cause the flood
   'The crops at Whakatane were always being destroyed by floods.' (Orbell 1992, 42)

It seems clear that one would want to say that the *he* in clauses like these occupies T. That would make it natural to view clauses with predicational noun phrase predicates as consisting of this T followed by an NP predicate (as proposed, in essence, by Reedy (1979, 61)).

On the other hand, there is also evidence that predicational noun phrase predicates are DP predicates headed by *he*. The evidence is that they can have a possessor introduced by one of the prepositions *a* or *o*. If we continue to assume that such possessors occupy the specifier of D (see section 2.1), that would make it natural to view the predicates in (63) as DPs headed by *he*. The bracketing in (63) is intended to suggest this.

(63) a. [He    momo mate    o  te  kiri] te  pāpaka.
        Pred.a type  sickness of the skin the eczema
        '*Eczema* is a skin ailment (lit. ailment of the skin).' (H. M. Ngata 1994, 120)
   b. [He    toa       taua o  Te Ati Awa] tēnei tangata a    Te
      Pred.a champion war  of Te Ati Awa  this  man     Pers Te
      Wharepouri.
      Wharepouri
      'This man Te Wharepouri was a warrior of Te Ati Awa.'
   c. [He    kaipeita rongonui] a    ia  o  te  taiwhenua.
      Pred.a painter  famous   Pers she of the landscape
      'She is a well-known landscape *painter* (lit. painter of landscapes).' (H. M. Ngata 1994, 321)

Conceivably, the most straightforward solution is that predicational noun phrase predicates have a dual syntactic analysis: the *he* that introduces them can be analyzed either as the content of T or as the indefinite article (see Bauer 1997, 29, for a similar conclusion). This solution may or may not be ideal. In any event, the important point for our purposes is that this *he* cannot be replaced by *tētahi*. Sentences such as *Tētahi kōrero ātaahua tēnā* (cf. (61a)) are ungrammatical.

Notice now that if we move away from the syntax and consider the semantics of these clauses, the situation seems much clearer. One would want T, whether its content is *he* or not overt, to have a meaning like the English predicational copula: it should express a two-place relation between an individual $x$ and a property $P$, as shown in (64).

(64) $\Pi(x, P) \leftrightarrow P(x)$

We are now in a position to show that depending on the syntax, the distribution of *he* and *tētahi* here either follows from our account or is consistent with it. Suppose that in clauses with predicational noun phrase predicates, T is not overt and the predicate is a DP. Then the ability of this DP to be a *he* indefinite follows from the fact that *he* indefinites are composed as properties. Similarly, the inability of this DP to be a *tētahi* indefinite follows from the fact that *tētahi* indefinites are composed as individuals, via Specify. On the other hand, suppose that *he* occupies T in clauses of this type. Then the fact that it is homophonous with the indefinite article *he* is presumably no accident: the two are alike in that the expression that is their NP complement must be composed as a property.

In sum, the uses of *he* and *tētahi* to introduce predicates might well follow from our account. At a minimum, they pose no difficulty for it.[16]

### 2.7 A Dash of Pragmatics

The theory of restriction and saturation has something to contribute to an understanding of the pragmatic differences between *he* and *tētahi*. Below, we discuss two differences in the discourse functions, broadly construed, of these indefinites as arguments. Although these differences involve preferences, not absolute requirements, they are nonetheless real, so it is significant that they fit comfortably into our analysis.

#### 2.7.1 In Narrative Discourse

According to CMM (1995, 434), *he* indefinites in narrative discourse cannot be used to introduce characters that are in the spotlight—central focuses of narration. Rather, these indefinites can only be used to introduce characters that are in the background—relatively minor figures. The correctness of this observation is borne out by textual sources (e.g., Orbell 1992; Jones and Biggs 1995; selected portions of *Ngā Tāngata Taumata Rau* 1990). In almost every instance, the characters introduced by *he* indefinites do not play a major role in the narration but are quite unimportant (out of focus). Their insignificance is revealed by the fact that they are usually nameless (though (18a) is an exception) and do not persist in the narrative beyond one or two subsequent mentions.

A typical example is (65), taken from a chapter of Jones and Biggs 1995 that tells the story of Whatihua and his first wife, Rua-pū-tahanga. After Whatihua takes a second wife, Rua-pū-tahanga becomes angry and runs off with their child. He pursues her; she abandons the child and keeps running; he reaches the child. The narrative continues:

(65) Tae    noa  mai    [he tāngata] hei    whakarere-nga iho    mā-na
     arrive only to.here a   people   so.as take-Nmlz      down  T.of-him
     i    tana tamaiti, kua tata te  whiti o  te   wahine ra   i  te
     DO   his  child    T   near the reach of the woman  that to the
     pūaha o Kāwhia.
     mouth of Kawhia
     'When others (lit. people) arrived to take the child, she was almost across the harbour mouth.' (Jones and Biggs 1995, 81 [8.4])

The people introduced by the *he* indefinite in (65) are minor figures, serving only to get the child out of the way as the pursuit continues. They are never referred to again. For similar examples, see CMM 1995, 433–435.

In contrast, *tētahi* indefinites can be used to introduce characters whether they are in the spotlight or in the background. The pair of examples in (66) and (67) is intended to suggest the range of possibilities. In (66), taken from the story of two cannibals, Whare-tīpeti and Tapaue, a *tētahi* indefinite is used to introduce a minor figure. After it is discovered that Whare' and Tapaue have killed people and eaten then, some other men resolve to kill them. The narrative continues:

(66) I tino  ū    ai  rāua      ki ta rāua   take, na   te  patu-nga a
     T very firm Pro they.du   at their.du cause T.of the kill-Nmlz of
     Whare' rāua     ko    Tapaue i   [tētehi], he       whanauga no
     Whare' they.du Ident Tapaue DO  a         Pred.a relative   T.of
     Te Ruinga.
     Te Ruinga
     'Their resolve was strengthened when Whare' and Tapaue killed yet another person, [who was] a kinsman to Te Ruinga.' (Jones and Biggs 1995, 283 [45.8])

Like the people introduced by *he* in (65), the kinsman of Te Ruinga introduced by *tētahi* in (66) is nameless and never mentioned again. The narrative reveals that to the extent that he matters at all, he matters not as a character but as a further instance of a cannibalistic act.

Compare this with (67), the beginning of the biography entry for Te Hiko Pīata Tama-i-hikoia in *Ngā Tāngata Taumata Rau* 1990, in which *tētahi* is used to introduce the central character: Te Hiko himself.

(67) Ko    Te Hiko Pīata Tama-i-hikoia [tētahi tino rangatira o  Te
     Ident Te Hiko Pīata Tama-i-hikoia a       very chief      of Te
     Wairarapa] mai i  te  tau  1840 ki 1880.
     Wairarapa  from at the year 1840 to 1880
     'One of the leading Wairarapa chiefs from the 1840s to the 1880s was Te Hiko Piata Tama-i-hikoia.' (*Ngā Tāngata Taumata Rau* 1990, 189)

These and similar examples make it clear that unlike *he*, *tētahi* in narrative discourse is insensitive to the issue of where the spotlight is focused.

One might wonder whether this particular contrast might follow from a more fundamental semantic contrast, such as the ability to introduce a discourse referent. Suppose, contrary to what we claimed earlier, that *he* indefinites were simply unable to introduce a discourse referent. Subsequent anaphoric reference to them would then be impossible, and they would effectively be limited to characters in the background.

We should emphasize that such a scenario cannot be right. All the evidence known to us argues that *he* and *tētahi* are equally able to introduce a discourse referent. The discourse referents introduced by the two types of indefinites can serve as the antecedents of discourse anaphora, as was shown in section 2.3.1. They can also antecede various kinds of bound variable anaphora, including the null subjects of infinitive clauses (represented as *PRO* in (68)), and donkey pronouns (69).

(68) a. ki te tū   [he wahine] ki te kōrero PRO
        if stand  a  woman    Infin speak
        'if a woman stands up to speak'
     b. Ka haere [ētahi] ki te hoko taonga PRO i  ngā    toa.
        T  go    a.pl    Infin buy  goods        at the.pl store
        'Some people went to buy goods in the stores.' (Waititi 1974, 98)

(69) a. Ki te hoatu e  te  tangata [he takoha] ki a    koe, e
        if    give  by the person  a  gift    to Pers you T
        pīrangi ana ia kia whakaaro koe he     tino tao              pro.
        desire  he  T  think        you Pred.a very precious.thing
        'If a person$_i$ gives you a present$_j$, he$_i$ usually wants you to think it$_j$ is valuable.'

b. Ka kite-a     he tohora e  [tētahi kaititiro], ka whakatū-ria pro
   T  see-Pass a whale    by a       lookout   T  raise-Pass
   te   haki o  tōna kāinga.
   the  flag of his  house
   'If a whale was spotted by a lookout$_i$, he$_i$ would raise the flag of his$_i$ house.' (Waititi 1974, 132)

We return to this issue in chapter 3.

Our theory offers a more promising approach to this difference in the narrative functions of *he* and *tētahi*. Most traditional narrative discourse is about individuals. In such narratives, the usual expectation is that a character in the spotlight is an individual. But it matters far less whether characters in the background are individuated. If we accept this, then the reason why *he* indefinites are not used to introduce characters in the spotlight is that these indefinites are never composed as individuals; they are composed as properties, via Restrict (see Bauer 1997, 148, for a similar suggestion). But because *tētahi* indefinites are composed as individuals, via Specify, they can introduce any of the cast of characters, major or minor.

### 2.7.2 In the Museum

A more minimalist kind of discourse can be found in the museum, on the identifying cards or labels accompanying objects on exhibit. In 1994, we briefly visited the Te Papa Tongarewa Museum of New Zealand in Wellington and spent an enjoyable hour or two in the Maori collection. Objects in the Maori collection are accompanied by identifying labels and descriptive text in two languages, Maori and English. It was the labels that caught our linguistic attention. Whereas the English-language labels almost always consisted of bare NPs (e.g., *Short Club Weapon*, *Shell Trumpet*), the Maori-language labels often consisted of DPs, and many were indefinite. Our informal impression was that there was a significant correlation between the type of indefinite on the label and the nature of the object(s) on display.

Though we have not returned to New Zealand to check the facts more systematically, we are fortunate to have had our initial impression solidified and expanded by some enlightening commentary from the museum staff.[17] On the basis of this, we tentatively characterize the situation as follows. When an object is exhibited alone in a display case or is the only object of its type on display, then it is typically labeled by an indefinite headed by *he*, not *tētahi* (e.g., *He Mere* 'Short Club Weapon',

*He Tiki* 'Greenstone Pendant').[18] On the other hand, when several objects of the same type are exhibited together in a display case, the entire display, or each object in it, is typically labeled by an indefinite headed by *tētahi*, not *he* (e.g., *Ētahi Tiki* 'Greenstone Pendants', *Tētahi Tiki* 'A Greenstone Pendant (in a display of several such pendants)').

Assuming that this contrast is real, it too can be given a rationale in terms of the theory of restriction and saturation. When an object is exhibited on its own, what is highlighted is the prototype that the object represents. Labeling such an object with *he* serves to reinforce this, because *he* indefinites are composed as properties, via Restrict. But when several objects of the same type are exhibited together, what is highlighted is the fact that each object is an (arbitrarily selected) instance of the prototype. Labeling such objects with *tētahi* is appropriate, because *tētahi* indefinites are composed as (relevant but arbitrarily selected) individuals, via Specify.

Given our limited grasp of the museum situation, these remarks are purely speculative. We include them here to make a larger point. There are other real-world situations outside the realm of narrative discourse proper where *he* and *tētahi* contrast. Subtle though these kinds of contrasts are, an analysis in terms of modes of composition has the potential to elucidate them.

## 2.8 Conclusion

We would like to close this chapter by placing our account of Maori indefinites in a somewhat broader perspective.

Our account of *he* and *tētahi* in terms of modes of composition is close in spirit to some other characterizations of these articles that have been offered previously. For instance, Polinsky (1992) attempts to unite the uses of *he* by claiming that it is underspecified for the features [referential] and [definite]. Bauer (1993, 357, and 1997, 172), in her discussions of *he* and *tētahi*, asserts that what is important about these articles is not their (in)definiteness but that *he* focuses on the type of object, whereas *tētahi* focuses on the individual object. Our approach differs from Polinsky's and Bauer's, most notably in affirming that *he* and *tētahi* are indeed indefinite determiners. Nonetheless, it should be clear that all three approaches have some conceptual common ground. Polinsky's characterization of *he* as nonindividuated and Bauer's characterization of *he* in terms of type are close to our notion of predicate restriction. Bauer's characterization of *tētahi* in terms of (the number of) individuals resonates with our appeal to choice functions. Viewed from this perspective, our principal contribution to the analysis of *he* and *tētahi* is to have developed a theory—the theory of restriction and saturation—within which the non-truth-conditional but strongly felt contrast between these articles can be understood.

Of course, if our theory is on the right track, it should generalize beyond *he* and *tētahi* to all cases of morphologically distinguished indefinites whose semantic distribution is more limited than that of indefinites in general. The observation raises a question: what sorts of limited distributions can a language-specific indefinite have, and how successful is our theory at accounting for them?

The question deserves more serious contemplation than we are prepared to give it here. Still, as the beginnings of a response, we now suggest how our approach would handle two further examples of language-specific indefinites with a limited semantic distribution. Our examples are bare plurals in English (see, e.g., Carlson 1977; van Geenhoven 1998) and the two types of indefinites in St'át'imcets (Lillooet Salish; see Matthewson 1999).

It has been known since Carlson 1977 that English bare plurals always have narrow scope with respect to (other) operators (see van Geenhoven 1998, 84–93, and the references cited there). For instance, (70) means that it was not the case that Maxie saw ghosts in the attic, not that there were ghosts in the attic that Maxie didn't see.

(70) Maxie didn't see ghosts in the attic.

In Carlson's view, English bare plurals are names of kinds that acquire an existential interpretation when they combine with a stage-level predicate. Because the predicate both relates the kind to the targeted argument and supplies the existential force of that argument, the bare plural cannot take scope beyond it—it must have narrowest scope. Building on this aspect of Carlson's approach, van Geenhoven (1998) develops a theory of indefinites in which English bare plurals are property-denoting expressions that undergo semantic incorporation: their meaning is "absorbed by a verb as the predicate of that verb's internal argument's variable" (1998, 132). Van Geenhoven's semantic incorporation is discussed further in chapter 3. The important point here is that for her approach, as for Carlson's, the narrow scope of bare plurals follows from the claim that their existential force is contributed by the predicate.

Our approach derives the distinctive narrow scope of bare plurals from their mode of composition. We claim that in English, bare plurals must be composed via the nonsaturating mode Restrict. From this hypothesis, it follows that bare plurals have essentially the same semantic distribution as *he* indefinites in Maori: they can introduce a referential argument in episodic sentences, they must have narrow scope with respect to operators, and so on (see section 2.5).[19] More generally, in recognizing Restrict as a distinct composition operation, our theory provides one way of accounting for language-specific indefinites that must have narrow scope.

A more intricate empirical challenge is presented by the two types of indefinites in St'át'imcets (Lillooet Salish), which are investigated in depth by Matthewson (1999). These indefinites contrast interestingly with the two types of Maori indefinites that have preoccupied us in this chapter. Wide scope indefinites, which are headed by a morphologically complex determiner, must have wide scope with respect to any operator present in the translation. Matthewson establishes convincingly that these expressions are indeed semantically indefinite but cannot have narrow scope, intermediate scope, or distributive readings. Polarity indefinites, which are headed by the determiner *ku*, must meet two requirements: they must occur within the c-command domain of an operator and they must have narrow scope.[20]

The focus of Matthewson's discussion is the wide scope indefinites. She argues for a choice function analysis in which these indefinites introduce a free variable over choice functions—a variable that must undergo existential closure, but only at the highest level. In this way, her analysis invokes the closure mechanism of Reinhart (1997) and Winter (1997), but achieves empirical results far closer to those of Kratzer (1998).

When Matthewson's analysis is recast in terms of our approach, what emerges is the following. We claim that wide scope indefinites in St'át'imcets must be composed via Specify, the type-shifting mode that composes the property supplied by the indefinite as a free variable over choice functions. These indefinites therefore have exactly the same mode of composition as *tētahi* indefinites in Maori. Their distributional differences from *tētahi* indefinites we propose to derive from the workings of existential closure in these two languages. Our hypothesis is that in Maori, closure must be freely available at any point (see section 2.5), whereas in St'át'imcets, closure can intervene only as a last resort, to rescue a composition that would otherwise be ill formed.

More generally, we view it as a language-specific option whether existential closure is implemented freely or only as a last resort. When closure is freely available, as in Maori, the result is the full range of scope possibilities predicted by Reinhart (1997) and Winter (1997) and exhibited by *tētahi* indefinites. When closure is available only as a last resort mechanism, as in St'át'imcets, the result is the obligatorily wide scope predicted by Kratzer (1998) and exhibited by the wide scope indefinites of that language.

The claim that existential closure is parameterized in this way bears on our account of the other indefinites of St'át'imcets: the polarity indefinites headed by *ku*. Recall that these indefinites must both occur within the c-command domain of an operator and have narrow scope. The narrow scope requirement is what is of interest here. According to Matthewson (1999, 122), "it is not yet clear whether *ku* unambiguously forces narrowest scope, or merely disallows widest scope." Significantly, once it is granted that existential closure in St'át'imcets is a last resort, our approach is flexible enough to handle either possibility.

If *ku* forces narrowest scope, we would analyze the narrow scope requirement in terms of mode of composition: polarity indefinites must be composed via Restrict. The narrowest scope of these indefinites would then follow in exactly the same way as for *he* indefinites in Maori. On the other hand, if *ku* merely disallows widest scope, we would analyze the narrow scope requirement in terms of closure: whatever their mode of composition, polarity indefinites must be existentially closed within the scope of an operator. Notice that both possibilities are consistent with the view of closure as a last resort mechanism, invoked only to evade compositional ill-formedness of one kind or another.

In short, our approach allows for a range of language-specific indefinites with limited distributions. The observation raises a question: are there any language-specific systems of indefinites that our approach would rule out? Tantalizingly, the answer seems to be yes. If existential closure is indeed parameterized as we have just proposed, then no language should simultaneously have indefinites of the *tētahi* type and wide scope indefinites of the St'át'imcets type. In other words, no language should have two types of morphologically distinguished indefinites, one of which can occur everywhere except as the pivot of the existential construction, and the other of which must invariably have wide scope. The reason is that in our theory, both types of indefinites would be composed via Specify, differing only in the details of existential closure. But in a given language, closure must either be freely available or be available only as a last resort—not both.

This strikes us as a clear prediction of our approach. We have no idea whether it is correct.

In sum, our approach to indefinites in Maori can be generalized to some other language-specific indefinites with a limited distribution. But it cannot account for every conceivable system of such indefinites. Whether this is a positive or negative aspect of our theory remains to be seen.

In this chapter, we presented some Maori evidence for our theory of restriction and saturation. We argued that the two types of indefinites in Maori differ in their mode of composition: indefinites headed by *he* are entered into composition via Restrict, whereas indefinites headed by *tētahi* are entered into composition via Specify. The difference explains the otherwise puzzling distribution of *he* and *tētahi*—a distribution that involves substantial overlap as well as some telling differences. The analysis confirms a key prediction of our theory. If semantically incomplete noun phrases can be composed via different operations, then one might expect that the morphosyntax could explicitly signal which composition operation to employ. Maori *he* versus *tētahi* offers just such a case.

# Chapter 3
## Object Incorporation in Chamorro

This chapter examines another key prediction of our theory, one introduced by our claim that a predicate can be semantically composed with a noun phrase in a way that does not completely saturate it. On the Fregean view described in chapter 1, semantic incompleteness is a necessary condition for semantic composition. Hence, saturation of a predicate's argument renders it unavailable for further semantic composition.

But our mode of composition Restrict does not saturate a predicate's argument; it only narrows its interpretive domain. The predicate's degree of unsaturation is not reduced. As a result, we might expect a restricted argument to remain available for semantic composition—for further restriction or even for saturation by an additional noun phrase.

Our theory thus leaves open a door usually assumed to be completely closed. Since Frege 1997[1862], semantic approaches to predication have assumed that the composition of an expression with a predicate's argument automatically saturates the argument—makes it semantically complete. The predicate's degree of unsaturation is reduced, and further composition with respect to the argument is precluded. The assumption is pervasive even in the strand of research that seeks to analyze indefinites as property-denoting (for recent examples, see Farkas 1997; van Geenhoven 1998; de Swart 2001).[1] In syntactic approaches to predication, roughly the same assumption can be discerned in the principles that ensure a one-to-one mapping between semantic roles and syntactically characterized expressions, such as Government-Binding's Theta Criterion (Chomsky 1981) and Lexical-Functional Grammar's Completeness and Coherence Principles (Bresnan 1982).

In contrast, we predict that it should be possible for an argument to be linked to, and coherently composed with, more than one expression—a scenario we refer to as *multiple linking*. The possibility arises because our theory distinguishes between composition operations on the one hand and the issue of semantic completeness on the other. But we also claim that the only nonsaturating mode of composition is Restrict, which composes an argument with the property supplied by a semantically incomplete noun phrase. The claim leads to a more refined prediction. For multiple linking to succeed, all expressions composed with the targeted argument, except the last, must be composed via Restrict and hence must be semantically incomplete. Otherwise, the result will be oversaturation of the argument—a forbidden outcome.

Multiple linking, as we have just characterized it, is obviously not the norm. Typically, the syntax and the semantics conspire to make available exactly one expression to be composed with a targeted argument, so that the mapping between arguments and expressions appears to be one to one. We nonetheless believe that multiple linking does occur, under just the conditions predicted by our theory. The purpose of this chapter is to support our contention with evidence from Chamorro, an Austronesian language of the Mariana Islands.

Like many other Austronesian languages, Chamorro has a version of the construction known as object incorporation. Consider (1), in which the incorporating verb is *gäi-* 'have' and the incorporated object is enclosed in brackets. (See appendix B for a list of abbreviations used in the Chamorro examples.)

(1) a. Man-gäi-[ga'] häm.
　　　 Agr-have-pet we
　　　 'We have pets.'
　　b. Hayi gäi-[patgun]?
　　　 who WH[nom].Agr.have-child
　　　 'Who has a child?'

What is distinctive about Chamorro incorporation from an Austronesian perspective is that the incorporated object can be doubled by an independent noun phrase, which we refer to as the *extra object*. In (2), the extra object is italicized.

(2) a. Gäi-[ga']　　 yu' *kätu*, lao matai.
　　　 Agr.have-pet I　 cat　 but Agr.die
　　　 'I had a pet cat, but it died.'
　　b. Hayi gäi-[patgun]　　　　 *hao*?
　　　 who? WH[nom].Agr.have-child you
　　　 'Whose child are you (lit. Who has a child, namely, you)?'

This chapter investigates the syntax and semantics of Chamorro object incorporation, with the goal of establishing three points. First, the incorporated object is semantically incomplete in our terms: it denotes a property rather than an individual or a generalized quantifier. It can therefore be composed via the nonsaturating mode Restrict. Second, the extra object is not a syntactic complement of V, but instead is an adjoined constituent. Third, both the incorporated object and the extra object are composed with the same argument: the verb's internal argument. This triad of results conforms perfectly to the expectations of our theory, since our theory predicts the possibility of compositions in which an argument is restricted by one expression—here, the incorporated object—and can then be saturated by another—the extra object.

Section 3.1 offers a bit of background on Chamorro grammar. Section 3.2 introduces incorporation in Chamorro, while section 3.3 establishes that the incorporated object is semantically incomplete. Sections 3.4 and 3.5 investigate the syntax and semantics of the extra object. Our strategy in these sections is to build a case that the extra object is not a syntactic complement of V but nonetheless is composed with the verb's internal argument. Section 3.6 presents our account and contrasts it with some alternatives offered by other approaches. Section 3.7 takes a closer look at restriction without saturation. We use evidence from Chamorro and Maori to identify the point in the compositional process at which unsaturation must be resolved and semantic completeness achieved. Finally, section 3.8 concludes.

A word about syntax before we begin. The analysis of Chamorro incorporation to be constructed in this chapter relies on evidence from syntax as well as semantics. But we do not fully explore the syntax of incorporation in this language. Nor do we take a firm stand on the issue that has engaged students of noun incorporation since Kroeber (1909, 1911) and Sapir (1911), namely, whether the incorporated noun has a syntactic life independent of the complex verb containing it. For our purposes, it does not much matter what module of grammar is responsible for deriving the complex verb of incorporation clauses. We discuss some of the evidence favoring a syntactic derivation in appendix A.

## 3.1 A Dash of Chamorro Grammar

Like its distant relative Maori, Chamorro is both a head-initial language and a null argument language. Clauses are projected from a category

Infl(ection) that occurs at the left and indicates tense-aspect-mood. This category is followed by the predicate, which can be of any category type, and then by the predicate's arguments. Consider the following examples, which illustrate various realizations of Infl as well as predicates that are verbs (3a–b), adjectives (3c), and nouns (3d):

(3) a. Ginin p*um*uti    i    kannai-ña.
Imperf Agr.be.hurt the hand-Agr
'His hand had gotten hurt.'
b. Debi di ta-abiba    maseha díkiki' na hatdin.
ought Agr-encourage any    small L garden
'We should all tend some sort of small garden.' (*Saipan Tribune* 12/15/98)
c. Parehu    ha'    yan iya Kagman yan Matuis.
Agr.same Emp with    Kagman and Matuis
'[As Gonno] is like Kagman and Matuis.' (*Saipan Tribune* 11/23/99)
d. Sais añus idat-ña i    pätgun.
six years age-Agr the child
'The child's age was six years.' (Onedera 1994, 21)

When the predicate is a noun or preposition, it is followed first by its complements and then by the subject. When the predicate is a verb or adjective, word order is more flexible, but the unmarked and most frequent order is Verb-Subject-Object-Other Arguments.

(4) a. Ha-konni' esti i    dos ma'estru istudianti-nñiha pära ufan-hanao
Agr-take this the two teacher    student-Agr    Fut Agr-go
pära Sadduk yan Milak Sigua.
to    River    and Falls Sigua
'These two schoolteachers took their students on an outing to Sigua River and Falls.' (Onedera 1994, 59)
b. P*um*oddung huyung dos na granu pugua' gi    ädyu i    matitik,
Agr.fall    out    two L piece betelnut Loc that    the torn
gi    kestat.
Loc sack
'Two betelnuts fell out of that torn thing, out of the sack.'

Following Chung (1998), we adopt a view of Chamorro clause structure in which the subject occupies Infl's specifier, which is projected to the right. Once again, we can afford to remain agnostic on the derivation of surface word order. But see Chung 1998 for evidence that VSO order arises when the subject is lowered to adjoin to the right of a verb or adjective.

The inflectional morphology of clauses will be important in what follows. Predicates in Chamorro are inflected for progressive aspect via reduplication. In addition, predicates that are verbs or adjectives are inflected for the person and number of the subject via agreement prefixes (or infixes) that also indicate tense, mood, and finiteness. It will be relevant later that there are two agreement paradigms: one for transitive verbs (i.e., verbs with a surface direct object) and the other for intransitive verbs and adjectives. In the examples in (5), the verbs *li'i'* 'see' and *tungu'* 'know' are inflected with agreement from the transitive paradigm, while the other predicates are inflected with agreement from the intransitive paradigm.

(5) a. Ha-li'i' si tata-hu na t*um*ótohgi gi päpa'
Agr-see Unm father-Agr Comp Agr.stand.Prog Loc under
trongku-n niyuk.
tree-L coconut
'She saw my father standing under a coconut tree.' (Cooreman 1982, 6)
b. Pues maolik yänggin ti ma'a'ñao hao sa'
so Agr.good if not Agr.afraid you because
maolek-ña ha' lokkui' na un-tungu'.
Agr.good-Compar Emp also Comp Agr-know
'So it's good if you're not afraid, because it's better too that you know (it).' (*Anakko' Despidida* 7)

Definite arguments and some adjuncts are inflected for morphological case, via particles that occur at the left edge of DP and are sometimes fused with the definite article. There are three morphological cases. The unmarked case is used for subjects, direct objects, possessors, and most objects of prepositions, as well as DPs that are topic or focus. The local case is used for locative and temporal phrases. The oblique case is used elsewhere. Some grammatical relations, including subject and direct object, are signaled by case marking alone. Others are signaled by case marking plus a preposition.

(6) Si Manglona ilek-ña na fuera ha' di i katta-nña
Unm Manglona say-Agr Comp besides Emp the letter-Agr
finene'na guätu gias Winkel gi Juniu, ha-tugi'i tä'lu i High
first there Loc Winkel Loc June Agr-write.to again the High
Commissioner.
Commissioner

'Manglona said that besides his first letter to Winkel in June, he had written to the High Commissioner again.' (*Marianas Variety* 12/4/79)

Also important will be the internal structure of noun phrases. Once again, we assume that the category informally known as the noun phrase is a DP, headed by the category D(eterminer), which occurs at the left. Chamorro has a standard inventory of determiners. Among the realizations of D are the definite article *i*, the null indefinite (nonspecific) article, the demonstratives, *pälu* '(contrastive) some', the strong quantifiers *todu* 'all' and *käda* 'each', and various weak determiners that also function as adjectives (see Chung 1998).

(7) a. i   fina'denni'
    the hot.sauce
    'the hot sauce'
  b. ädyu i   palao'an
    that the woman
    'that woman'
  c. meggai na biahi
    many L time
    'many times'

To the right of D is its complement, NP, which we take to consist of N followed by N's complements. Notice that adjectives, relative clauses, and other nominal modifiers must follow D but can adjoin to either side of NP. These word order options are evidence that N and its complements form a maximal projection from which D is excluded.

(8) a. ädyu i   [yä-hu]         na lepblu
    that the WH[obj].like-Agr L book
    'that book which I like'
  b. ädyu i   lepblu [ni     yä-hu]
    that the book  Comp WH[obj].like-Agr
    'that book which I like'
  c. i  [yänggin mattu    i   batku siha] na hotnát
    the if     Agr.arrive the ship Pl L work
    'the work when the ships came in' (Cooreman 1983, 88)
  d. ni háfafa ha'  na distrosu    [fi*na*'tinas-ña      i   gera]
    not any   Emp L destruction WH[obj].make-Agr the war
    'no destruction that the war had wrought' (Cooreman 1983, 176)

Farther to the right within DP is the possessor, which bears a certain morphosyntactic resemblance to the subject of a clause. Like a subject, the possessor occurs in the unmarked morphological case, and N is inflected for its person and number via agreement suffixes. Further, just as the subject typically separates V from its complements in surface word order, so the possessor must separate N from its complements. The word order of arguments within DP, in other words, is N-Possessor-Other Arguments.

(9) a. i   haga-nmami
the daughter-Agr
'our daughter'
   b. i   bisita-ña si   Francisco as   Teresa
the visit-Agr Unm Francisco Obl Teresa
'Francisco's visit to Teresa'

Following Abney (1987) (see also Chung 1998), we claim that the possessor occupies the specifier of D, which is the position within DP analogous to the subject's position within IP. This claim will be crucial later.

## 3.2 Incorporation

We turn next to object incorporation.

Chamorro has two existential verbs, *guäha* 'exist' and *taya'* 'not exist', which occur in a familiar kind of impersonal construction (see Chung 1987). In this construction, the subject is a null expletive, and the existential verb has an internal argument that exhibits the definiteness effect.

(10) a. Guäha   famagu'un gi   giput.
Agr.exist children   Loc party
'There were children at the party.'
   b. Gi mismu tiempu, guäha   lokkui' parehu na sinisedi   giya
at same   time,   Agr.exist also   same   L  experience Loc
Solomon Islands.
Solomon Islands
'At the same time, there's a similar thing happening in the Solomon Islands.' (*Saipan Tribune* 6/20/00)
   c. Debi u-guäha más   industria fuera   ki turista yan magagu.
ought Agr-exist more industry except   tourist and clothing
'There should be more industries aside from tourism and the garment industry.' (*Saipan Tribune* 8/3/99)

d. Gi paingi taya' guini ni únunu ha'.
   Loc last.night Agr.not.exist here not one Emp
   'No one was here last night.'

When the verb's internal argument is a DP with a possessor in its specifier, the construction expresses existential 'have' (see, e.g., Keenan 1987).

(11) a. I taotao mo'na guäha tanu'-ñiha yan lugat-ñiha.
       the people first Agr.exist land-Agr and place-Agr
       'The ancient spirits have their lands and places (lit. As for the ancient spirits, there are their lands . . .).' (Cooreman 1982, 1)
   b. Guäha gä'-ña kätu si Jose.
      Agr.exist pet-Agr cat Unm Jose
      'Jose has a pet cat.'
   c. Taya' chansa-kku mu-nä'lu tatti.
      Agr.not.exist chance-Agr Infin-return back
      '[The doctors kept saying that] I had no chance of coming back [to life].' (*Saipan Tribune* 8/12/99)

Existential 'have' can also be expressed by two verbs of possession, *gäi-* 'have' and *täi-* 'not have', which are morphologically related to *guäha* and *taya'*. These verbs of possession select two arguments, a possessor and an internal argument corresponding to the possessed. The possessor argument is linked to the subject DP. The internal argument, we claim, is linked to an object that must be incorporated. Consider:

(12) a. Gäi-[famagu'un] ädyu na palao'an.
       Agr.have-children that L woman
       'That woman has children.'
   b. Käna ha' todus man-gäi-[kommun sanhälum].
      almost Emp all Agr.have-toilet inside
      'Almost all [residents] have indoor toilets.' (*Saipan Tribune* 5/30/00)
   c. Täi-[prublema] i próhimu.
      Agr.not.have-problem the fellow
      'The guy had no problem [spelling *Saipan*].' (*Saipan Tribune* 12/16/99)

From a crosslinguistic standpoint, object incorporation in Chamorro conforms to some familiar patterns. To begin with, incorporation is productive. Although the verbs of possession are the only two Chamorro verbs to serve as hosts of incorporation, the construction is fully productive as far as the incorporated object is concerned. The N of the incorporated object can be any common noun at all, including relational nouns as well as a wide range of other concrete and abstract nouns, whether indigenous or borrowed words. The list in (13) is intended to give some sense of the range of possibilities.

(13) täi-[familia]       'have no family'
     gäi-[nana]          'have a mother'
     gäi-[tali]          'have a rope'
     gäi-[balakbak]      'have luggage'
     gäi-[hugeti]        'have a toy, have toys'
     gäi-[iyu]           'have a possession'
     gäi-[tiyan]         'have a stomach'
     täi-[tanu']         'have no land'
     gäi-[giput]         'have a party'
     gäi-[salappi']      'have money'
     gäi-[malinik]       'have a headache'
     gäi-[nina'siña]     'have power'
     täi-[rispetu]       'have no respect'
     gäi-[madduk]        'have a hole'
     gäi-[tiempu]        'have time'
     täi-[bali]          'have no value'

Further, as in Greenlandic (see, e.g., Sadock 1980), incorporation has phonological consequences: the verbs of possession are realized not as independent words but as stressed prefixes attached to the N of the incorporated object. The resulting complex word is a verb, since it has all the morphological trappings of verbs, including inflection for tense-aspect-mood and finiteness, morphological agreement with the subject, and so on (14a–b). It also, like other verbs, has a morphological causative form (14c).

(14) a. Un dia siña ha'   g*um*äi-[familia]   hao.
        one day can Emp Agr.have-family you
        'One day you might come to have a family.' (*Saipan Tribune* 8/31/99)
     b. Kumu mohon un-é'kunguk yu', un-täi-[problema]     pa'gu.
        if    Unreal Agr-listen   me  Agr-not.have-problem now
        'If you had listened to me, you wouldn't have problems now.'

c. Hagu ha' yu' mu-na'-gägai-[salappi'].
you Emp me WH[nom]-make-have-money.Prog
'It's because of you that I have money (lit. You cause me to have money).'

Finally, incorporation clauses are intransitive, and this is transparently revealed by the morphosyntax. The complex verb's agreement with the subject must be chosen from the intransitive paradigm.

(15) a. Man-gäi-[famagu'un].
Agr-have-children
'They have children.'
b. Lämeggai pära ufan-täi-[che'chu'] dispues.
a.little.more Fut Agr-not.have-work later
'Even more people will have no work later.' (*Saipan Tribune* 6/13/00)

Compare the realizations of agreement in (15) with those exhibited by the intransitive verbs in (16) and the transitive verbs in (17).

(16) a. Man-malagu.
Agr-run
'They ran.'
b. Pära ufan-malagu.
Fut Agr-run
'They will run.'

(17) a. Ma-bäba i petta.
Agr-open the door
'They opened the door.'
b. Pära uma-bäba i petta.
Fut Agr-open the door
'They will open the door.'

Further, if the subject is pronominal, it can be realized as a weak pronoun (see (18)). This is an option available only to subjects of *intransitive* clauses, as the examples in (19) are intended to suggest.

(18) a. Man-gäi-[kareta] häm.
Agr-have-car we
'We own a car.'
b. Täi-[pasiensia] hao!
Agr.not.have-patience you
'You have no patience!'

(19) a. Man-mamokkat häm tatti.
 Agr-walk    we   back
 'We walked back.'
 b. In-silélebra    (*häm) i   giput.
 Agr-celebrate.Prog  we   the party
 'We were celebrating the party.'

The intransitivity of incorporation clauses argues that the incorporated object is not a surface direct object—not, in other words, a DP complement of V. The intuition has been explored many times in the literature (see, e.g., Mithun 1984; Baker 1988). Let us now try to flesh it out for Chamorro.

### 3.3 The Incorporated Object Is Semantically Incomplete

Crucial to the account of Chamorro developed in this chapter is our claim that the incorporated object is semantically incomplete: it denotes a property rather than an individual or a generalized quantifier. This claim is supported by syntactic evidence that reveals that the incorporated object—more precisely, the nominal phrase in which the incorporated N originates—is NP but not DP. We present the evidence here.

To begin with, the incorporated object can be larger than just N. It can be a compound noun, as (20) shows.

(20) a. Kao gäi-[batku-n    airi] hao?
 Q   Agr.have-ship-L air   you
 'Do you have an airplane?'
 b. yänggin täi-[insurance     hinemlu'] hao
 if    Agr.not.have-insurance health   you
 'if you don't have health insurance' (*Saipan Tribune* 8/19/99)

The incorporated object can also consist of a noun followed by modifiers of various sorts. In (21), the modifier is the noun phrase *hayu* 'wood'. Notice that we have bracketed the entire incorporated object, including the modifier.

(21) Man-gäi-[guma' hayu].
 Agr-have-house wood
 'They have a wood house.'

In (22), the modifiers are adjective phrases: a simple adjective in (22a) and adjective phrases with more elaborate internal structure in (22b-c).

(22) a. Si     Miguel täi-[kareta         asút].
       Unm Miguel Agr.not.have-car blue
       'Miguel doesn't have a blue car.'
   b. Malägu' yu' gumäi-[amigu      siha taiguennao giya hagu].
      Agr.want I  Infin.have-friend Pl  like.that   Loc you
      'I want to have friends like you.'
   c. Ti  prisisu        na   un-gäi-[kabesanti kalaktus taiguihi i
      not Agr.necessary Comp Agr-have-mind     sharp    like.that the
      scientist] pära un-kumprendi.
      scientist  Fut  Agr-understand
      'It's not necessary for you to have a mind as sharp as a
      scientist's for you to realize [this].' (*Saipan Tribune* 12/8/98)

In (23), the modifiers are relative clauses.

(23) a. Sueddu-n i    nuebu na man-utuhun ni
       salary-L the new  L   AP-start   Comp
       täi-[edukasion                    ni    maolik].
       WH[nom].Agr.not.have-education Comp WH[nom].Agr.good
       '[The minimum wage] is the salary of new starting [workers]
       who don't have an education that is good.' (*Saipan Tribune*
       9/14/99)
   b. Täi-[amiga                   ni    yä-hu]              si  Carmen.
      Agr.not.have-friend Comp WH[obj].like-Agr Unm Carmen
      'Carmen has no women friends who I like.'
   c. Taya'           ha'   gäi-[sapatus              ni
      Agr.not.exist Emp WH[nom].Agr.have-shoe Comp
      omlat-hu].
      WH[obl].fit-Agr
      'There's no one whose shoes (lit. who has shoes that) I fit.'

If we assume that modifiers of these sorts must be adjoined to maximal projections, then examples such as those in (21)–(23) argue that the incorporated object is a maximal projection.

Consistent with the idea that the incorporated object is a maximal projection, it can consist of a noun followed by complements. This is shown in (24).

(24) a. Ni    bangku täi-[kunfiansa              gi   check gubietnu].
       even bank    Agr.not.have-confidence Loc check government
       'Even banks don't have confidence in government checks.'
       (*Saipan Tribune* 3/6/01)

b. Todu i taotao ni man-gäi-[nisisidat put gualu'],
all the person Comp WH[nom].Agr-have-need for farm
ha-midídiyi.
Agr-survey.for
'All the people who had need for farmland, they would survey for.' (Cooreman 1983, 53)
c. Ni unu gäi-[aturidat mam-a'tinas areklu].
not one WH[nom].Agr.have-authority Infin.AP-make rule
'No one has authority to make rules.' (*Saipan Tribune* 6/1/99)

The incorporated object can even contain a coordinate structure. Depending on how (25a) is parsed, the incorporated object is either a noun modified by conjoined nominals or itself a coordinate NP. In examples of type (25c), which are acceptable to some speakers, the incorporated object is unambiguously a coordinate NP.

(25) a. ädyu siha i man-gäi-[chetnut kurasón yan diabetes]
that Pl the WH[nom].Agr-have-wound heart and diabetes
'those who have heart disease and diabetes' (*Saipan Tribune* 1/20/00)
b. Kao man-gäi-[fotgun kandit yan kahun ais] siha?
Q Agr-have-stove electricity and box ice they
'Do they have an electric stove and a refrigerator?'
c. Gäi-[rilos oru yan guäguan na alahas siha].
Agr.have-watch gold and expensive L jewelry Pl
'She has a gold watch and expensive jewelry.'

The full range of expansions points to the conclusion that the incorporated object has at least the internal structure of NP.

At the same time, the incorporated object is smaller than DP. It cannot be headed by an overt determiner, such as the demonstrative in (26a) or the universal quantifier in (26b).

(26) a. *Kao hagu gäi-[ädyu na kareta]?
Q you WH[nom].Agr.have-that L car
('Do *you* own that car?')
b. *Si Juan gäi-[todu i läpis].
Unm Juan Agr.have-all the pencil
('Juan has all the pencils.')

Nor can it consist of any of the pro-forms widely assumed to occupy D, such as personal pronouns (see, e.g., Postal 1969b) or interrogative pronouns.

(27) a. *Pära un-gäi-[häm].
    Fut Agr-have-us
    ('You would have us.')
  b. *Gäi-[hafa]?
    Agr.have-what?
    ('What does he have?')
  c. *Gäi-[kuantu         na famagu'un] hao?
    Agr.have-how.many? L children    you
    ('How many children do you have?')

Finally, the incorporated object cannot contain a possessor, even one whose presence is signaled only by morphological agreement (see (28b)).

(28) a. *Si   Antonio gäi-[kareta-n]   Dolores.
    Unm Antonio Agr.have-car-L Dolores
    ('Antonio has Dolores's car.')
  b. *Gäi-[lepblo-mmu]   yu'.
    Agr.have-book-Agr I
    ('I have your book.')

If we maintain that possessors occupy the specifier of D, then the ungrammaticality of the null possessor in (28b) serves to confirm that the incorporated object is not DP—or, for that matter, any projection of D.

In short, as far as internal structure is concerned, the incorporated object is NP but not DP. Let us continue to assume that this NP is composed with the verb's internal argument, but finesse all related syntactic questions, including the question of how the N of the incorporated object comes to combine morphologically with V. (For some evidence that syntactic head movement is involved, see appendix A.) This minimal commitment to the syntax puts the focus on the point of greatest relevance to us: as an NP, the incorporated object is property-denoting and therefore semantically incomplete.

### 3.4 The Extra Object

The plot now thickens. Alongside the structures just exhibited, Chamorro also permits the incorporated object of *gäi-* or *täi-* to be doubled by an independent noun phrase. This amounts to saying that Chamorro has a version of what Mithun (1984) has called classificatory noun incorporation (CNI).[2] Consider the following examples, which are also intended to suggest that the extra object has all the internal structure of DP. In (29a), the extra object is *un ga'lagu* 'a dog'; in (29b), the bare indefinite *kadena* 'necklace'; and in (29c), *i finañagumu* 'your offspring'.

(29) a. Gäi-[ga']    *un ga'lagu* ennao na patgun.
      Agr.have-pet a dog    that    L  child
      'That child has a pet dog.'
   b. Si    Margarita täi-[iyu]       *kadena.*
      Unm Margarita Agr.not.have-possession necklace
      'Margarita doesn't have a(ny) necklace.'
   c. Lao hayi  gäi-[patgun]       *i   finañagu-mu*?
      but who? WH[nom].Agr.have-child the offspring-Agr
      'But who *does* your child belong to (lit. Who has your offspring as child)?' (*Saipan Tribune* 8/10/99)

As is typical of CNI, the extra object in these incorporation structures looks morphologically like a direct object—more precisely, like a DP complement of the complex verb. The extra object occurs in the unmarked morphological case, which is spelled out as *si* for proper nouns but not overtly realized otherwise. Compare the extra objects in (30) with the ordinary direct objects in (31).

(30) a. Hämi gäi-[ga']      *ennao na ga'lagu.*
      we   WH[nom].Agr.have-pet that  L  dog
      '*We* own that dog.'
   b. Hayi gäi-[patgun]      si   Carmen?
      who? WH[nom].Agr.have-child Unm Carmen
      'Whose child is Carmen?'

(31) a. I  ma'estra siha ma-tätaitai    ennao na lepblu.
      the teacher  Pl  Agr-read.Prog that   L  book
      'The teachers are reading that book.'
   b. Ha-fa'bäba si    Carmen.
      Agr-deceive Unm Carmen
      'He deceived Carmen.'

Further, if the extra object is pronominal, it can be realized as a weak pronoun. Compare the extra objects in (32) with the ordinary direct objects in (33).

(32) a. Hayi gäi-[ma'estra] *hao*?
       who? WH[nom].Agr.have-teacher you
       'Whose teacher are you?'
    b. Si Julia *yu'* gäi-[patgun].
       Unm Julia me WH[nom].Agr.have-child
       'Julia has me as child.'
(33) a. Hayi um-ayuda *hao*?
       who? WH[nom]-help you
       'Who helped you?'
    b. Ni unu yu' um-é'e'kunguk.
       not one me WH[nom]-listen.Prog
       'No one was listening to me.' (*Saipan Tribune* 7/1/99)

Although the morphological profile just illustrated is not unique to direct objects, it is limited to argument DPs—subjects and direct objects in particular. That might make it tempting to assume that the extra object simply *is* the direct object of an incorporation clause. We argue below, however, that such an assumption cannot be correct. Other morphological evidence, and all the syntactic evidence, converges to reveal that the extra object is not a complement of V.

Consider, to begin with, the evidence against direct objecthood that is supplied by verb agreement. If the extra object were a DP complement of the complex verb, we would expect the verb's agreement with the subject to be chosen from the transitive paradigm. But the verb is consistently inflected with agreement from the intransitive paradigm, whether or not an extra object is present. Compare (15) with (34).

(34) a. Hämi man-gäi-[magagu] *i gaigi gi*
       we WH[nom].Agr.have-clothes the WH[nom].Agr.be Loc
       *hilu' siya.*
       top chair
       'We are the ones whose clothes are on the chair.'
    b. Man-gäi-[ga'] häm *nuskuantus ga'lagu* yan in-pépeksai siha.
       Agr.have-pet we several dog and Agr.raise.Prog them
       'We have several dogs and are raising them.'

The agreement pattern suggests that the extra object is not a direct object after all.

The conclusion is confirmed by three pieces of syntactic evidence that the extra object is not a complement of V.

First, the extra object differs from a complement of V in that it is inaccessible to movement. Like English, Chamorro freely allows complements of V to undergo *wh*-movement (see Chung 1998 and the references cited there). Direct objects are eligible for movement in the standard *wh*-constructions, which in Chamorro include constituent questions (such as (35a)), focus constructions (35b), and relative clauses (35c).

(35) a. Hafa na atumobit i   chi'lu-mu  lahi
     what? L  car     the sibling-Agr male
     ha-súsugun              ____?
     WH[obj].Agr-drive.Prog
     'Which car was your brother driving?'
  b. Tres na famagu'un Dolores in-li'i'     ____.
     three L  children   Dolores WH[obj].Agr-see
     'It was three of Dolores's children that we saw.'
  c. Kao guäha  [siha más  [ni    ti  fina'na'gue-mmu   ____]]?
     Q   Agr.exist Pl   more Comp not WH[obj].teach-Agr
     'Is there anyone who you haven't taught?'

PP complements of V can undergo *wh*-movement in constituent questions (36a) and focus constructions (36b), although they cannot be relativized.

(36) a. Ginin hayi na    ma-sakki ennao i   kareta ____?
     from  who? Comp Agr-steal that   the car
     'From whom did they steal that car?'
  b. Ginin i  famagu'un na    in-kenni' i   ga'lagu ____.
     from  the children   Comp Agr-take the dog
     'From the children we took the dog.'

Now if the extra object were a complement of V, then it too should be eligible for *wh*-movement. But, contrary to expectations, when the extra object is moved, the result is ungrammatical—almost unparsable. Consider:

(37) a. *Manu  gäi-[kareta]        ____ si   Antonio?
     which? WH[obj].Agr.have-car    Unm Antonio
     ('Which car does Antonio own (lit. Which does Antonio have as car)?')
  b. *Hafa na lepblu gäi-[iyo]-mmu        ____?
     what? L  book  WH[obl].have-possession-Agr
     ('Which books do you have?')

92                                                                    Chapter 3

c. *Tres guihi na kätu gäi-[ga']                    ___.
   three there L cat WH[obj].Agr.have-pet
   ('Three of those cats, he has (as pets).')
d. *Kao guäha    [famagu'un siha guini [ni    pära
   Q    Agr.exist children    Pl   here   Comp Fut
   un-gäi-[istudianti]           ___]]?
   WH[obj].Agr-have-student
   ('Are there any children here who you will have as students?')
e. *Guäha   [tres  ha'  na taotao [ni    si   Antonio
   Agr.exist  three Emp L  person  Comp Unm Antonio
   täi-[parentis]               ___]].
   Agr.not.have-relative
   ('There are just three people who Antonio isn't related to.')

The inaccessibility of the extra object to movement argues that it is not a complement of V.

Second, the extra object differs from a complement of V in that it is an island. Although Chamorro does not freely allow movement out of noun phrases, possessors can escape from the DP whose specifier they occupy under certain well-defined circumstances. Movement of the possessor is permitted, for instance, when the host DP is a complement of V and D happens to be null. The fact that such movement is possible reveals that DP complements of V are not, in general, islands. (For further discussion, see Chung 1998.)

(38) a. Hafa na klasi-n pitsonas siña un-na'maolik [sininte-nña ___]?
        what? L sort-L person    can Agr-improve  feeling-Agr
        'What kind of person's feelings can you improve?'
     b. Hayi un-amti [addeng-ña ___] ni     ämut?
        who? Agr-treat leg-Agr         Obl medicine
        'Whose leg did you treat with the medicine?'

If the extra object were a DP complement of V, then its possessor ought to be accessible to movement under just the same circumstances. But in fact, nothing can be moved out of the extra object, even the possessor, and even when D happens to be null.

(39) a. *Hayi un-gäi-[ma'estra] [chi'lu-ña    ___ palao'an]?
        who? Agr-have-teacher sibling-Agr      female
        ('Whose sister will you have as teacher?')

b. *Si  Dolores ädyu na palao'an i  [gäi-[doktu]
   Unm Dolores that L  woman  the Agr.have-doctor
   hao [chi'lu-ña ____]].
   you sibling-Agr
   ('Dolores is the woman whose brother is your doctor.')

The ungrammaticality of (39a–b) is evidence that the extra object is an island. Islandhood is, of course, more characteristic of adjuncts than of complements—a point we will come back to.

Third, the extra object does not have the combinatorial possibilities of a complement. Like many other languages, Chamorro permits conjoined verbs to share a complement, as long as the complement satisfies the subcategorization and selection requirements imposed by each verb. This familiar pattern is illustrated in (40).

(40) a. [Ha-chiku yan ha-toktuk] si  Juan i  famagu'un.
        Agr-kiss and Agr-hug  Unm Juan the children
        'Juan kissed and hugged the children.'
     b. [Man-ritótoka       yan mam-a'mámaolik] mákina.
        Agr.AP-repair.Prog and Agr.AP-fix.Prog  machine
        'He repairs and fixes machines.'

If the extra object were indeed a complement, then it should be able to participate in constructions of this sort. More precisely, it should be able to be shared by conjoined verbs, at least one of which is a complex verb with an incorporated object. But as might be expected by now, such a pattern is forbidden. (41) shows that the extra object cannot be shared by conjoined verbs. This is so even when every conjunct is a complex verb with an incorporated object, as in (41a).[3]

(41) a. ?*Guahu [gäi-[amiga]                yan
        I       WH[nom].Agr.have-friend and
        gäi-[doktu]]              si   Rita.
        WH[nom].Agr.have-doctor Unm Rita
        ('Rita is my friend and my doctor (lit. It's me who has Rita as friend and doctor).')
     b. *Hämi [man-gäi-[ga'] yan in-pépeksai]  ädyu siha na ga'lagu.
        we    Agr-have-pet and Agr-raise.Prog that Pl L  dog
        ('We own and are raising those dogs.')

In short, the extra object lacks some of the morphology and all of the syntax of a DP complement of V. We take this to indicate that it is not, after all, a complement of V. It follows from this that the extra object is not a complement of *gäi*-, of *täi*-, or of the complex verb that includes the incorporated object.

The conclusion raises the question of where the extra object fits in the phrase structure of incorporation clauses. Following the clear precedent set by Baker (1988, 1996), we hypothesize that the extra object is a syntactic adjunct—a hypothesis consistent with its islandhood. Further details of the phrase structure are discussed in appendix A. For our purposes, what matters is that the extra object is not a complement, but rather syntactically adjoined.

### 3.5 The Extra Object Is a Semantic Argument

We are now ready for the surprise in our triad of results. Despite its status as an adjoined constituent, the extra object is not semantically an adjunct—not (merely) a restrictive modifier. Instead, it is composed with the verb's internal argument and can, in fact, saturate that argument.

The line of reasoning that brings us to this conclusion runs as follows: We investigate three semantic restrictions exhibited by the extra object. Each restriction is best accounted for by assuming that the verb imposes semantic demands on its internal argument and the extra object must satisfy those demands. But that hypothesis amounts to the claim that the extra object is composed with the internal argument—the same argument with which the incorporated object is composed.

Section 3.5.1 discusses a definiteness effect exhibited by the extra object. Section 3.5.2 examines the distribution of *un* 'a, one', which we claim is an affirmative polarity item. Finally, section 3.5.3 probes the relation between the extra object and the verb's other argument: the possessor.

#### 3.5.1 A Definiteness Effect

One kind of evidence that the extra object is composed with the verb's internal argument comes from an unexpected contrast between *gäi*- 'have' and *täi*- 'not have'. The reader might already have noticed that the extra object associated with *gäi*- 'have' can be any kind of DP at all. The extra object can be a pronoun or proper noun, for instance.

(42) a. Kao si    Rita gäi-[patgun]    hao?
     Q   Unm Rita Agr.have-child  you
     'Are you Rita's child?'

b. Guahu gäi-[istudianti]     si    Sally.
   I    WH[nom].Agr.have-student Unm Sally
   'Sally is *my* student.'

It can also be a DP headed by the definite article or a demonstrative. These options are illustrated in (43).

(43) a. Hayi gäi-[diskuidu]               *i*
        who? WH[nom].Agr.have-negligence the
        *ma-susésedi*                *pa'gu.*
        WH[nom].Agr.Pass-experience.Prog now
        '[I keep on asking myself] whose fault the current situation is.'
        (*Saipan Tribune* 2/22/01)
     b. Hayi gäi-[isao]              *esti.*
        who? WH[nom].Agr.have-fault this
        '[We can't trade accusations about] whose fault this is.' (*Saipan Tribune* 10/26/99)
     c. Si   Miguel gäi-[che'lu    lä'amku' na palao'an] esti i
        Unm Miguel Agr.have-sibling older   L  woman   this the
        *gaigi       gi   akague-kku.*
        WH[nom].Agr.be Loc left-Agr
        'Miguel's older sister is this person on my left.'

The extra object of *gäi-* can be a DP headed by a strong quantifier. Consider:

(44) a. Gäi-[iyu]           *todu klasi-n atumobit.*
        Agr.have-possession all   kind-L car
        'He owns all kinds of cars.'
     b. Si   Dolores gäi-[amiga]     guennao na iskuela *käna  ha'*
        Unm Dolores Agr.have-friend there  L  school almost Emp
        *todu ma'estra.*
        all  teacher
        'Almost all teachers are Dolores's friends at that school.'

Finally, the extra object can be a weak DP, such as a bare indefinite or a DP headed by a numeral or a weak quantifier like *meggai* 'many'.

(45) a. Meggai na taotao man-gäi-[gima']        *guma' simentu.*
        many   L  person  WH[nom].Agr-have-house house cement
        'Many people have concrete houses.'

b. Kao gäi-[iyu]     hao *dos na kareta?*
   Q   Agr.have-possession you two L car
   'Do you own two cars?'
c. Gäi-[parentis]   *meggai* si   Antonio.
   Agr.have-relatives many Unm Antonio
   'Antonio has many relatives.'

What is unexpected is that the extra object associated with *täi-* 'not have' does not pattern the same way. Instead, it exhibits a definiteness effect. Pronouns and proper nouns are not permitted, as (46) is intended to suggest.

(46) a. *Si   Julia täi-[patgun]     *yu'*.
        Unm Julia Agr.not.have-child me
        ('I'm not Julia's child.')
     b. *Hagu, kao guäha    siha ni
        you   Q   Agr.exist Pl   Comp
        man-täi-[ma'estra]    *hao?*
        WH[nom].Agr-not.have-teacher you
        ('As for you, are there any people who haven't had you as teacher?')
     c. *Hämi man-täi-[patgun]     si   Rita.
        we   WH[nom].Agr-not.have-child Unm Rita
        ('Rita isn't *our* child.')

DPs headed by the definite article, a demonstrative, or a strong quantifier are not permitted either.

(47) a. *Si   Antonio täi-[kareta]    *ennao.*
        Unm Antonio Agr.not.have-car that
        ('Antonio doesn't own that car.')
     b. *Si   Carmen täi-[ga']    *esti na ga'lagu.*
        Unm Carmen Agr.not.have-pet this L dog
        ('Carmen doesn't have this dog.')
     c. *Si   Antonio täi-[iyu]    *todu klasi-n kareta.*
        Unm Antonio Agr.not.have-possession all   kind-L car
        ('Antonio doesn't own all kinds of cars.')

The only sorts of DPs that can serve as extra objects of *täi-* are the weak DPs. Among these are bare indefinites and DPs headed by a numeral or a weak quantifier.[4]

(48) a. Täi-[ga']            yu' *ga'lagu.*
       Agr.not.have-pet I   dog
       'I don't have a dog.'
   b. Si    Carmen täi-[primu]            *pali'.*
       Unm Carmen Agr.not.have-cousin priest
       'Carmen has no priests as cousins.'
   c. Täi-[ga']            *dos na ga'lagu.*
       Agr.not.have-pet two L  dog
       'He doesn't have two dogs.'
   d. Si    Julia täi-[amiga]           *meggai na ma'estra.*
       Unm Julia Agr.not.have-friend many L  teacher
       'Julia doesn't have many teacher friends.'

Also included among the weak DPs, significantly, are negative concord items. Some relevant examples are these:

(49) a. Täi-[familia]           *ni hayi*    si    Antonio.
       Agr.not.have-family not anyone Unm Antonio
       'Antonio has no family at all.'
   b. Si    Joaquin täi-[amigu]           *ni   hayi na ma'estru.*
       Unm Joaquin Agr.not.have-friend not one L   teacher
       'Joaquin doesn't have any teacher friend.'
   c. Täi-[lateria]                   esti na tenda *ni   háfafa   ha'   na*
       Agr.not.have-canned.goods this L  store  not anything Emp L
       *lateria,*        ädyu ha'  i   lateria-n             gollai.
       canned.goods that  Emp the canned.goods-L vegetables
       'This store doesn't have any canned goods, except canned vegetables.'
   d. Si    Dolores täi-[patgun]           *ni un granu.*
       Unm Dolores Agr.not.have-child not a   piece
       'Dolores has no children at all.'
   e. Esti na patgun täi-[iyu]               *ni   sikera dos na hugeti.*
       this L child   Agr.not.have-possession not even   two L  toy
       'This child doesn't have even two toys.'

The ability of negative concord DPs to occur as extra objects of *täi-* is instructive in two respects. First, because Chamorro does not permit negative concord items to serve as predicates of clauses, we can be sure that the DPs in (49) are indeed extra objects and not part of an embedded or conjoined clause of some sort (see note 4). The examples in (49) thus make it completely clear that an extra object *can* be associated with *täi-*, even though many conceivable sorts of extra objects are ungrammatical (see (46)–(47)). Second, because negative concord in Chamorro is licensed by sentential negation, (49) confirms that it is sentential negation that is included in the meaning of *täi-*. (The same is true of the negative existential verb *taya'* 'not exist' and the negative locative verb *taigui* 'not be (in a location)'.) This point will be useful later.

The definiteness effect illustrated in (46)–(49) is quite robust. It is reminiscent of restrictions on the internal argument of 'have' that were observed within the European structuralist tradition by Benveniste (1966) and within the generative tradition, broadly construed, by Keenan (1987), Freeze (1992), Szabolcsi (1994), Partee (1999), and others. The challenge is to account for the fact that in Chamorro, the extra object of *täi-* 'not have' exhibits a definiteness effect, but the extra object of *gäi-* 'have' exhibits no such restriction. Notice that matters are made more complicated by the fact that the existential verbs *guäha* 'exist' and *taya'* 'not exist', which are morphologically related to *gäi-* and *täi-*, do not contrast in a similar way (see section 3.2). Both existential verbs impose a definiteness effect on their internal argument, as can be seen from the following examples:[5]

(50) a. Guäha tres na tinekcha' kalamasa.
      Agr.exist three L fruit pumpkin
      'There were three pumpkins.' (*Mannge' na Alaguan Kalamasa* 3)
   b. Taya' dos pat tres simana disdi ki um-ätungu'.
      Agr.not.exist two or three week since Agr-know.each.other
      'There hadn't been two or three weeks since they'd known each other.' (Cooreman 1982, 7)

(51) a. *Guäha todu man-malangu.
      Agr.exist all WH[nom].Agr-sick
      ('There was everyone who was sick.')
   b. *Taya' todu klasi-n hugeti-ña si Joe.
      Agr.not.exist all sort-L toy-Agr Unm Joe
      ('Joe doesn't have all sorts of toys (lit. There aren't all sorts of toys of Joe's).')

What explains these patterns? We can begin to construct an account by recalling the approach to the existential construction pursued by McNally

(1992), Musan (1996), Dobrovie-Sorin (1997), and others, according to which the definiteness effect is traced ultimately to argument structure. The key idea is that existential verbs demand an internal argument that is a property—a demand that in the normal case is satisfied only by composition with the meaning of an indefinite or other weak DP.

Within our theory, there are two ways of expressing the generalization that a predicate demands an argument that is a property. We could assume that the predicate's semantic type encodes this information directly. On such a view, the type of a one-place predicate that demands a property as argument would not be $\langle e,t \rangle$, but rather $\langle \langle e,t \rangle,t \rangle$. Alternatively, we can assume that the predicate has one of the standard semantic types, but imposes the further requirement that the argument must be composed via the nonsaturating mode Restrict. On this view, the generalization that the argument must be a property follows from the fact that properties are the only expressions that Restrict can compose.

Although these assumptions lead to the same result in simple cases, their theoretical repercussions are quite different. The first assumption raises the troubling issue of the proliferation of semantic types. But the second assumption seems benign from the standpoint of the type theory. Notice further that the second alternative is expected within our approach; the predicate's demand that an argument be composed via Restrict is fully analogous to the demand imposed within argument expressions by Maori *he*, discussed in chapter 2. Finally, the second assumption has empirical advantages, as we will show soon. It is therefore the second assumption that we adopt.

We propose the following. The existential verbs *guäha* 'exist' and *taya'* 'not exist' are alike in requiring their internal argument to be composed via Restrict. But the verbs of possession differ from one another precisely along this dimension. *Täi-* 'not have' requires its internal argument—the argument corresponding to the possessed—to be composed by Restrict; *gäi-* 'have' makes no such demand. Finally, and crucially, the extra object is composed with the internal argument and can saturate it.

Such a proposal accounts right away for the contrast we are interested in. *Gäi-* permits its extra object—an adjoined constituent—to be any kind of DP at all, whereas *täi-*'s extra object must be semantically incomplete; it must exhibit a definiteness effect. But if we accept this, then we are led directly to the conclusion that the internal argument of the verbs of possession is multiply linked. The reason is that the internal argument is linked not only to the extra object but also to another expression, the incorporated object—or so we have assumed from the beginning.

Importantly, it does not seem possible to alter the argument structures of the verbs of possession to negotiate around this result. Assuming, as seems reasonable, that a verb with the meaning 'have' or 'not have' has at most two arguments, the possessor and the possessed, it is clearly the second of these arguments that corresponds to the extra object *and* the incorporated object. The only way to maintain the full analysis that we have built up so far is to accept multiple linking: the extra object is composed with the same argument that the incorporated object is composed with.

### 3.5.2 An Affirmative Polarity Item

Further evidence that the extra object is composed with the verb's internal argument comes from the distribution of *un* 'a, one'. This determiner is apparently an affirmative polarity item, by which we mean that it cannot fall under the scope of sentential negation (see Ladusaw 1979).[6]

The inability of affirmative polarity DPs to fall under the scope of sentential negation should, in principle, give rise to two empirical patterns. On the one hand, in negative contexts in which the DP can take wide scope with respect to the negation, that reading should be forced. On the other hand, in negative contexts in which the DP is, for some reason, prevented from taking wide scope, ill-formedness should result.

It has proved surprisingly difficult to determine the status of Chamorro *un*—or, for that matter, English *some*—with respect to the first of these patterns. We have encountered one or two speakers whose judgments are firm that in sentences of type (52), the indefinite headed by *un* must take wide scope with respect to negation.

(52) a. Ti ma-prensa un chinina-hu.
 not Agr-iron a shirt-Agr
 'They didn't iron a shirt of mine (= There was a shirt of mine that they didn't iron).'
 b. Si Jose ti man-ayuda un palao'an.
 Unm Jose not Agr.AP-help a woman
 'Jose didn't help a woman (= There was a woman who Jose didn't help).'

Compare the sentences in (53), which illustrate that *un* need not take wide scope with respect to other operators, such as the universal quantifier or the intensional operator. In (53a), every child asked me for a potentially different penny; in (53b), they want us to seek some new car or other, not a particular car.

(53) a. Käda patgun ha-gagao yu' un séntimus.
    each child Agr-beg me a penny
    'Each child begged a penny from me.'
 b. Man-malägu' siha na pära bai infan-man-aligao un nuebu
    Agr-want they Comp Fut Agr-AP-seek a new
    na kareta giya Guam.
    L car Loc Guam
    'They want us to look for a new car in Guam.'

For most speakers, however, judgments on the scope of *un* with respect to negation are far less consistent than what is reported in (52). Various factors might contribute to this. To begin with, speakers' intuitions about the meaning might conceivably be obscured by morphosyntactic uncertainty over what verb form—transitive or antipassive—to employ in sentences of type (52) (see Chung 1998, 114–115 and note 19, for discussion). Further, judgments are complicated by the fact that in Chamorro—as in English—the same negatives that express sentential negation can be used instead to express denial of the proposition. But affirmative polarity items are sensitive only to sentential negation, not to denial of the proposition. We have not yet managed to find a path around these complications. With that said, we will proceed as though the judgments in (52) were fully general.

Fortunately, the status of *un* with respect to the second empirical pattern is much clearer. We demonstrate this by returning briefly to the existential construction. It is well known that the internal argument of an existential verb is scopeless: it must take narrowest scope with respect to all operators, including negation (see Heim 1987). In the McNally-style approach that we have adopted, the scopelessness of the internal argument follows from the claim that it must be composed via Restrict. It must therefore be a property, and properties are scopeless. The analysis leads to the expectation that in negative existential sentences, the internal argument should never be linked to an affirmative polarity DP. The reason is that such a DP could not satisfy the existential verb's demands and its own demands at the same time: it could not simultaneously be composed via Restrict and take wide scope with respect to negation.

*Un* conforms straightforwardly to this expectation. Recall that negative existential sentences in Chamorro are formed from the verb *taya'* 'not exist'. The meaning of this verb includes sentential negation, as can be seen from the fact that it licenses negative concord.

(54) Taya'     ni  unu man-aitai          put   ni
     Agr.not.exist not one WH[nom].Agr.AP-read about not
     háfafa   ha'.
     anything Emp
     'There wasn't anyone who read about anything.'

The point of interest is that *taya'* cannot have an internal argument that is an *un* indefinite. This is exactly what we expect.

(55) a. *Taya'       un prublema.
        Agr.not.exist a  problem
        ('There isn't a problem.')
     b. *Taya'       un gä'-ña   ga'lagu.
        Agr.not.exist a  pet-Agr dog
        ('He doesn't have a dog (lit. There isn't a pet dog of his).')

In contrast, the other existential verb, *guäha* 'exist', also demands an internal argument that is composed via Restrict, but that argument can be an *un* indefinite. We claim that the difference is that *guäha* presents no sentential negation for *un* to contend with.

(56) a. Guäha    un letchun gi  päpa' kareta.
        Agr.exist a  piglet  Loc under car
        'There's a piglet under the car.' (*Lechon! Lechon! Lechon!* 1)
     b. Guäha    un kareta-ña si    Antonio ni      nuebu.
        Agr.exist a  car-Agr  Unm Antonio Comp WH[nom].Agr.new
        'Antonio has a new car (lit. There's a car of Antonio's that's new).'

The overall pattern confirms that *un* is indeed an affirmative polarity item.

What is the distribution of this affirmative polarity item in incorporation clauses? Interestingly, the same contrast emerges as in the existential construction, but this time with respect to the extra object. In clauses formed from the verb *täi-* 'not have', whose meaning includes sentential negation, it is impossible for the extra object to be an *un* indefinite. This is shown in (57).

(57) a. *Si Carmen täi-[patgun]    un lahi.
       Unm Carmen Agr.not.have-child a  son
       ('Carmen has no son.')
    b. *Täi-[ga']    un ga'lagu ennao na patgun.
       Agr.not.have-pet a  dog   that  L child
       ('That child doesn't have a dog.')

But in clauses formed from the other verb of possession, *gäi-* 'have', the extra object is not restricted in this way.

(58) a. Un taotao gäi-[patgun]   un lahi.
       a  person Agr.have-child a  son
       'A man had a son.'
    b. Gäi-[ga']    un ga'lagu ennao na patgun.
       Agr.have-pet a  dog   that  L child
       'That child has a dog.'

The parallel between the existential sentences in (55)–(56) and the incorporation clauses in (57)–(58) invites us to give the same account for *täi-* in (57) as we gave for *taya'* in (55). Specifically, suppose we continue to maintain that the internal argument of *täi-* must be composed via Restrict. That demand ought to conspire with the presence of sentential negation to predict the impossibility of the affirmative polarity DPs in (57). But for the account to succeed, we must also maintain—crucially—that the extra object is composed with the internal argument and can saturate it. The hypothesis is one that we have arrived at before. It amounts to the claim that the internal argument of *täi-* is multiply linked: both the incorporated object and the extra object are composed with it.

### 3.5.3 A Curious Restriction

Our last piece of evidence that the extra object is composed with the verb's internal argument comes from pronominal anaphora.

The incorporation clauses that we have been investigating obey what seems at first glance to be a rather curious restriction on anaphora. The restriction can be stated as follows: the subject of the verb of possession cannot be coindexed with the possessor of the extra object.

This curious restriction can be seen at work in the sentences in (59). In these—and, for that matter, in many other examples cited in this chapter—the subject is topicalized in order to neutralize the information structure constraints that take effect when both subject and object occur to the right of the verb (see Chung 1998). Even so, the results here are ill formed, because the subject is coindexed with the possessor of the extra object. The subject in (59a) is the definite noun phrase *i antigu na rai Ihiptu* 'the ancient king of Egypt', the subject in (59b) is the quantified noun phrase *käda patgun* 'every child', and so on. Throughout, the possessor of the extra object is a null pronoun whose presence is overtly signaled by morphological agreement. Notice that for convenience, we have chosen not to represent the null pronoun as *pro*, but instead simply coindex the possessor agreement with the subject.

(59) a. *I antigu na rai Ihiptu$_i$ gäi-[asagua]   i   mismu
    the ancient L king Egypt Agr.have-spouse the own
    *chi'lu-ña$_i$*.
    sibling-Agr
    ('The ancient king$_i$ of Egypt was married to (lit. had as spouse) his$_i$ own sister.')
 b. *Käda patgun$_i$ gäi-[ma'estra]   si   nana-ña$_i$.
    each child   Agr.have-teacher Unm mother-Agr
    ('Every child$_i$ has his$_i$ mother as a teacher.')
 c. Si   Bill Gates$_i$ gäi-[iyu]   batku-n airi / *i   batku-n
    Unm Bill Gates Agr.have-possession ship-L air /   the ship-L
    *aire-nña$_i$*.
    air-Agr
    'Bill Gates$_i$ owns an airplane/*his$_i$ airplane.'
 d. Si   Joe$_i$ täi-[iyu]   meggai na hugeti(*-ña$_i$).
    Unm Joe Agr.not.have-possession many L toy-Agr
    'Joe$_i$ doesn't have many toys (*of his$_i$).'

What is the evidence that this restriction specifically excludes coindexing between the subject and the possessor of the extra object? To begin with, we can restore grammaticality by removing the possessor and its associated agreement, as shown in (59c–d). But the problem with the ungrammatical examples in (59) is not just that a possessor is present. We have already seen that the extra object, like all other DPs, permits a possessor in its specifier (see (29c)). In (60a), the possessor is the proper name *Antonio*; in (60b), it is a null pronoun whose presence is signaled only by agreement.

(60) a. Kao hagu gäi-[istudianti]   i   patgun Antonio?
    Q   you WH[nom].Agr.have-student the child Antonio
    'Do *you* have Antonio's child as student?'

b. Hinasso-kku    na    [i   lahi-hu]$_i$ gäi-[ma'estra]    i
   WH[obj].think-Agr Comp the son-Agr Agr.have-teacher the
   asagua-ña$_j$.
   spouse-Agr
   '[Did Jose$_j$ move to Guam?] What I thought was that my son$_i$
   had his$_j$ wife as teacher.'

Further, the problem with the ungrammatical examples in (59) is not just that coindexing holds between the subject and some other subconstituent of the clause. Coindexing with the subject is generally allowed, of course. And coindexing with the subject is possible in incorporation clauses that are semantically quite close to the ungrammatical examples in (59), as long as the relation does not also involve the possessor of the extra object. Here are two illustrations of the point.

Consider first (61).

(61) a. Si    Carmen$_i$ gäi-[haga        ni    gofatungo'-ña$_i$].
        Unm Carmen Agr.have-daughter Comp very.friend-Agr
        'Carmen$_i$ has a daughter who is her$_i$ best friend.'
     b. Taya'      ni   unu$_i$ gäi-[ma'estra           ni    más
        Agr.not.exist not one WH[nom].Agr.have-teacher Comp more
        hobin na chi'lu-ña$_i$    palao'an].
        young L sibling-Agr female
        'No one$_i$ has a teacher who is his$_i$ younger sister.'

In these examples, the incorporated object is a complex noun phrase containing a relative clause, and the predicate of the relative clause is a DP with a possessor in its specifier. Even though the subject of the verb of possession is coindexed with the possessor, the result is grammatical, presumably because no extra object is involved.

Consider next (62). Under special discourse circumstances, it is possible for the complex verb of incorporation to be modified by an adjunct that expresses location. The most obvious difference between this location phrase and an extra object is that the location phrase surfaces in the oblique morphological case.

(62) Täi-[patgun]      si Dolores nu  guahu.
     Agr.not.have-child Dolores Obl me
     'Dolores has no child in me [said to dissociate the speaker from Dolores].'

In (63), the location phrase has a possessor in its specifier, and that possessor is coindexed with the subject. Even though the surface pattern differs minimally from (59b), the result is grammatical, because—as before—no extra object is involved.

(63) Käda patgun$_i$ gäi-[ma'estra]     as    nana-ña$_i$.
     each  child    Agr.have-teacher Obl mother-Agr
     'Every child$_i$ has a teacher in his$_i$ mother.'

The conclusion seems clear that what is specifically excluded is coindexing between the subject and the possessor of the extra object.

The account that we tentatively suggest of this curious restriction proceeds from two assumptions, one particular and the other general. The particular assumption is that a verb of possession expresses the meaning that its two arguments are related as possessor to possessed. The general assumption is that the assertion of a predicate is informative only when its meaning is not already presupposed. Some such pragmatic principle, we believe, lies behind the observation that a sentence like (64) is strange when uttered with neutral, noncontrastive intonation but acceptable when the subject receives contrastive stress.

(64) Jane killed the dead person.

Uttered with neutral intonation, (64) is infelicitous, because there is a component of the meaning of the asserted predicate, *killed*, that also occurs in the presupposition, as part of the meaning of the internal argument: namely, the meaning expressed by *dead*. But when the subject *Jane* is focused, then the meanings of both *killed* and *dead* are relegated to the presupposition, and no conflict arises.

From these assumptions, it is immediately obvious in outline how to account for the restriction illustrated in the ungrammatical examples in (59). In order for a verb of possession to be asserted felicitously, the information that its two arguments are related as possessor to possessed should not form part of the presupposition (see de Jong 1987). We claim that this is precisely what goes wrong in the ungrammatical examples in (59). As a consequence of the coindexing between the subject and the possessor of the extra object, the subject and the extra object are presupposed to be related as possessor to possessed.[7]

Observe now that a third assumption—familiar by now—is needed to complete the picture. In order for the account to work, the extra object must actually be composed with an argument of the verb: the argument corresponding to the possessed. This assumption is crucial. Notice that we cannot achieve the desired results by maintaining merely that the argument is composed with the *incorporated object*. The reason is that the incorporated object and the extra object need not have the same denotation, and it is the extra object whose possessor participates in the coindexing.[8]

To sum up, multiple linking occurs in incorporation clauses. The extra object is composed with the verb's internal argument—the same argument that the incorporated object is composed with.

### 3.6 Our Account

We consider it established, then, that multiple linking occurs in object incorporation in Chamorro. Both the incorporated object and the extra object are composed with the verb's internal argument. From the standpoint of familiar approaches to predication, this is a surprising—almost unprecedented—result. But it is completely expected within the theory of restriction and saturation that we have developed in this monograph.

This section presents the specifics of our account. We first show how our analysis handles the Chamorro facts discussed so far. We then briefly compare it with some other semantic approaches to incorporation, notably, those offered by van Geenhoven (1998) and Bittner (2001).

There are three main ingredients to our account of incorporation in Chamorro. First, the theory of restriction and saturation. Second, the claim that the incorporated object is semantically incomplete. And third, the idea that the Chamorro verbs of possession, *gäi-* 'have' and *täi-* 'not have', are two-place predicates that differ in the following way: *täi-* demands that its internal argument must be composed via Restrict, but *gäi-* does not.[9]

To see how our account works, consider first how semantic composition proceeds in the simplest incorporation clauses—clauses that contain an incorporated object but no extra object, such as (65).

(65) Gäi-[kareta] si Antonio.
  Agr.have-car Unm Antonio
  'Antonio has a car.'

Because the incorporated object *kareta* 'car' is semantically incomplete, the property that it supplies is composed with *gäi-*'s internal argument via Restrict. Importantly, this operation does not reduce the predicate's degree of unsaturation. See (66). (For convenience, English rather than Chamorro words are used in (66) and following representations.)

(66) $\lambda y \lambda x \lambda e$ [have$'$(y)(x)(e)]    car$'$
     $\langle e, \langle e, t \rangle \rangle$              $\langle e, t \rangle$

$\lambda x \lambda y \lambda e$ [have$'$(y)(x)(e) $\wedge$ car$'$(y)]
$\langle e, \langle e, t \rangle \rangle$

Next, the individual supplied by *si Antonio* is composed with the external argument via function application, an operation that saturates that argument and reduces the predicate's degree of unsaturation by one. Finally, at the event level, the unsaturation of the internal argument is amnestied by existential closure, and semantic completeness is achieved. What emerges is (67).

(67) $\exists e \exists y$ [have$'$(y)(a)(e) $\wedge$ car$'$(y)]
     $\langle t \rangle$

We have given a Davidsonian rendering of *have*. We assume that the existential closure of the event argument in (67) represents temporary location, and that in the stronger sense of possession, the verb is inherently generic (see Chierchia 1995b). In the examples below, we show the inherent generic.

The compositional process has the same outlines when the verb of the incorporation clause is *täi-* 'not have', as in (68).

(68) Täi-[kareta]    si    Antonio.
     Agr.not.have-car Unm Antonio
     'Antonio doesn't have a car.'

There are two relevant differences. First, *täi-* demands that its internal argument must be composed via Restrict. This demand is met when the property supplied by *kareta* is composed, as (69) shows. Second, *täi-* expresses sentential negation, which must be entered into semantic composition at the sentential level, after the predicate has achieved semantic completeness. In a system in which semantic composition tracks syntactic structure, there are various ways of arranging this; see Ladusaw 1992 for one proposal. What is of interest here is the outcome: the incorporated object must have narrow scope with respect to the negation.

(69)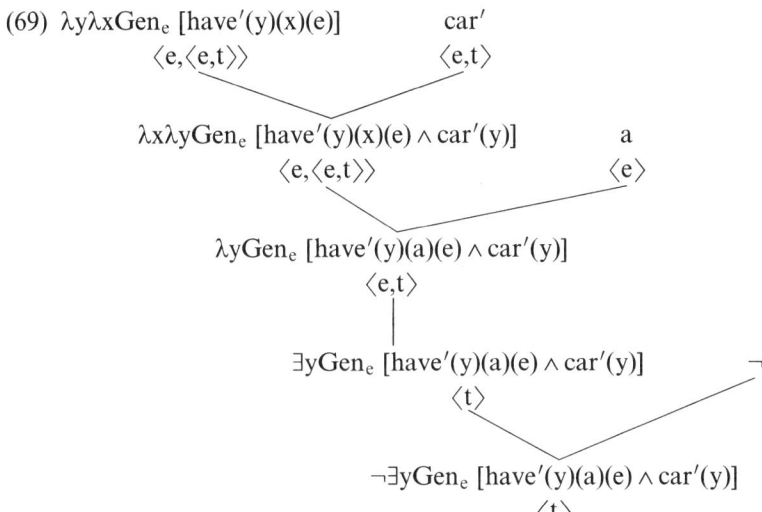

Consider next incorporation clauses in which the incorporated object is doubled by an extra object, such as (70).

(70) Si Carmen gäi-[ga'] i ga'lagu.
Unm Carmen Agr.have-pet the dog
'Carmen has the dog as pet.'

For our purposes, the key stage in the semantic composition of this example occurs after Restrict has composed the expression *gä'* 'pet' with *gäi-*'s internal argument. At that point, the internal argument is (still) unsaturated, so it can be targeted by a further composition operation. Function application composes it with the individual supplied by *i ga'lagu* 'the dog', saturating the argument and reducing the predicate's degree of unsaturation by one. This is shown in (71). (In section 1.3, we introduced the notational convention of demoting an argument's lambda prefix after Restrict has applied, to allow composition of other arguments to proceed. In (71), it is crucial to note that this is a possibility rather than a necessity, since the extra object saturates the argument after Restrict, but before the subject is targeted.)

(71)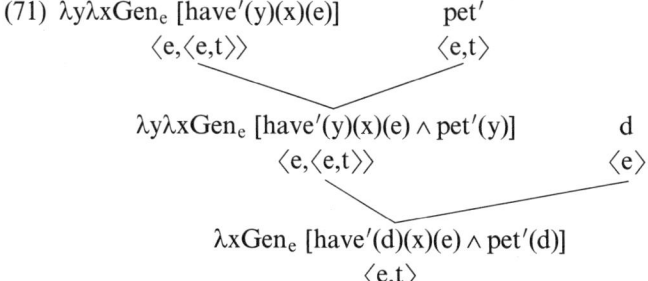

The result is multiple linking: more than one expression has been coherently composed with the argument.

It is important that multiple linking can succeed only if predicate restriction precedes saturation. No other order of composition will allow a given argument to be targeted by more than one composition operation (see section 1.2). Compare (71) with the failed derivation (72), in which an attempt is made to reverse the order. Once function application composes the individual supplied by *i ga'lagu* 'the dog' with the internal argument, the argument becomes saturated and is unavailable for further composition. It is then impossible for the property supplied by *gä'* 'pet' to be composed with it.

(72)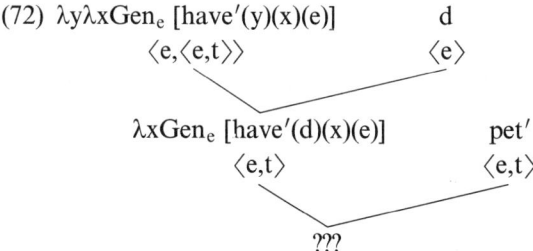

The only workable order is one in which saturation is delayed until the argument is composed with the last expression to which it is linked (or until even later, when existential closure occurs). Before then, it can be targeted only by the nonsaturating mode Restrict.

Finally, let us turn to the corresponding incorporation clauses in which the verb is *täi-* 'not have'. Here the spotlight shifts to *täi-*'s demand that its internal argument must be composed by Restrict—a demand that is responsible for some subtle contrasts.

Consider, for instance, the grammaticality contrast illustrated in (73).

(73) a. Si   Antonio täi-[ga']        *ga'lagu.*
Unm Antonio Agr.not.have-pet dog
'Antonio doesn't have a(ny) dog as pet.'
b. *Si   Antonio täi-[ga']       *esti na ga'lagu.*
Unm Antonio Agr.not.have-pet this L dog
('Antonio doesn't have this dog as pet.')

We claim that the difference between these examples is that (73a) has a well-formed semantic composition but (73b) does not. In (73a), both *gä'* 'pet' and *ga'lagu* are semantically incomplete expressions, so they can be composed with *täi-*'s internal argument via Restrict, as shown in (74). Each instance of composition conforms to the demand that Restrict must be employed.

(74)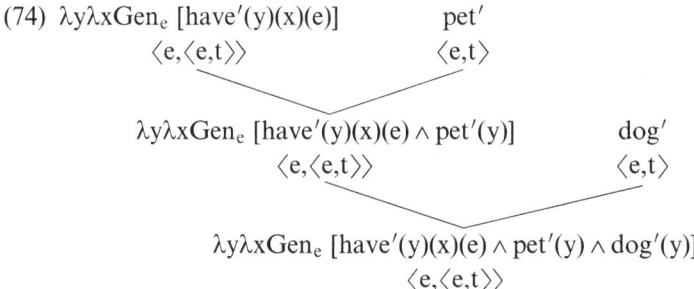

In (73b), however, *esti na ga'lagu* 'this dog' cannot be composed via Restrict, because it denotes an individual. It therefore cannot be composed with *täi-*'s internal argument at all, even though it is linked to this argument, and even though the argument is (still) unsaturated at the relevant point in semantic composition. The end result, shown in (75), is that there is simply no way to integrate this expression into the interpretation without violating the condition on *täi-*.

(75)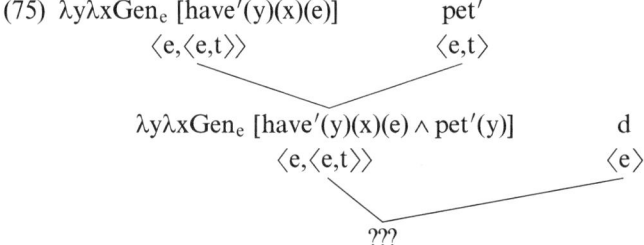

112                                                                Chapter 3

The contrast illustrated in (76) is similar.

(76) a. Täi-[ga']         *ni un ga'lagu* ennao na patgun.
        Agr.not.have-pet not a dog    that L child
        'That child doesn't have any dogs at all as pets.'
     b. *Täi-[ga']        *un ga'lagu* ennao na patgun.
        Agr.not.have-pet a dog     that L child
        ('That child doesn't have a dog as pet.')

As before, what separates these examples is that (76a) has a well-formed semantic composition but (76b) does not. In (76a), semantic composition proceeds in essentially the same way as was just discussed for (73a). The only difference—which we ignore—is that the negative concord determiner *ni un* has a domain-widening effect on the denotation of *ga'lagu* 'dog' (see Kadmon and Landman 1993). In (76b), on the other hand, the composition becomes problematic when we attempt to compose the indefinite *un ga'lagu* 'a dog' with *täi-*'s internal argument. The operation that combines the two must be Restrict, because that is what *täi-* demands. But if Restrict is employed, then the property supplied by *un ga'lagu* will ultimately fall under the scope of sentential negation, contrary to what is demanded by the affirmative polarity determiner *un*. See (77).

(77)

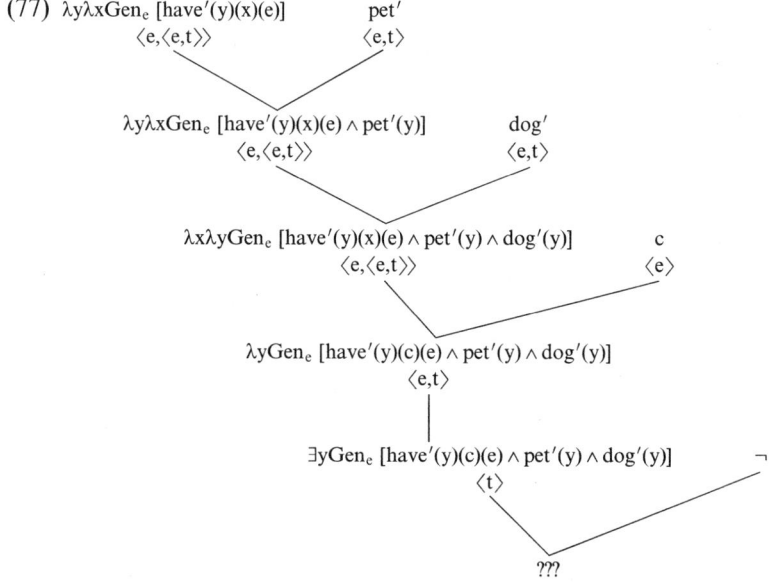

By this point, it should be evident that Restrict, with its ability to compose without saturating, is the key to our account of incorporation in Chamorro. The observation leads to a worry. In our theory, what would prevent an incorporation clause in Chamorro from containing absurdly many extra objects, all semantically incomplete and therefore able to be composed via Restrict? To restate the worry in crosslinguistic terms, what would prevent an incorporated object from being doubled by one or more extra objects even in languages, such as Greenlandic or Maori, that simply do not permit this?

While these are legitimate questions, we see no reason to expect the answer to be found in the theory of restriction and saturation—or, for that matter, in any other aspect of semantic theory. The research tradition in which our approach is grounded assumes that the role of semantics is to interpret syntactic structure, not to dictate what structure is presented for interpretation. But in the troubling scenarios just described, there are no interpretation issues in the strict sense. The problem is rather that the wrong structure—more accurately, too elaborate a structure—has been presented for interpretation.

Putting matters this way suggests that it is the responsibility of the syntax, broadly construed, to determine whether incorporation in a given language is an instance of CNI. And, in fact, it is easy to imagine the kinds of language-specific considerations that might come into play. For example, suppose that a language has incorporation but does not allow DPs to be adjoined. In such a language, the Chamorro route to extra objects would automatically be closed off. Considerations of this sort could well lie behind the fact that semantically incomplete noun phrases in Maori—whether indefinites headed by *he* or incorporated objects—are never doubled by an independent DP (see sections 2.4.1 and A.2.2.1). On the other hand, in languages that have incorporation and independently allow free adjunction of DPs, such as Mohawk (see Baker 1996), one might well expect to find CNI.

It is harder to tell a convincing story about why the syntax might prevent an incorporated object in Chamorro from being doubled by more than one extra object. Given that extra objects are syntactically adjoined, the limitation to one seems mysterious. Nonetheless, such limitations are known to occur elsewhere. In the theory of polysynthetic languages developed by Baker (1996), overt DP "arguments" are actually adjuncts coindexed with, and licensed by, a null argument. The relevant point is that a given null argument can license no more than one DP adjunct—

a stipulation that Baker builds directly into his adjunct licensing condition (1996, 139–142). Further, as a reviewer observes, a DP argument in English generally cannot license more than one adjunct. Compare *They parted angry* and *They parted friends* with *??They parted friends angry*.

Syntactic licensing might ultimately be responsible for the Chamorro limitation on extra objects as well. In this connection, we should note that extra objects differ from other DP adjuncts in Chamorro—for instance, appositives—in that they occur in the unmarked morphological case (see section 3.4). Revealingly, this case is used to signal various grammatical relations that cannot be iterated: subject, direct object, possessor, topic, focus, and the like.

In short, in the system we envision, the syntax and the semantics work together to prevent the overgeneration of extra objects. The syntax is responsible for excluding extra objects that are syntactically ill formed; the semantics is responsible for excluding extra objects, such as those in (73b) and (76b), whose meanings cannot be coherently composed.

We close this section by briefly comparing our account with two other semantic approaches to incorporation: van Geenhoven's (1998) analysis in terms of semantic incorporation and Bittner's (2001) analysis in terms of surface composition as bridging. These other accounts are designed to handle incorporation in Greenlandic, which differs crucially from Chamorro incorporation in not being a version of CNI. Incorporated nouns in Greenlandic can be associated with stranded modifiers, but they cannot be doubled by an independent DP. Given this, it is unsurprising and in no way negative that these other accounts do not generalize immediately to Chamorro. The comparison is nonetheless instructive, because it serves to highlight the distinctive contribution of the theory of restriction and saturation to our account.

Van Geenhoven's (1998) analysis of incorporation in Greenlandic is representative of her overall approach to indefinites that must take narrow scope. In her approach, the incorporated noun supplies a predicate that is absorbed by the verb as a restriction on its internal argument. This semantic incorporation bears some resemblance to our operation Restrict. Where van Geenhoven's approach differs from ours is in her claim that the existential force of the incorporated noun is contributed lexically, by the verb meaning. The result is that "the internal argument's variable is existentially bound" from the beginning, although "the verb leaves a slot for a predication over this variable" (van Geenhoven 1998, 143).

# Object Incorporation in Chamorro 115

This is what prevents semantic incorporation from generalizing smoothly to incorporation in Chamorro. To appreciate the point, consider how van Geenhoven's system would assemble a semantic translation for the Chamorro sentence (70), which is repeated here.

(70) Si    Carmen gäi-[ga']    i    ga'lagu.
     Unm Carmen Agr.have-pet the dog
     'Carmen has the dog as pet.'

One would begin by combining the meaning of the incorporating verb *gäi-* 'have' with the meaning of the incorporated object *gä'* 'pet', as shown in simplified form in (78). Notice especially the translation of 'have', which conforms fully to van Geenhoven's view of the semantics of incorporating verbs.

(78) λPλx∃y [have'(y)(x) ∧ P(y)]           pet'
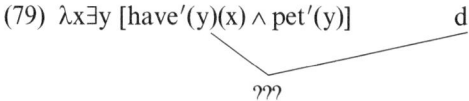
     λx∃y [have'(y)(x) ∧ pet'(y)]

Even at this point in the process, the internal argument is saturated. The existential quantifier that makes it semantically complete has been present from the start, in the verb meaning, and the property that supplies its restriction has now been composed. We therefore expect the internal argument to be unavailable for further composition. But if that is so, then there is no way to integrate the meaning of the extra object *i ga'lagu* 'the dog' appropriately into the translation. See (79).

(79) λx∃y [have'(y)(x) ∧ pet'(y)]           d
         ???

We mentioned earlier that incorporated nouns in Greenlandic can be associated with stranded modifiers, although they cannot be doubled by an independent DP. Interestingly, stranded modifiers pose a compositional problem for van Geenhoven's system similar to what we have just shown. As she says in discussing the incorporation clause whose meaning is 'Ester bought fresh fish', "there is no way to combine the complex verb 'fish-buy' with the property supplied by 'fresh'" (1998, 148). The repair strategy that she suggests is to undo the previous step of the composition, type-shift the incorporated object so that it will (ultimately) accept a modifier, and then recompose the verb meaning with the type-shifted incorporated object.

Whatever the merits of such a strategy for stranded modifiers in Greenlandic, it would be tricky to extend it to the extra object in Chamorro. The reason is that the extra object is not a restrictive modifier, as we have already shown.

Stepping back a bit, we can see why semantic incorporation does not generalize well to incorporation in Chamorro. The idea that the existential force of the incorporated object is contributed by the verb leaves no room for predicate restriction (i.e., absorption) to occur without saturation. But exactly that flexibility, we claim, is what Chamorro incorporation demands.

In contrast to van Geenhoven's discussion, Bittner's (2001) treatment of Greenlandic incorporation is quite brief. It is presented as one illustration of her theory of surface composition as bridging, a theory whose leading idea is that semantic composition within the clause is, like discourse, fundamentally dynamic. In Bittner's theory, the central mechanisms of clause-internal composition are dynamic anaphora and type-driven bridging. These work together to resolve type mismatches by "fill[ing] in predictable anaphoric links between basic meanings that come from the lexicon as rough approximations of what is actually needed" (2001, 128). One argument that Bittner gives for her approach is that it enables semantic composition to be "both universal and faithful to overt surface structures" (2001, 133).

The formal implementation of Bittner's theory is quite intricate, and we cannot do justice to it here. Very informally, and in greatly simplified form, here are the outlines of her analysis of Greenlandic (see Bittner 2001, 149–152).[10]

Bittner assumes that in general, the local context for an affix is established by the stem to which it is attached. Therefore, in Greenlandic incorporation, the local context for the verb—an affix—is established by the incorporated noun. The incorporated noun supplies a property and the verb meaning has an unsaturated internal argument. When the two are combined, the type mismatch is resolved by existential closure, a bridging mechanism that makes the internal argument semantically complete and ensures that it has narrow scope.

If there is a stranded modifier associated with the incorporated noun, its meaning is composed next. Its local context is established by the complex verb whose meaning we have just calculated, and the type mismatch between the two is resolved by base-elaboration bridging. This mechanism treats the property supplied by the modifier as an elaboration of the discourse referent introduced by the internal argument. The result is that the meaning constructed for the Greenlandic incorporation clause 'Ester bought fresh fish' resembles 'Ester fish-bought and it was fresh'.

Can this style of approach be extended to incorporation in Chamorro? Up to a point, the answer seems to be yes. The dynamic existential closure invoked to bridge the meanings of the incorporated object and the affixal verb in Greenlandic can be applied right away to Chamorro. Moreover, even though closure saturates the verb's internal argument, base-elaboration bridging provides a route by which the meaning of the extra object might be folded into the composition.

To see this, consider first incorporation clauses in which the extra object supplies a property, such as (45a) or (73a). In such clauses, the property can be accommodated via base-elaboration bridging just as stranded modifiers are accommodated in Greenlandic. Of course, when the incorporating verb is *tāi-* 'not have', care must be taken to ensure that the sentential negation has scope over the anaphoric link. The meaning constructed for (73a) should be 'It is not the case that [Antonio has a pet and it is a dog]', not the deviant '?*[Antonio doesn't have a pet] and it is a dog'. We will return to this in a moment.

In incorporation clauses in which the extra object supplies an individual, such as (70), matters are more complicated. Here it is tempting to invoke a generalized version of base-elaboration bridging that would link either a property *or an individual* to a discourse referent in the context. If that could be done, an interpretation could be constructed for (70)—one close to 'Carmen has a pet and it is the dog'.

The difficulty that we see with such a dynamic account is that it would be too successful. If base-elaboration bridging could be generalized as we have just suggested, there would be nothing to prevent it from linking the individual supplied by the extra object in (73b) to the discourse referent of the internal argument. The type mismatch seems the same as in (70). But (73b), repeated here, is ill formed.

(73) b. *Si    Antonio täi-[ga']        esti na ga'lagu.
       Unm Antonio Agr.not.have-pet this L  dog
       ('Antonio doesn't have this dog as pet.')

Notice that we cannot dismiss the problem by claiming that the interaction of dynamic anaphora with negation is what is at fault. Earlier, in discussing (73a), we assumed that the sentential negation would have scope over the anaphoric link introduced by base-elaboration bridging.

That assumption should lead to a sensible interpretation here, namely, 'It is not the case that [Antonio has a pet and it is this dog]'. So the ill-formedness of (73b) remains a mystery.

More generally, the style of analysis that we have just sketched seems to offer no satisfactory explanation of the pattern documented in section 3.5.1: the extra object of *täi-* exhibits a definiteness effect, whereas the extra object of *gäi-* does not. Here is what goes wrong: once base-elaboration bridging is generalized to handle the full range of well-formed extra objects, it can accommodate even the type mismatches that we know are unresolvable.

It may be that some other extension of Bittner's dynamic theory might succeed in circumventing this dilemma. Meanwhile, we conclude that her theory too does not generalize comfortably to incorporation in Chamorro. The underlying reason is that the incorporated object and the extra object are not anaphorically related. Instead, we claim, the two are composed with the same argument: one merely restricts the argument, while the other can saturate it.

### 3.7 Restriction without Saturation

Incorporation in Chamorro confirms what is perhaps the most surprising prediction of our theory: if all other conditions are right, a given argument can be linked to, and coherently composed with, more than one expression. The fulfillment of this prediction is noteworthy whatever one's views of predication and saturation happen to be. The fact that no other theory known to us handles the evidence as well offers a powerful argument for distinguishing the notion of semantic composition from the concept of saturation. Even for arguments, the two need not coincide.

Let us, then, take the theory of restriction and saturation for granted and go on to investigate its consequences for the dynamics of discourse. The most obvious question can be posed very simply. What are the discourse ramifications of restriction without saturation? To restate the question in incorporation-specific terms, what would it mean for the incorporated object in Chamorro to introduce a discourse referent?

This is an issue that we have already begun to discuss. Above, in considering Bittner's surface composition as bridging, we in essence argued that any discourse referent introduced by the incorporated object cannot be referred to anaphorically by the extra object. Our argument was based on the definiteness effect documented earlier in section 3.5.1. We now show that it is also possible to arrive at the same conclusion via a different route. The route that we have in mind involves class inclusion relations.

Stenning (1978) observes that discourse anaphora is sensitive to what he calls the hierarchy defined by class inclusion. In this hierarchy, common nouns and pronouns are ordered according to class inclusion relations, so that *cat*, for instance, is subordinate to *creature*, because "if something falls under the denotation of *cat*, then it falls under the denotation of *creature*" (1978, 167). Stenning's observation is that either an antecedent can be subordinate to its discourse anaphor on the hierarchy, or the two can be coextensional. What is forbidden is for a discourse anaphor to be subordinate to its antecedent.

Thus, *cat* can serve as the antecedent for *creature* in (80a), because *cat* is subordinate to *creature*. But it is strange or impossible for *creature* to serve as the antecedent for *cat* (80b).

(80) a. The cat$_i$ went out. Sandy fetched the creature$_i$ in.
    b. ?*The creature$_i$ went out. Sandy fetched the cat$_i$ in.

Significantly, the hierarchy of class inclusion also plays a role in Chamorro incorporation, as can be seen if we inspect the relation between the incorporated object and the extra object when both are common nouns. Of interest is that this relation is the opposite of what we would expect if the incorporated object were an antecedent and the extra object were its discourse anaphor. The facts are that the incorporated object *cannot* be subordinate to the extra object.

The point emerges clearly from the contrast between (81) and (82). Notice, to begin with, that *kätu* 'cat' is subordinate to *ga'ga'* 'animal'; *lahi* 'son' is subordinate to *patgun* 'child'; and *unpesu* 'dollar' is subordinate to *salappi'* 'money'. In the examples in (81), the incorporated object is subordinate to the extra object, which would be the standard arrangement if the extra object were a discourse anaphor referring back to the incorporated object. Revealingly, this pattern is ungrammatical.

(81) a. *Gäi-[katu]   si   Jose *ga'ga'*.
       Agr.have-cat Unm Jose animal
       ('Jose has a càt pét.')
    b. *Täi-[lahi]   i   dos *patgun*.
       Agr.not.have-son the two child
       ('The two don't have a child as son.')

c. *Si   Rita täi-[unpesu]      *ni  háfafa   ha' na salappi'.*
      Unm Rita Agr.not.have-dollar not anything Emp L  money
      ('Rita has no dollars [in] money.')

In the examples in (82), the two common nouns have been reversed, so that the extra object is now subordinate to the incorporated object. This pattern is well formed.

(82) a. Gäi-[ga']        si     Jose *kätu.*
        Agr.have-pet Unm Jose cat
        'Jose has a pèt cát.'
     b. Täi-[patgun]        i    dos *patgun lahi.*
        Agr.not.have-child the two child  son
        'The two don't have a son as child.'
     c. Si    Rita täi-[salappi']      *ni  háfafa   ha' na unpesu.*
        Unm Rita Agr.not.have-money not anything Emp L  dollar
        'Rita has no money [in] dollars.'

Importantly, it is by no means required for the extra object to be subordinate to the incorporated object. The two can have intersecting denotations; in other words, they can be located on independent branches of the hierarchy.[11]

(83) a. Hämi man-gäi-[ga'lagu]      *ädyu siha i*
        we   WH[nom].Agr-have-dog that Pl  the
        *in-pépeksai.*
        WH[obj].Agr-raise.Prog
        'We are the ones who own those dogs that we are raising.'
     b. Si    Carmen täi-[primu]      *pali'.*
        Unm Carmen Agr.not.have-cousin priest
        'Carmen doesn't have priests as cousins.'
     c. Si    Joaquin täi-[amigu]     *ni  hayi   na ma'estru.*
        Unm Joaquin Agr.not.have-friend not anyone L  teacher
        'Joaquin does not have any teachers as friends.'

The incorporated object and the extra object can also, it seems, be coextensional. Speakers are sometimes hesitant about examples such as those in (84), possibly because they find it hard to imagine a convincing context of use. We do not know why such examples are worse when the extra object is definite (as in (84c)) than when it is a bare indefinite or a negative concord DP (84a–b).

(84) a.  Gäi-[guma']   yu' *guma'*.
         Agr.have-house I   house
         'I have a house (as a house).'
   b.    Täi-[lateria]            esti na tenda *ni   háfafa   ha'*
         Agr.not.have-canned.goods this L store  not anything Emp
         *na lateria*.
         L canned.goods
         'This store has no canned goods at all.'
   c.    ?/*Si  Juan gäi-[kareta]  *i   kareta*.
         Unm Juan Agr.have-car  the car
         ('Juan has the car as car.')

What is expressly prohibited is for the incorporated object to be subordinate to the extra object.

The restriction illustrated in (81)–(84) is not unique to Chamorro. It is well documented for CNI in other languages, although there it is usually described in terms of specificity rather than class inclusion (see, e.g., Woodbury 1975; Mithun 1984; S. Rosen 1989; and for a characterization close to ours, Anderson 2000). For us, the relevance of this restriction is that it confirms a conclusion that we had reached earlier: any discourse referent introduced by the incorporated object cannot be referred to anaphorically by the extra object.

Such a conclusion might lead one to assume that incorporated objects—and, more generally, noun phrases composed via Restrict—do not introduce any discourse referent at all. That is, in fact, what Farkas (1997) proposes for the property-denoting noun phrases that she calls predicate modifiers. In her typology of noun phrases, predicate modifiers are like so-called full arguments in that they saturate the argument with which they are combined. What differentiates them from full arguments is that they do not introduce a discourse referent.

Our theory takes exactly the opposite position. One of our fundamental claims is that noun phrases composed via Restrict do not saturate the argument with which they are composed. But we also contend that, even for such noun phrases, a discourse referent is ultimately introduced.

Donkey anaphora supplies some persuasive evidence for our claim that discourse referents are introduced even for noun phrases composed via Restrict.

In incorporation clauses in which no extra object is present, the incorporated object can antecede a donkey pronoun. This generalization, which is supported by extremely robust judgments, is illustrated in (85).

These examples involve the sorts of constructions in which donkey anaphora is typically found: quantificational sentences with complex subjects, such as (85a–b), and conditional sentences, such as (85c). As the translations indicate, in every case the pronoun is anaphoric to the incorporated object.[12]

(85) a. Käda taotao ni    gäi-[kareta$_i$]         ha-diséseha
       each person Comp WH[nom].Agr.have-car Agr-wish.Prog
       na    siña ha-bendi pro$_i$.
       Comp can Agr-sell
       'Each person who owns a car$_i$ wishes that he could sell it$_i$.'
    b. Käda unu ni    gäi-[haga$_i$],         siempri
       each one Comp WH[nom].Agr.have-daughter surely
       ha-po'lu    na    bunita    gui'$_i$.
       Agr-assume Comp Agr.pretty she
       'Everyone who has a daughter$_i$ thinks that she$_i$ is beautiful.'
    c. Yänggin gäi-[guma'$_i$]    i    dos taotao, siempri malägu'
       if      Agr.have-house the two person surely   Agr.want
       na    uma-na'bunitu  pro$_i$ todu i    tiempu.
       Comp Agr-make.pretty    all  the time
       'If two people own a house$_i$, they always want to make it$_i$ nice.'

Further, these pronouns have the characteristic interpretation of donkey pronouns. The meaning of (85a), for instance, is 'Everyone who owns a car wishes that he could sell the car that he owns'.

As is well known, donkey anaphora obeys an intricate set of conditions that have been described and analyzed in various ways (see, e.g., Heim 1982, 1990; Partee 1984; Haïk 1984; Reinhart 1987; Chierchia 1995a). One such condition requires the discourse referent of the antecedent to be accessible to the pronoun, where the precise characterization of "accessible" depends on the overall analysis. In (86), this condition is evidently not met, because the life span of the incorporated object's discourse referent is cut short by sentential negation. The result is that donkey anaphora is just as ungrammatical in the Chamorro example as in its English translation.

(86) *Käda taotao ni    täi-[computer$_i$]
     each person Comp WH[nom].Agr.not.have-computer
     ha-diséseha    na    siña ha-fahan pro$_i$.
     Agr-wish.Prog Comp can Agr-buy
     (*'Each person who doesn't have a computer$_i$ wishes that he could buy it$_i$.')

The ill-formedness of (86) lends further weight to the claim that donkey anaphora is involved in (85). But if so, then a discourse referent must ultimately be introduced for the incorporated object, because that is what the donkey pronoun refers to.

The point can be taken further. Notice that if we are correct that noun phrases composed via Restrict have discourse referents associated with them, then all such noun phrases—not just incorporated objects—should be able to serve as antecedents for donkey anaphora. The line of thought leads to two predictions. Pivots of existential sentences in Chamorro should be able to antecede donkey pronouns. And so should indefinites headed by *he* in Maori.

Very significantly, these predictions are borne out. The pivot of a Chamorro existential sentence can antecede a donkey pronoun, as (87a) shows. Compare (87b), which suggests that donkey anaphora is possible only if the pivot's discourse referent is accessible to the pronoun. (The antecedents in these examples appear in italics.)

(87) a.  Käda taotao ni    guäha    *[kareta-ña]$_i$*  ha-diséseha
         each  person Comp Agr.exist car-Agr          Agr-wish.Prog
         na   siña ha-bendi *pro$_i$*.
         Comp can  Agr-sell
         'Each person who has a car$_i$ (lit. of whom there is a car) wishes that he could sell it$_i$.'
  b. *Käda taotao ni    taya'         *[iyo-nña         computer]$_i$*
      each  person Comp Agr.not.exist  possession-Agr computer
      ha-diséseha   na   u-fahan *pro$_i$*.
      Agr-wish.Prog Comp Agr-buy
      (*'Each person who doesn't have a computer$_i$ (lit. of whom there isn't a computer) wishes that he could buy it$_i$.')

Further, in Maori, indefinites headed by *he* can antecede donkey anaphora, as (88a) shows. In this respect, they are no different from indefinites headed by *tētahi* (88b).

(88) a. Ki te mea ka hari-a   *he kai$_i$*  ma  taua            wahine, me
        if         T bring-Pass a  food T.of the.aforem woman   T
        hoatu *pro$_i$* ki te  pononga tuatahi, mā-na   e hoatu *pro$_i$* ki te
        give            to the attendant first  T.of-her T give           to the
        tuarua.
        second
        'If food$_i$ was brought to the woman, it$_i$ was given to a first attendant, who gave it$_i$ to a second.' (Orbell 1992, 67)

b. Ka kite-a   he tohora e   *tētahi kaititiro$_i$*, ka whakatū-ria *pro$_i$*
   T  see-Pass a  whale   by a           lookout  T  raise-Pass
   te   haki o tōna$_i$ kāinga.
   the flag of his    house
   'If a whale was spotted by a lookout$_i$, he$_i$ would raise the flag of his$_i$ house.' (Waititi 1974, 132)

The conclusion seems unavoidable that when a noun phrase is composed via Restrict, a discourse referent is ultimately introduced for it. At the same time, as we showed earlier, this discourse referent must be inaccessible to the extra object.

These twin conclusions offer a window into the discourse contribution of restriction without saturation and the role of existential closure in securing that contribution. Here is how we interpret the evidence.

Discourse referents are introduced only at the point at which arguments are saturated. We claim that when a semantically incomplete noun phrase is composed with an argument via Restrict, there are two paths by which that argument can achieve semantic completeness: (a) through the composition of some further expression, or (b) through existential closure.

Path (a) is taken in incorporation structures in which the incorporated object is doubled by an extra object that is semantically complete. In such structures, once the meaning of the extra object is composed and the argument is saturated, it introduces a discourse referent.

Path (b) is taken in incorporation structures lacking an extra object, as well as all other structures in which predicate restriction is not followed by further composition that would saturate the argument. In these structures, existential closure steps in to amnesty the unsaturation and make the argument semantically complete. Once that happens, a discourse referent is introduced.

Crucially, path (b) cannot be taken if the composition of some further expression would saturate the argument—for instance, in incorporation structures in which there is an extra object of type e. Otherwise, the judgments in (81) and (82) would be the opposite of what we actually find: the cases in (81) would be grammatical, contrary to fact. But path (b) must be taken if further composition does not lead to saturation. Otherwise, donkey anaphora ought to be impossible in (85), (87a), and (88), but it is well formed.

We can now see that the full range of evidence reveals both that existential closure is necessary and that it cannot be allowed to amnesty semantic incompleteness immediately after an initial attempt at saturation has failed. Rather, closure must be delayed until a point in the compositional process when further attempts at saturation are impossible in principle. We take this point to be the event level.

The view of existential closure that we have arrived at is not new. It is essentially the view advanced originally by Heim (1982) and adopted by Diesing (1992), Kratzer (1995), and numerous others. What we have done is to deconstruct existential closure within our theory, making clear why it must work in exactly the way it has always been assumed to. Its raison d'être and its exact location in the compositional process seem quite reasonable, if we assume that unsaturation must be amnestied and semantic completeness achieved, but only after it is clear that saturation cannot occur via the normal compositional means.

## 3.8 Conclusion

Two natural questions arise at this point, and it seems only right to conclude by addressing them. First, how general is the account of incorporation that we have offered in this chapter? And second, are there constructions besides incorporation in which multiple expressions are linked to, and coherently composed with, the same argument?

As far as we can tell, our approach can extend to a range of incorporation constructions in natural language, once it is recognized that much of the crosslinguistic variation exhibited by these constructions is not fundamentally semantic. Here is what we have in mind.

Previous studies of incorporation (see, among many others, Mithun 1984; Baker 1988) suggest that the prototypical incorporated constituent consists of some projection of N that is linked to an internal argument. In our approach, constituents of this sort are semantically incomplete—property-denoting. Because they are not DPs but merely projections of N, they must be composed via Restrict, just as we claimed for Chamorro.

It is well known that languages differ in whether they permit an incorporated constituent to be doubled by an independent DP—in other words, whether they exhibit some version of CNI (see, among many others, Sadock 1980; Mithun 1984). When doubling is possible, we claim that both the incorporated constituent and the independent DP are linked to the internal argument, and semantic composition proceeds essentially as in Chamorro. First, the meaning of the incorporated constituent is composed with the argument via Restrict, and then the meaning of the extra DP is composed with the same argument via some appropriate composition operation. Because Restrict leaves the argument unsaturated, this order of composition has a well-formed outcome: it does not lead to oversaturation.

When doubling by an independent DP is prohibited, we contend that the prohibition arises not from semantics but from language-particular syntax or perhaps language-particular morphology. For instance, as observed in section 3.6, a language might permit incorporation but simply not allow DPs to be adjoined. If Baker (1988) is right that the extra DP in CNI must be adjoined, the result in such a language would be that CNI would be ruled out. Possibilities of this sort strike us as reasonable. More to the point, the alternative—that language-particular *semantics* might dictate whether incorporation permits doubling by an independent DP— strikes us as implausible.

Cross-cutting the issue of doubling is the question of whether the incorporated constituent has an impact on discourse. Since at least Sadock 1980, 1986, and Mithun 1984, 1986, it has been known that languages differ in whether they permit an incorporated constituent to be associated with a discourse referent, and if they do, whether the discourse referent must satisfy Heim's (1982) Novelty Condition. Some of the relevant data are controversial (see the references just cited and Baker 1996). Still, if we step back and try to make sense of the material available, four basic patterns can be discerned.

(a) In Chamorro and other languages (e.g., Greenlandic—see, e.g., Sadock 1980; van Geenhoven 1998), the incorporated constituent can introduce a discourse referent that must be novel. Our analysis of this pattern was presented in section 3.7. After the meaning of the incorporated constituent is composed via the nonsaturating mode Restrict, the unsaturation of the argument is amnestied by existential closure. Crucially, we claim, arguments that are existentially closed must obey Heim's (1982) Novelty Condition.

(b) In languages with canonical versions of CNI (e.g., Mohawk—see Baker 1996), the incorporated constituent can evidently be associated with a discourse referent that is novel or familiar (see Sadock 1986, 25; Baker 1996, 287–291; and—for a different view—Mithun 1984, 859– 871). One way of describing this pattern would be to assume that these languages handle the semantics of incorporation essentially as in (a), but recognize an extra route by which unsaturated arguments can achieve semantic completeness: their variable can be existentially closed or supplied with a value from the common ground. When the latter route is chosen, the result would be a familiar discourse referent (see, e.g., Kratzer 1995, 160). Notice that such an account would attribute the discourse contrast between incorporation in Chamorro and incorporation in Mohawk to a difference in the mechanisms available in these languages for resolving unsaturation.[13]

(c) In languages such as Maori, the incorporated constituent cannot introduce a discourse referent by any means other than accommodation. We claim that these languages too handle the semantics of incorporation essentially as in (a). Further, we maintain that the incorporated constituent's inability to introduce a discourse referent—except through accommodation—does not follow from semantics but rather has some other source. Several sorts of other sources are conceivable. For instance, in languages in which the complex verb of incorporation is derived via compounding or some other morpholexical process, it would be reasonable for the complex verb to be a word and hence an anaphoric island, in the sense of Postal (1969a). But then the incorporated constituent, lacking any independent syntactic status, would be unable to introduce a usable discourse referent. We think Maori is a language of this sort; see appendix A. Similarly, there may well be languages in which discourse referents can be introduced only by DPs with overt determiners (for related discussion, see Chierchia 1998). Given that incorporated constituents are merely projections of N, in such a language they would be unable to introduce a discourse referent.

(d) Finally, there seem to be languages in which the incorporated constituent can introduce a discourse referent only when the predicate explicitly asserts the introduction of such a referent. We take Massam (2001) to have established that Niuean is a language of this sort. The focus of Massam's discussion is the Niuean construction often identified as object incorporation—a construction much like incorporation in Maori, a closely related language. Although Massam argues that the Niuean construction does not involve incorporation after all, her evidence is consistent with an incorporation analysis like our account of Maori in appendix A. Consequently, we believe that Niuean *does* have incorporation. What interests us here is Massam's discussion of whether incorporated objects in Niuean introduce a discourse referent. As she shows, the incorporated objects of transitive verbs do not introduce a discourse referent that persists past their own NP. But the incorporated pivots of existential verbs do introduce a discourse referent. In our view, her discussion reveals that lexical semantics can cause the incorporated constituent to introduce a discourse referent, even when other factors prohibit such a referent from being introduced as a by-product of semantic composition.[14]

The speculative character of this discussion is obvious. But we think the overall point is clear: our theory generalizes to other prototypical incorporation constructions by handling their semantic composition essentially as it handles incorporation in Chamorro. Language-specific differences in (prototypical) incorporation pose no obstacle to this approach, because almost all such differences can—and should—be traced to morphology or syntax, not to semantics.

Let us now turn to the second question—whether there are constructions besides incorporation in which multiple expressions are composed with the same argument.

One obvious candidate for a construction of this type is the split topic construction in German (see, among many others, Fanselow 1988; van Riemsdijk 1989; Diesing 1992; van Geenhoven 1998; Kuhn 2001). In this construction, an argument of the predicate is realized by two distinct DPs, one in topic position and the other internal to the clause. The topic DP is a bare plural—or, in some dialects, a singular indefinite—that occupies the specifier of C or forms part of a VP that surfaces in this position. The clause-internal DP cannot have an overt N and in this sense resembles the remnant of NP ellipsis. Some representative examples are cited in (89).

(89) a. Ameisen haben ja einen Postbeamten viele gebissen.
       ants have Prt a postman many bitten
       'As for ants, many have bitten a postman.' (Diesing 1992, 33)
   b. Einen Frosch glaube ich, dass er einen kleinen sah.
       a frog believe I that he a small saw
       'As for frogs, I believe he could see a small one.' (Kuhn 2001, 185)
   c. Einen Wagen gekauft hat er sich noch keinen.
       a car bought has he himself yet none
       'As for cars, he has not yet bought one.' (Kuhn 2001, 181)

The syntactic dilemma posed by the split topic construction can be stated very simply. Island effects argue that the topic DP has achieved its position via movement (see van Riemsdijk 1989). That, plus the fact that the topic DP and the clause-internal DP correspond to the same argument, suggests that the two should be derived via some movement that splits up a DP into two independent constituents. But phrase-structural considerations—for instance, the ability of each DP to exhibit its own distinct determiner—make any straightforward analysis in terms of movement problematic.

On the semantic side, van Geenhoven (1998) asserts that both halves of the split topic construction must be interpreted as narrow scope indefinites (see also Diesing 1992). In her analysis, the topic DP and the clause-internal DP are generated as independent subconstituents of VP and interpreted via semantic incorporation: the properties they denote are absorbed by the verb as restrictions on the targeted argument.

While our approach to split topics is in many ways a reinterpretation of van Geenhoven's approach, we differ from her and follow Kuhn (2001, 210) in our semantic characterization of the two DPs. In our view, the topic DP must be interpreted as a narrow scope indefinite, but the clause-internal DP need not be: it can be a wide scope indefinite or—in Swiss German—even a universal quantifier, if conditions are right (see Spaelti 1995). Consider:

(90) Orthographische Fehler waren ihm sogar drei nicht
 spelling mistakes were to.him even three not
 aufgefallen.
 noticed
 'As for spelling mistakes, there were even three that he didn't recognize.' (van Geenhoven 1998, 33, n. 15)

Once this view is adopted, our approach to split topics becomes clear in outline. This is another construction in which multiple expressions are linked to, and composed with, the same argument. Further, the evidence argues that the topic DP must be composed via Restrict, whereas the clause-internal DP can in principle be composed by a wider range of composition operations. The topic DP has a profile fully consistent with the semantics of predicate restriction. It can be interpreted only as a narrow scope indefinite, and it can evidently be iterated (Kuhn 2001, 191–192). On the other hand, the clause-internal DP has none of these characteristics.

For these suggestions to be crystallized into an analysis, we would have to respond to some challenging questions. What forces the meaning of the topic DP to be composed via Restrict? Further, assuming that semantic composition tracks syntactic structure, what syntactic structure will ensure that the targeted argument is restricted by the meaning of the topic DP before it is (potentially) saturated by the meaning of the clause-internal DP? The contemplation of these questions must remain a project for the future. Meanwhile, split topics give some reason to believe that multiple linking is not limited to incorporation but can occur in other constructions as well.

# Appendix A
# The Syntax of Chamorro Incorporation

Since Kroeber 1909, 1911, and Sapir 1911, most discussions of the phenomenon of incorporation have approached it from the standpoint of the morphology-syntax interface. The fundamental issue concerns the status of the incorporated noun. Does this noun have a syntactic life independent of the complex verb containing it, or is it merely a subpart of a complex word formed by compounding or some other morphological process?

The issue has continued to be controversial, as can be seen from Sadock 1980, 1986, Mithun 1984, 1986, Di Sciullo and Williams 1987, Baker 1988, 1996, S. Rosen 1989, Anderson 2000, and others. But it is firmly in the background for the purposes of this monograph. To emphasize this, we have relegated our discussion of the phrase structure of Chamorro incorporation to this appendix.

Section A.1 surveys the lexical and syntactic approaches to incorporation, with particular attention to the phenomenon that Mithun has called classificatory noun incorporation (CNI). Section A.2 discusses some Chamorro evidence that narrows the range of possibilities but does not settle the status of the incorporated object. Section A.3 presents some evidence that bears directly on this question. Much of the evidence favors a syntactic analysis like Baker's (1988, 1996), in which the incorporated N combines with V via head movement. Section A.4 returns to the extra object, which was shown in section 3.4.1 to be a syntactic adjunct, and discusses its attachment site.

## A.1 Previous Approaches

The issues raised by incorporation have a special slant in CNI, when the incorporated noun is doubled by an independent noun phrase. In essence, the independent noun phrase seems to offer an additional window into the status of the incorporated noun.

Proceeding for simplicity's sake as if the only (relevant) incorporation is object incorporation, we can frame two questions about the phrase structure of CNI. First, does the incorporated object function as an independent noun phrase in the syntax? And second, is the extra object a complement of the verb?

The lexical approach to incorporation answers "no" to the first question and "yes" to the second. In this approach, the predicate of CNI is a transitive verb whose DP complement is the extra object. The incorporated object is a "qualifier" (Mithun 1984, 859, 863; Di Sciullo and Williams 1987, 64) or "classifier" (S. Rosen 1989, 297) that imposes additional selectional restrictions on the extra object but has no independent syntactic status (see the references just cited; Anderson 1992, 33; and—for commentary—Sadock 1991, 92–93, and Baker 1996, 306–314). Semantically, such an approach has much in common with our view that the incorporated object is semantically incomplete and composed via Restrict. As far as the syntax goes, it assumes the phrase structure for CNI sketched in (1).

(1)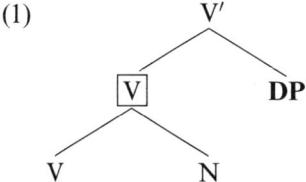

In this structure, the V in the box is a morphologically complex verb consisting of the verb plus the incorporated object. The complex verb is transitive: its DP complement, in boldface, is the extra object.

On the other hand, the syntactic approach to incorporation answers "yes" to the first question and "no" to the second. The standard generative version of this approach was developed by Baker (1988) and investigated in detail by Baker (1996) for CNI in Mohawk and other polysynthetic languages. In Baker's system, the incorporated object originates as the head of an NP complement to V. This N raises to adjoin to V via head movement, thereby enabling its NP to satisfy universal principles (e.g., the Case Filter (Baker 1988) or the Theta Criterion (Baker 1996)). The extra object is an adjunct, adjoined to VP and coindexed with

# Syntax of Chamorro Incorporation 133

the NP complement of V (see Baker 1996, 306–326). In such an analysis, the structure before head movement is essentially (2).

(2)
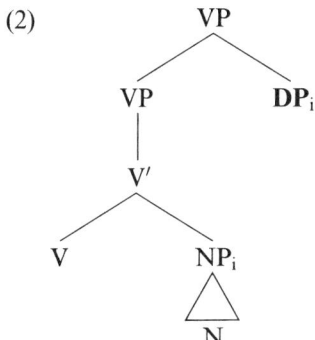

Previous discussions of CNI that are explicit about phrase structure are generally committed to one of these two structures. It should be obvious, though, that (1) and (2) do not exhaust the possibilities. One can easily imagine a lexical approach to incorporation in which the extra object is not a DP complement of the verb, but an adjunct. Such an approach might assume a phrase structure for CNI like (3).

(3)
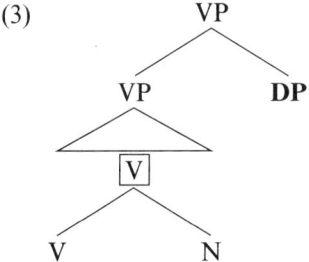

One can also imagine a syntactic approach to incorporation in which head movement operates on a phrase structure different from (2). For instance, the verb might take a small clause complement projected from some functional head F, where F's complement is the maximal projection of the incorporated object and F's specifier, the extra object. Before N raises, ultimately to adjoin to V, such a structure would look like (4).

(4)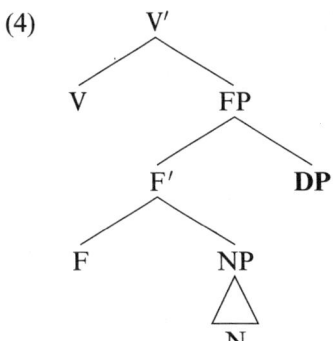

Though (3) and (4) have not, as far as we know, been seriously proposed by anyone, they nonetheless serve to make the point that the extra object might not reveal as much about the status of the incorporated object as one might have hoped. Even so, the two are connected in one respect. Suppose we accept the idea that a head can have at most one complement, and suppose further that there is exactly one verb in the canonical incorporation clause. Then if the extra object is a complement of the verb, the incorporated object cannot be; and vice versa.

## A.2 Some Preliminary Results

With this much background, let us now revisit the syntactic results of chapter 3. We begin with some results that help to clarify the phrase structure of incorporation.

### A.2.1 The Extra Object Is a Syntactic Adjunct

In section 3.4.1, we established that the extra object in Chamorro incorporation is not a complement of V, but rather is syntactically adjoined. The evidence came from the extra object's inaccessibility to *wh*-movement, its islandhood, and its inability to be shared by conjoined verbs.

The conclusion that the extra object is an adjunct argues that incorporation clauses in Chamorro cannot have (1) as their phrase structure. Nor can they have (4) as their phrase structure, because in (4) the extra object is the specifier of a complement to V and therefore equivalent to a complement of V for movement purposes (see Chomsky 1986). The range of possible phrase structures is thus narrowed significantly, although the status of the incorporated object remains unresolved.

### A.2.2 The Incorporated Object Originates within NP

In section 3.3, we established that the incorporated object originates within a maximal projection that we identified as NP but not DP.

One might be tempted to see this as evidence for the superiority of the syntactic approach to incorporation. The line of thought would go as follows: It is assumed by virtually everyone that the complex verb of incorporation consists of V plus an incorporated *noun*. In the syntactic approach, this N originates as the head of an NP complement to V and then raises to V via head movement. In the lexical approach, the N forms a morphological compound with V, where the process of compound formation is assumed to be restricted to heads. Consequently, only versions of the syntactic approach have assumed that the incorporated N originates within its own NP.

There is, however, nothing necessary about this state of affairs. It is easy to conceive of a lexical approach to incorporation in which the compound verb would consist of V plus the phrasal constituent NP. In such a scenario, the so-called incorporated noun would be an NP, but for morphological purposes alone. It would still have no syntactic life independent of the complex verb containing it.

We introduce this scenario because it strikes us as quite plausible, both in general and for Austronesian languages in particular.

Consider the general issue first. Numerous generative linguists have observed that morphological compounds sometimes consist of a head plus a phrase. One classic example involves so-called N-N compounds in English. It has been known since Chomsky and Halle 1968, 21–22 and n. 9, that N-N compounds can exhibit a nonhead constituent that is an N with modifiers or, more rarely, an N with complements but without a determiner—NP but not DP in current terms (see, e.g., Hoeksema 1985; Lieber 1988; Spencer 1991, 321; Cinque 1993; Jackendoff 1997). Some of these NP-N compounds are widely accepted and very familiar.

(5) a. [rare book] dealer
    b. [second language] acquisition
    c. [civil rights] bill
    d. [excess profits] tax

Others are new creations that suggest that the formation of NP-N compounds is productive.

(6) a. [high net worth] individuals (from the *Santa Cruz Sentinel*)
    b. [UCSC students of color] activists (from the *Santa Cruz Sentinel*)

c. [small enrollment] courses (from a UCSC administrative memo)
d. [eligibility for review] policy (from a UCSC administrative memo)
e. [control of dogs] act (from a sign about the leash law in Dublin, Ireland)

Opinions differ on what theoretical conclusions should be drawn from complex words of this type (see the references cited above for a range of views). But whatever the broader implications, it seems clear that morphological theory must recognize that compounds can consist of a head plus a phrase. A lexical approach to incorporation that treats the complex verb as a compound of V plus NP would thus be permitted on general grounds.

We think it significant that some Austronesian languages distantly related to Chamorro seem to have incorporation of just this sort (see Mithun 1984; Massam 2001).[1] One of these languages, we believe, is Maori (though see Pearce 2001 for a different view). Below we present the Maori facts in detail, both to fill out the picture of semantically incomplete noun phrases in this language and to facilitate comparison with Chamorro.

**A.2.2.1 Incorporation in Maori**  In Maori, object incorporation offers an alternative to *he* for dealing with internal arguments that are semantically incomplete. In this construction, which is fully productive, a semantically incomplete noun phrase that is linked to the verb's internal argument does not surface as an independent DP but instead is incorporated: it appears to the immediate right of V, unaccompanied by any determiner. Compare the transitive clauses in (7) with the incorporation clauses in (8).

(7) a. Kei te whāngai a   Rewi i   ngā   poaka.
    T    feed      Pers Rewi DO the.pl pig
    'Rewi is feeding the pigs.' (Waititi 1962, 23)
  b. He      karanga i   aua          manuhiri.
     Pred.a call      DO the.pl.aforem visitor
     '[The local women's task] is to welcome those visitors.' (Karetu 1974, 3)
  c. I muri mai   ka whānau  a   Koata i   a   Kāwharu.
     at after to.here T give.birth Pers Koata DO Pers Kāwharu
     'Koata then gave birth to Kāwharu.' (Jones and Biggs 1995, 253 [40.2])

(8) a. He    tino pai   a   Rewi ki te whāngai [poaka].
       Pred.a very good Pers Rewi Infin feed    pig
       'Rewi is very good at feeding pigs.' (Waititi 1962, 23)
   b. E karanga [manuhiri] ana ia.
      T call     visitor        she
      'She is welcoming visitors.' (Bauer 1997, 199)
   c. Tērā       anō  ia  e whānau   [tamariki].
      over.there again she T give.birth children
      'She would have more children.' (Jones and Biggs 1995, 109 [13.2])

Incorporation in Maori is an instance of what Mithun (1984) has called incorporation of the compounding type: the incorporated object cannot be doubled by an independent noun phrase and the construction is, for all practical purposes, intransitive. Semantically, the incorporated object is interpreted as a narrow scope indefinite that happens not to set up a discourse referent. In our terms, it is composed with the verb's internal argument via Restrict.

Evidence from word order suggests that the verb and the incorporated object form a complex verb in Maori. Particles usually identified in Maori grammars as occurring in a fixed order to the right of V occur instead to the right of the incorporated object in incorporation clauses. Among these forms are the adverbial particles (shown in (9a)), the imperfective particle *ana* (9b), and the locative pro-form *ai* (9c).

(9) a. I whai [uri]        anō  tēnei tangata.
       T have descendant again this  person
       '[The writer does not know whether] this man has any descendants.' (Jones and Biggs 1995, 39 [3.54])
   b. E kiriweti [wāhine] ana ia.
      T hate      women       he
      'He hates women.' (Bauer 1997, 161)
   c. Ka haere atu    rāua    ki reira, mahi [māra kūmara]    ai.
      T  go    away  they.du to there  make farm sweet.potato Pro
      'They would soon be coming to make kuumara plantations there.' (Jones and Biggs 1995, 281 [45.1])

Pronominal subjects, which occur to the right of V but to the left of nonpronominal argument and adjunct phrases, also occur to the right of the incorporated object in incorporation clauses.

(10) a. Kei te ruku [kōura]   rātou.
         T    dive   crayfish  they
         'They are diving for crayfish.' (Bauer 1997, 44)
     b. Kei te kōrero [whakataukī] māua    ko    Koro.
         T    speak   proverb     we.du  Ident  Father
         'Father and I are discussing proverbs.' (Karetu 1974, 59)

These word orders represent the only relevant possibilities. More generally, nothing, not even pro-forms, can separate the verb from the incorporated object in surface structure.

If we take at face value the claim that postverbal particles and pronominal subjects are positioned to the immediate right of V, then (9) and (10) suggest that the verb and the incorporated object form a complex verb—perhaps one created by morphological compound formation (see Bauer 1997, 315). Let us provisionally assume this, though other analyses are possible (see especially Massam 2001), and go on to scrutinize the internal structure of the incorporated object.

In the examples cited above, the incorporated object is simply a noun. But a much wider range of possibilities is attested in the literature. (For a different set of judgments, see Pearce 2001.) The incorporated object can be a compound noun (see Bauer 1993, 479).

(11) a. He      aha    hoki koutou i   mau [rau rākau] ai?
         Pred.a what? also you.pl  T   wear leaf tree   Pro
         'Why do you (pl) wear leaves of trees?' (Karetu 1974, 4)
     b. I muri mai    i     nga    whakaongaonga, kai te hiahia [kapu
         at after to.here DO the.pl excitement    T    want     cup
         tī] ahau.
         tea I
         'After all the *excitement*, I need a cup of tea.' (H. M. Ngata 1994, 137)

The incorporated object can also consist of conjoined nouns. In the examples in (12), the conjoined Ns are juxtaposed, sometimes with an adverb such as *hoki* 'also' following the rightmost conjunct.

(12) a. I moe [tāne, wāhine atu]  ki reira.
         T sleep man  women  away at there
         'They married husbands and wives there.' (Jones and Biggs 1995, 339 [58.15])

b. Haere ki tāwāhi   ki te kitekite [whenua, iwi   hoki].
   go   to other.side Infin see   land   people also
   'Go abroad to see lands and people.' (Karetu 1974, 137)
c. Me haere koe ki te uta  [kūmara,   rīwai, kāpeti, kāreti,
   T  go   you Infin load  sweet.potato potato cabbage carrot
   mātene hoki], ki runga i    te taraka.
   mutton also   to top    DO the truck
   'You should go load sweet potatoes, potatoes, cabbage, carrots, and mutton onto the truck.' (Waititi 1974, 40)

The incorporated object can consist of a noun modified by an adjective, as Bauer (1993, 479) has observed. Notice that in (13c), the imperfective particle *ana* and the pronominal subject occur to the right of the adjective. This word order argues that the complex verb includes both N and its adjective modifier.

(13) a. Ka hanga [pā   wehe]    mo rātou ki runga i    tētehi puke.
       T  build  fort separate for them at top   DO a    hill
       'They built themselves a separate fort on a hill.' (Jones and Biggs 1995, 305 [50.3])
    b. Ka kōrero [kupu tohutohu] a   Hata ki a    ia.
       T  speak  word guide     Pers Hata to Pers him
       'Hata said words of advice (lit. guiding words) to him.' (Waititi 1974, 165)
    c. E rukuruku [kōura   nunui] ana ia.
       T dive     crayfish big    she
       'She is diving for big crayfish.' (Bauer 1997, 316)

The incorporated object can consist of a noun followed by other types of modifiers, including relative clauses. In (14a), the noun is modified by a finite relative clause; in (14b), by a nonfinite relative clause; and in (14c), by both an adjective and a relative clause.

(14) a. Nā reira i tahuri ai  te wahine rā  ki te kimi [huarahi e
       therefore T turn  Pro the woman that Infin find  way     T
       ea         ai ōna     wawata].
       be.satisfied Pro her.pl desire
       'Therefore the woman set about finding a way by which she could realize her goal.' (Karetu 1974, 97)

b. Ko tēnei, ko te whai [wāhi hei tangi-hanga tūpāpaku].
   Ident this  Ident the have place so.as mourn-Nmlz corpse
   '[One of the main reasons] is this, to have a place for mourning
   the dead.' (Karetu 1974, 153)
c. He rerekē te whai [matua kēkē e rua tekau tau te
   Pred.a funny the have parent different T two ten year the
   tamarikitanga atu i a koe].
   being.young more than Pers you
   'It's *funny* to have an uncle twenty years younger than you.'
   (H. M. Ngata 1994, 171)

The incorporated object can consist of a noun followed by a PP modifier. Notice that in (15) the pronominal subject occurs to the right of the PP. This word order confirms, as before, that the complex verb includes the entire phrase consisting of N plus modifier.

(15) Hai nga hōtoke ka purei [pirori ki rō whare] ahau.
     in the.pl winter T play bowl at inside house I
     'In winter, I play *indoor* bowls.' (H. M. Ngata 1994, 226)

Finally, the incorporated object can consist of a phrase that expresses coordination. In the examples in (16), the incorporated object ends with an indefinite DP that is headed by *tētahi* and preceded by the preposition or conjunction *me* 'and, with'. Whether the relevant constituent is a comitative PP or a DP conjunct preceded by a conjunction, its status as a maximal projection strongly suggests that the entire incorporated object is not a head but a phrase.

(16) a. Ko Pētera mā i tono-a ki te moana ki te ruku [kuku,
        Ident Peter et.al T send-Pass to the ocean Infin dive mussel
        kōura, kina, me ētahi atu kai moana].
        crayfish sea.egg and a.pl other food sea
        'Peter and his friends were sent to the ocean to dive for mussels,
        crayfish, sea-eggs, and other seafood.' (Waititi 1974, 29)
    b. Kāore he mahi hoko [paraikete, hīti, pera, naihi, pāoka,
       T.not a work buy blanket sheet pillow knife fork
       pune, tauwera, me ētahi atu taonga mō te whare].
       spoon towel and a.pl other possession T.of the house
       'There's no need to buy blankets, sheets, pillows, knives, forks,
       spoons, towels, and other things for the house.' (Waititi 1974,
       74)

Syntax of Chamorro Incorporation                                       141

In short, there is ample evidence that the incorporated object in Maori can be more than just N. It is a phrase that can be coordinated and that consists of N plus modifiers but without a determiner—NP but not DP, in other words. There is also evidence that the complex verb includes this entire NP (e.g., (13c) and (15)). Semantically, the results are fully consistent with the idea that the incorporated object is property-denoting and therefore semantically incomplete. Morphosyntactically, we can say this: if the complex verb of incorporation is, as we have proposed, a morphological compound in Maori, then the process of compound formation must be able to combine V with NP.

**A.2.2.2 Summary** There are thus theoretical and empirical reasons to believe that morphological compounds can consist of a head plus a phrase. But if that is so, then the Chamorro evidence that the incorporated object originates within NP does not distinguish a syntactic approach to incorporation from a lexical approach.

## A.3 Some More Conclusive Results

Fortunately, there is evidence that bears more directly on the status of the incorporated object in Chamorro. We can set the stage for the evidence by observing that head movement—the cornerstone of the syntactic approach—is widely viewed as an operation that targets heads and only heads. Such a view makes some clear predictions about the surface constituency of the incorporated noun. If the syntactic approach is correct for Chamorro incorporation and the complex verb is derived by head movement, then the incorporated N should form a surface constituent with V that is separate from the rest of its original NP. On the other hand, if the lexical approach is correct, then there is no reason to expect N to be separated from the rest of NP, because—as we have just shown—morphological compounds can consist of a head plus an entire phrase.

We know of three empirical patterns that bear on the surface constituency of the incorporated noun and therefore on the issue of whether incorporation is morpholexical or syntactic. The first pattern favors a lexical approach to incorporation; the other two favor a syntactic approach.

### A.3.1 Coordinate NPs
As was observed in section 3.3, there are speakers of Chamorro who permit the NP of the incorporated object to be a coordinate NP. Some

examples were given in (25) of chapter 3; another example appears here.

(17) Esti i pätgun gäi-[bula asút yan agäga' na biskleta].
    this the child Agr.have-ball blue and red L bicycle
    'This child has a blue ball and a red bicycle.'

Incorporated objects that are coordinate NPs are also permitted in Maori, as we have just shown, and in Greenlandic (Bittner 1998). This is remarkable, given that the incorporation constructions found in these languages are, in other respects, quite dissimilar.

The ability of the incorporated object to be a coordinate NP argues for a lexical approach to incorporation in Chamorro. The reason is this: If the complex verb is a morphological compound consisting of V plus NP, then structures like (17) can be produced straightforwardly, as long as the process of compound formation has access to coordinate NPs. Such access would be difficult to rule out in principle. However, if the complex verb were derived by head movement, then structures like (17) could be produced only by violating the Coordinate Structure Constraint—by moving an N that is a proper subpart of a coordinate structure. The problem is diagrammed in (18).

(18)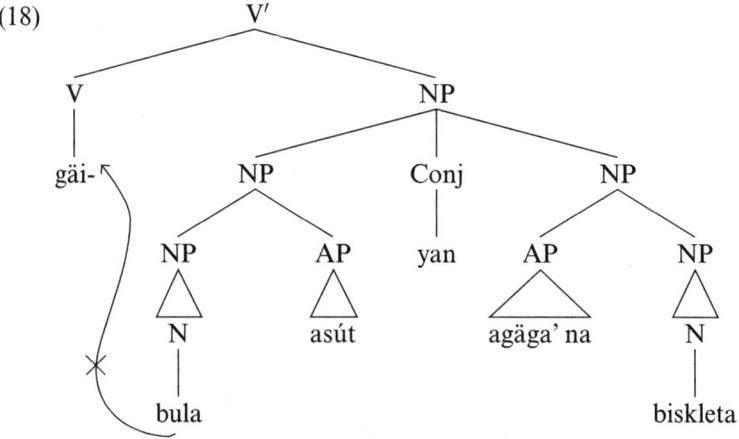

Similar problems would arise if the complex verb were derived in the syntax by some operation that combined V and N but did not involve movement—Merge, for instance (Chomsky 1995).

Considerations of this sort led Bittner (1998, 21–22) to reject a syntactic approach to Greenlandic incorporation for a lexical approach (more precisely, a base-generation approach). There are two reasons why we are

Syntax of Chamorro Incorporation

reluctant to make a similar move. First, not all Chamorro speakers find sentences like (17) to be grammatical, although some clearly do. Second, it is not obvious to us how a lexical approach would handle the two patterns that we discuss next.

### A.3.2 The Word Order of the Incorporated Object

As has been amply illustrated by this point, the incorporated noun in Chamorro always precedes the rest of the NP in which it originates. This amounts to saying that the NP of the incorporated object appears to be N-initial in surface structure.

The observation is important because Chamorro NPs are not generally required to be N-initial. Modifiers can routinely adjoin to either side of NP (see section 3.1), and when adjunction is to the left, the resulting NP begins with a modifier, not with the head N. Nonetheless, the modifiers of an incorporated object must occur to the right of N. Compare:

(19) a. Man-gäi-[kareta tres] i famalao'an.
Agr-have-car three the women
'The women have three cars.'
b. Si Juan gäi-[kareta agäga'].
Unm Juan Agr.have-car red
'Juan owns a red car.'
c. Täi-[amiga ni yä-hu] si Carmen.
Agr.not.have-friend Comp WH[obj].like-Agr Unm Carmen
'Carmen has no women friends who I like.'

(20) a. *Man-gäi-[tres kareta] i famalao'an.
Agr-have-three car the women
('The women have three cars.')
b. *Gäi-[agäga' na kareta] yu'.
Agr.have-red L car I
('I own a red car.')
c. *Gäi-[yä-hu na kareta] si Juan.
Agr.have-WH[obj].like-Agr L car Unm Juan
('Juan owns a car that I like.')

The fact that the incorporated noun must precede the rest of its NP in surface structure argues for a syntactic approach to incorporation. This is because head movement automatically produces the word order of (19). In a head-initial language like Chamorro, general constraints on movement will always cause a moved head to raise to the left. Consequently, an N that raises to V in an incorporation clause must surface outside, and to the left of, its original NP—just the surface arrangement shown in (19). Assuming that head movement is obligatory in incorporation clauses, what is wrong with (20) is simply that no movement has occurred.

Notice that the same facts would be mysterious in a lexical approach—more precisely, in an approach in which the complex verb was a morphological compound consisting of V plus NP. Given that NPs are not generally required to be N-initial in Chamorro, it would be stipulative to impose such a requirement on NPs that are members of compound verbs. One could try to rationalize the requirement by assuming that the verbs of possession are prefixes that must attach to N. But such an assumption would not account for the verb's inability to attach to an N modifier of the incorporated object. Consider (21), in which the incorporated object *guma'* 'house' has an NP modifier consisting of the noun *hayu* 'wood'. The order of the incorporated object and the modifier cannot be reversed, as (22) shows, even though this is allowed elsewhere.

(21) Man-gäi-[guma' hayu].
Agr-have-house wood
'They have a wood house.'

(22) *Man-gäi-[hayu na guma'].
Agr-have-wood L house
('They have a wood house.')

Overall, these facts seem to suggest that a syntactic approach to incorporation is preferable to a lexical approach.

### A.3.3 The Word Order of the Subject

A similar kind of evidence favoring the syntactic approach is provided by the position of the subject in incorporation clauses.

We have already observed that various word orders are possible in Chamorro clauses whose predicate is a verb, but the unmarked word order is Verb-Subject-Object-Other Arguments. What is relevant here is that VSO order, however produced, combines with the syntactic approach to make a prediction. If the complex verb is derived by head movement, then the subject should be able to surface between this derived verb and the original NP of the incorporated object. The subject should, in other words, be able to separate the incorporated N from the rest of its NP.

For reasons that we do not fully understand but that probably involve information packaging, the subject of an incorporation clause typically occurs at an edge of the clause rather than in the middle. Even so, the subject can occur clause-internally, and then it can separate the incorporated N from the rest of its NP.[2] Consider the following examples. In (23a), the subject intervenes between the incorporated N and the NP modifier *ga'lagu* 'dog'; in (23b), between the incorporated N and the AP modifier *asút* 'blue'; and in (23c), between the incorporated N and a modifier or modifiers including a relative clause.

(23) a. Ginin gäi-[ga'] i chi'lu-hu palao'an [ga'lagu].
Imperf Agr.have-pet the sibling-Agr female dog
'My sister had a dog.'
b. Täi-[atumobit] si Joaquin [asút].
Agr.not.have-car Unm Joaquin blue
'Joaquin doesn't own a(ny) blue car.'
c. Gäi-[patgun] si Miguel [palao'an akuentuse-ñña
Agr.have-child Unm Miguel female WH[obl].talk.to-Agr
si Anna].
Unm Anna
'Miguel has a daughter who Anna was talking to.'

Perhaps the most telling of these examples is (23b), which means 'Joaquin doesn't own a(ny) blue car'. The sentential negation included in the meaning of *täi-* 'not have' makes it highly unlikely that *asút* 'blue' could be the predicate of a clause independent from the incorporation clause. (In other words, (23b) does not mean 'Joaquin doesn't own any car and it is blue'.) The only plausible analysis is one that treats *asút* as an AP modifier of the incorporated noun. Consistent with this, (23b) can be used to describe a situation in which Joaquin owns cars but none of them happens to be blue.

The syntactic approach can account straightforwardly for the word order shown in (23). But the facts would be more troublesome in a lexical approach in which the complex verb was a compound consisting of V plus NP. In order for such an approach to maintain that the incorporated N and its modifier(s) in (23) constituted a single NP, the subject would have to occur in the middle of the compound verb formed from that NP—a clear violation of lexical integrity. Thus, these facts, like those discussed in the previous subsection, seem to favor a syntactic approach over a lexical approach.

### A.3.4 The Overall Situation

Where does this leave us? The two word order patterns just described seem to favor a syntactic approach to Chamorro incorporation over a lexical approach. For the lexical approach, the challenge would be to develop a coherent analysis of the modifiers and other dependents accompanying the incorporated N. The evidence we have just presented argues that certain modifiers of the incorporated N do not form part of a compound verb. At the same time, the analytic alternative that would fit most comfortably into a lexical approach is not plausible—namely, to treat the full range of dependent constituents documented in section 3.3 as extra objects. One reason is that not all such constituents are attested independently as DPs. Another reason is that such constituents can *co-occur* with an extra object. But in general, the extra object cannot be iterated; see section 3.6.

On the other hand, the coordination pattern described at the beginning of this section seems to favor a lexical approach to incorporation over a syntactic approach. For the syntactic approach, the challenge would be to reconcile the obligatory character of head movement in incorporation clauses (see (19)–(22)) with the fact that such movement in (17) would violate the Coordinate Structure Constraint. This is a substantial challenge, made more so by the recurrence of the coordination pattern in languages such as Maori and Greenlandic.

We leave the matter here, aware that the evidence—so far—could be viewed as evenly balanced between the two approaches.

### A.4 The Attachment Site of the Extra Object

Let us, finally, return to the question of where the extra object is adjoined in the structure of incorporation clauses. We will suggest an answer that, surprisingly, seems to weigh in favor of a syntactic approach to incorporation.

Chamorro is a language in which the only adjuncts that are completely inaccessible to movement are those adjoined to NP (see Chung 1998, chap. 9). For instance, a prepositional phrase adjoined to VP (such as (24a)) or IP (24b) can undergo *wh*-movement as long as no island boundaries are crossed. But a prepositional phrase adjoined to NP (24c) cannot undergo *wh*-movement at all.

(24) a. Hafa pukka'-ña         i  pätgun ni bintana ___ antis di
       what? WH[obl].break-Agr the child  Obl window      before
       u-falagu?
       Agr-run
       'What did the child break the window with before he ran
       away?'
   b. Disdi ngai'an nai    mediku-n nana-mu    si Juan ___?
       since when? Comp doctor-L mother-Agr   Juan
       'Since when has Juan been your mother's doctor?'
   c. *Pära hayi na      guäha   [chinina ___]?
       for  who? Comp Agr.exist shirt
       ('Who was there a shirt for?')

Suppose we take this descriptive generalization at face value. Then our demonstration that the extra object, an adjunct, is inaccessible to movement suggests that it must be adjoined to NP, where the relevant NP is presumably the NP in which the incorporated object originates. In effect, the strategy of this proposal is to embed the extra object so deeply in the structure that movement is impossible. The result is the rather unusual structure sketched in (25). Here X represents a category that would be V′ in a syntactic approach to incorporation, but V—the compound verb—in a lexical approach.

(25)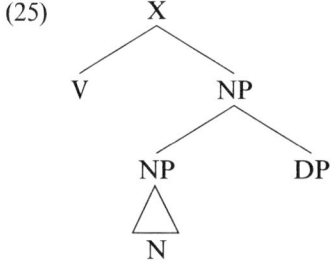

Interestingly, there is a sense in which (25) seems more plausible in a syntactic approach to incorporation than in a lexical approach. In the lexical approach that we have been pursuing, the complex verb is a compound consisting of V plus NP. If the extra object is adjoined to NP, it presumably would form part of that same compound. Now it is generally assumed that the nonhead constituents of compounds do not refer specifically, to individuals, but only generically, to properties or kinds (see, e.g., Spencer 1991, 312). The incorporated object is well behaved in this respect, because it is semantically incomplete. But the extra object is not: it *can* refer to a specific individual, as we have already shown (in section 3.4). The observation argues that the extra object should not be embedded in the compound verb after all. But then the lexical approach is left with no straightforward account of the fact that the extra object is inaccessible to movement.

In contrast, no comparable problems arise with (25) in a syntactic approach. One might wonder whether (25) would—in either approach—violate the universal prohibition against adjunction to arguments (see McCloskey 1992). No violation occurs, however, if we assume that what is prohibited by this principle is adjunction to syntactic expressions that are semantically complete—expressions whose meaning would saturate the argument with which they are composed.

We conclude that the attachment site of the extra object provides some reason to favor a syntactic approach to incorporation after all. After head movement, (25) would look like (26).

(26)
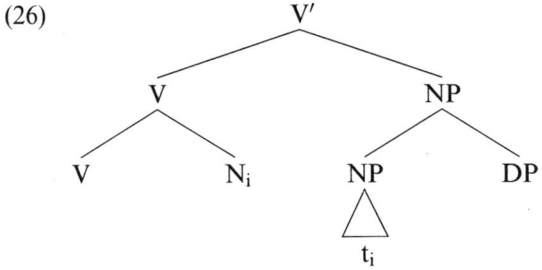

Importantly, assuming that semantic composition tracks syntactic structure, (26) accords almost perfectly with the formal account of the semantics of incorporation that we offered in chapter 3. In that account, the verb's internal argument is first restricted by the meaning of the incorporated object and can then be saturated by the meaning of the extra object. The only detail to be worked out is how to reconcile the semantic story with a syntactic structure in which V forms a constituent with the incorporated noun, but not with its entire NP. We leave this final detail as a project for the future.

# Appendix B
## Maori and Chamorro

The two languages that are the empirical focus of this study, Maori and Chamorro, belong to different branches of the Austronesian family and are therefore distantly related to each other.

Maori is a Polynesian language of New Zealand. The number of highly fluent speakers of Maori has clearly declined over the last half-century— to just over 8% of the adult Maori population in 1995. But the language has also been the focus of intense revitalization efforts, beginning with the Kohanga Reo (Language Nest) movement in 1981. Maori was recognized as an official language of New Zealand in 1987. For discussion of language maintenance efforts, the current situation of the Maori language, and prospects for the future, see Reedy 2000.

Maori is a well-documented language. Most of our Maori examples come from twentieth-century published sources: narratives, grammars, dictionaries, teaching materials, and journal articles. Some examples are from nineteenth-century sources (e.g., Orbell 1992; H. W. Williams 1971[1844]; W. L. Williams 1923[1862]). We have not changed the orthography of the original sources except to convert the double vowels sometimes used to represent long vowels (e.g., *aa*) to vowels with a macron (e.g., *ā*). In examples cited from H. M. Ngata 1994, an English-Maori dictionary, italics are used to indicate the dictionary entry cited.

Maori examples not attributed to a published source were generously supplied in 1994 by J. W. Milroy and Te Haumihiata Mason, both of the University of Waikato, and T. S. Karetu, then Head of the Maori Language Commission. We are greatly indebted to them.

Chamorro is a Western Austronesian language of the Mariana Islands, an archipelago consisting of Guam (an unincorporated U.S. territory) and the U.S. Commonwealth of the Northern Mariana Islands (CNMI). In the CNMI, Chamorro is a language of daily communication for most

Chamorro adults, but the percentage of children and young adults who are fluent speakers has declined rapidly. The situation perhaps resembles that in Guam in the 1970s or "the late 1960s when English began to replace Chamorro as the main language in a majority of island homes" (Rogers 1995, 245). Chamorro was recognized as an official language of Guam in 1972 and as an official language of the CNMI in 1985.

Chamorro is an underdocumented language with little written literature. Some examples cited in chapter 3 are from published sources (e.g., newspaper articles or teaching materials); others are from Ann Cooreman's two unpublished collections of Chamorro narratives (Cooreman 1982, 1983). But most of our Chamorro material has been generously supplied over the years by speakers in California and in Saipan. Among those whose insights and expertise we especially want to recognize are Priscilla Anderson, Antonio Atalig, Manuel F. Borja, Teresina Garrido, Ray P. Lujan, Maria T. Quinata, Maria P. Mafnas, Anicia Q. Tomokane, and Francisco Tomokane. We also wish to thank Carmen S. Taimanao, former director of the Chamorro Bilingual Program of the CNMI Public School System, and William I. Macaranas, former executive director of the Chamorro/Carolinean Language Policy Commission of the CNMI, for their advice and assistance.

There are various Chamorro spelling systems in use, including two official orthographies and a spelling that is widely used but not standardized (see appendix A of Chung 1998). All of our Chamorro examples, including those from published sources, are cited in a uniform orthography that gives a faithful representation of surface phonemes but inherits some unusual features from the other spelling systems. We use *a* to represent the low back vowel and *ä* to represent the low front vowel. Following the other orthographies, we also use *ch* to represent the voiceless alveolar affricate /ts/, *y* to represent its voiced counterpart /dz/, *ng* to represent the velar nasal, and the apostrophe to represent glottal stop. Also following the other orthographies, we use *ao* to represent the combination of the low back vowel plus /w/, and the vowel symbols *u* and *i* to represent the glides /w/ and /y/ elsewhere.

Below are the abbreviations used in the morpheme-by-morpheme glosses.

*Abbreviations Used in the Maori Glosses*

aforem    aforementioned
DO        direct object marker
du        dual

| Ident | identificational |
| Infin | infinitive |
| Nmlz | nominalization |
| Pass | passive |
| Pers | personal article |
| pl | plural |
| Pred | predicational |
| Pro | oblique clitic pronoun |
| Q | question particle |
| T | Tense |
| yo | younger |

*Abbreviations Used in the Chamorro Glosses*

| Agr | subject-verb agreement or possessor-noun agreement |
| AP | antipassive |
| Comp | complementizer |
| Compar | comparative |
| Emp | emphatic |
| Fut | future |
| Imperf | imperfect |
| Infin | infinitive |
| L | linker |
| Loc | local morphological case |
| nom | nominative (form of *wh*-agreement) |
| Obl | oblique morphological case |
| obj | objective (form of *wh*-agreement) |
| obl | oblique (form of *wh*-agreement) |
| Pass | passive |
| Pl | plural |
| Prog | progressive |
| Q | question |
| Unm | unmarked morphological case |
| WH | *wh*-agreement |

# Notes

**Chapter 1**

1. Note that we are not claiming that it is impossible to make them cohere, only that the available composition operation of function application is not able to compose them. If we returned to the definition of existential closure and made it "dynamic," then it would be possible to interpret (6) as cohering, by stipulating the additional condition that the witness of the existential closure is restricted to being the individual introduced. We do not view this as undermining the truth of (4). Instead, to the extent that the modified dynamic existential closure is viewed as an available mode of semantic composition, it is not saturating. The use of dynamic quantification in discourse interpretation is, in our view, crucially not about semantic composition: the definition of the contents of individual linguistic expressions.

2. Similarly, shifting the property into an existential generalized quantifier, or mapping it onto an entity of the kind sort, would accomplish the same thing: assimilate the offending content to an element in the domain of the function.

3. For our purposes, the representations that we give for the result of Restrict assume that this is an additional truth condition. Alternatively, we could give a presuppositional interpretation of Restrict, which returns a partial function with respect to the original total function, so that the property acts as a kind of selectional restriction. This is a presuppositional interpretation of predicate restriction. We do not think that anything in what we say here distinguishes between these two versions of Restrict.

4. Our decision to shift to Davidsonian notation at this point is not a substantive assumption. We think that for purposes of exposition these representations will be more perspicuous in tracking the effects of the assumption that we make below about saturation at the event level.

5. Because (27) is a theorem of the assumption that closure happens at the point of targeting (or must happen before another argument is targeted), the results of the next section apply to the traditional theory as well.

6. We do not rule out the possibility that some apparently quantificational DPs can be interpreted as group entities that directly saturate a position. In such cases,

the existential quantification over events can have scope over the content of the determiner. Crucially, however, in these cases the group entity is taken to directly saturate the predicate.

7. We set aside for the time being the case of a predicate that seeks a type $\langle e,t \rangle$ argument. No type mismatch occurs, because the property can directly saturate such a predicate by function application. The relation between Restrict and such second-order arguments will be discussed further in chapters 2 and 3.

8. Shifting into the type of generalized quantifiers is a logical possibility under the assumption that the predicate can combine with an expression of type $\langle \langle e,t \rangle, t \rangle$. In this discussion, we set aside this possibility by assuming that generalized quantifiers are interpreted on structures that are the output of quantifier raising. However, this assumption is not essential to our argument. A composition operation that would directly combine a generalized quantifier with the predicate would also be saturating.

9. In this chapter, we concentrate on DP arguments. As will become clear later, we assume that NPs, which denote properties, can be composed via Restrict. We further assume that the domain of Specify is restricted to DPs and that the fact that NPs cannot compose in this mode is principled.

**Chapter 2**

1. Standard grammars and dictionaries of Maori translate both *he* and *tētahi* as English 'a'. Whether the literature considers these articles to be indefinite is a more complex issue. While A. T. Ngata (1926, 13) explicitly identifies both articles as indefinite, W. L. Williams (1923[1862], 16–17) refers to them as definitives. Williams's full list of definitives reveals that he uses this term as generative linguists use the term *determiner*. Biggs (1969) uses the term *definitive* to refer to morphologically complex determiners formed from the definite article *te* 'the'. In his classification, *tētahi* is a definitive but *he* is not. It is unclear whether Biggs thought of this as a morphological term, a semantic term, or both. Bauer (1993, 110) refers to both *he* and *tētahi* as indefinite. However, in later work (1997, 164–169), she suggests that the primary function of Maori determiners is not to signal (in)definiteness but to signal the contrast between type of object and individual object(s).

2. Two points. First, it is often observed that cardinal numerals in Maori can precede or follow N within the noun phrase. In fact, cardinal numerals have the syntax of adjective predicates. When a cardinal numeral follows the head noun, it is, as Bauer (1997, 279) notes, typically the predicate of a relative clause. When a cardinal numeral precedes the head noun, it can usually be analyzed as a higher predicate that takes the noun phrase as its subject. We say "usually" because the syntax of numerals, already a complex area of Maori syntax, has been complicated further by interference from English; for discussion, see Bauer 1997, 275–289. Second, the entry for *tahi* in H. W. Williams's dictionary of Maori (1971[1844], 359) gives the meaning of *te tahi* as (not 'the one' but) 'the first (month)'.

3. A further syntactic difference between *he* and *tētahi* is that *tētahi*'s complement can undergo NP ellipsis, but *he*'s complement cannot. Among the other Maori determiners whose complements can undergo NP ellipsis are the demonstratives and the possessive pronouns but not the definite articles. The pattern is reminiscent of the English pattern of NP ellipsis.

4. Bauer (1997, 33–34) identifies a further construction used to express 'have', which she refers to as the existential possessive. Her discussion reveals that this construction differs from other existentials in that there is no argument that exhibits a definiteness effect. Instead, the subject is a definite noun phrase that includes a possessor and the predicate is a noun phrase introduced by *he*. If the possessor combines with the definite article to form a complex determiner, NP ellipsis is possible.

(i) He  hōiho tōna.
 Pred.a horse his
 'He has a horse (lit. His (possession) is a horse).' (Bauer 1997, 33)

5. Sentences that contain the nonverbal predicate *tērā* 'over there' are sometimes translated as existential sentences in English. But we do not analyze them as existential sentences in Maori, since—among other things—they do not exhibit a definiteness effect. A related sentence type containing *tērā* is analyzed by Bauer (1997, 660–661) as a preposed adverb construction in which the subject can raise to a position right after the adverb. As Bauer points out, this construction is sometimes used to introduce new protagonists into the discourse. But it too does not exhibit a definiteness effect. Consider:

(i) Tērā   [te ara pōharuharu] e ahu ana ki te one.
 over.there the road muddy   T lead   to the beach
 'There is a *muddy* road leading to the beach.' (H. M. Ngata 1994, 290)

(ii) Tērā    anō [ia] e whānau tamariki.
 over.there again she T give.birth children
 '(This was her way of saying that) she would have more children.' (Jones and Biggs 1995, 109 [13.2])

(iii) Tērā   [te hungawai tāne o Toa-angina] kua mau     herehere i
 over.there the in.law   male of Toa-angina T be.taken prisoner Cause
 a   rātou i mua tata atu.
 Pers them at front near away
 'Shortly before this they had captured Toa-angina's father-in-law.' (Jones and Biggs 1995, 293 [46.14])

6. The verb *ai* occurs in several fixed expressions in Modern Maori, such as *e ai ki te kōrero* 'it is said, people say'.

7. The negative *kāhore* is also the negative most often stranded in the Maori version of stripping, the ellipsis process that otherwise leaves behind only a noun phrase. (The English version of stripping produces sentences of the type *Jill likes pizza, but not Jack.*) Though Maori examples of stripping involving a negative may look superficially like negative existentials, they are not existential sentences and do not exhibit a definiteness effect.

8. For their judgments on the use of indefinites in negative existential sentences, we are indebted to J. W. Milroy, Tamati Reedy, and the late Bruce Biggs. We also acknowledge Ray Harlow and the late Bruce Biggs for ensuring that this information reached us.

Two further points. (a) The claim that *he* indefinites but not *tētahi* indefinites can be pivots of the existential construction is implicitly supported by our reading of many hundreds of pages of Maori material (most of it accompanied by English translation). These sources contain hundreds of examples of existentials in which a *he* indefinite serves as the pivot. But we have found only one example in which a *tētahi* indefinite serves as the pivot.

(i) Ka kai a    au i    te    mātene mehemea anake kaore [tētahi atu    momo
    T    eat Pers I    DO the mutton if        only    T.not a    away kind
    mīti].
    meat
    'I only eat *mutton* if there is no other kind of meat available.' (H. M. Ngata 1994, 292)

Notice that *tētahi atu momo mīti* 'another kind of meat' denotes a kind. If kinds are analyzed as properties, as suggested by McNally (1992), this example is not problematic for the proposal in the text.

(b) In Maori, noun phrases with plural preposed possessors can occur as pivots of the existential construction. An example is (ii).

(ii) Kaore aku    moni.
    T.not pl.my money
    'I've got no money.' (H. M. Ngata 1994, 246; *kind*)

Ray Harlow has observed (personal communication) that noun phrases of this sort have an indefinite construal as well as a definite construal. We claim that the indefinite construal is required in examples like (ii).

9. Though the classification of predicates as unaccusative or unergative has semantic correlates, it is not a purely semantic classification (see Perlmutter and Postal 1984; C. Rosen 1984; Levin and Rappaport Hovav 1995). Bauer's (1997, 148–149) remarks concerning the ability of the motion verb *rere* 'run, rush' to have a subject introduced by *he* should be read in this light.

10. Although (53a) is grammatical as a cleft construction, that is irrelevant. Bauer (1991) argues that cleft constructions in Maori are complex constructions in which the focus (introduced by *ko*) is a higher predicate and the rest of the construction is its subject, a null-headed relative clause (see also Bauer 1993, 220–221, and 1997, 665–667). On this analysis, the grammatical reading of (53a) is one in which *he* introduces the noun phrase *predicate* of the null-headed relative clause, so the sentence literally means 'It was Kawiti who was a true leader of Nga Puhi'. See section 2.6.2.

11. Biggs (1997, 3) observes that the internal argument of a transitive verb in the actor-emphatic construction can be a *he* indefinite.

(i) Mā-u    pea    e tiki    he wai    mo tātau?
    T.of-you perhaps T fetch a    water T.of us
    'Won't you fetch some [water] for us?' (Orbell 1992, 43)

This construction is probably a complex sentence type and the internal argument is probably a derived subject (see, e.g., Chung 1978, 175–183; Bauer 1997, 501–507).

12. As shown by CMM but not discussed in the text, the specificity constraint does not hold in quantificational constructions. One example is given here; see CMM 1995 for others.

(i) Kōrero ana [he wahine], whakaturi ana ia i a ia.
    speak      a woman make.deaf    he DO Pers himself
    'When a woman speaks, he makes himself deaf.'

One way of accounting for this is to reconfigure the specificity constraint as a constraint on judgment types, in the sense of Brentano (see Ladusaw 1994). We would say that in Maori, every sentence with an external argument must express a categorical judgment. Obviously, to pursue this here would take us too far afield.

13. Some of the English translations of the examples in this subsection have been altered from the original to make it more transparent which Maori constituent is the subject and which is the predicate.

14. The first *ko* in (59b) marks the topic (see Bauer 1993, 236–237, and 1997, 654–657).

15. The only clear independent evidence that *ko* is a preposition is that it marks future location in North Auckland dialects (Bauer 1997, 222). Some apparent morphosyntactic evidence that *ko* is a preposition is provided by the fact that, like some other prepositions, it cannot be followed by the personal article *a* (Bauer 1997, 28). However, the latter fact can also be described in purely phonological terms: immediately following a proclitic that ends in a vowel other than /i/, the personal article is not pronounced.

16. Notice that the discussion in sections 2.6.1 and 2.6.2 makes a prediction about the ability of the two types of indefinites to occur as subjects of predicational noun phrase predicates—that is, predicates introduced by *he*. Recall that in our system such predicates are individual-level, so their subjects are external arguments. We therefore predict that these subjects can be *tētahi* indefinites. But, thanks to the specificity constraint, they should be able to be *he* indefinites only in quantificational constructions (see note 12).

Initial investigation suggests that this prediction is realized. *Tētahi* indefinites can indeed be the subjects of noun phrase predicates introduced by *he*. One example is (52b) in the text; another is given in (i).

(i) He      tītī      tētahi kai tino reka ki te korokoro Māori.
    Pred.a muttonbird a    food very sweet to the throat    Maori
    'A food quite tasty to Maori palates is muttonbird.' (Waititi 1974, 117)

On the other hand, the only textual examples we have found in which a *he* indefinite serves as the subject of a *he* predicate are quantificational constructions. One example is cited here.

(ii) He    aha    kē atu    he kōrero māku?
    Pred.a what? else away a    speech T.of.me
    'What *else* could I say?' (H. M. Ngata 1994, 123)

17. We are grateful to Tamahou Temara, Information Officer at the Te Papa Tongarewa Museum of New Zealand, for answering our e-mail questions about the use of *he* and *tētahi* on identifying labels for exhibit objects.

18. In addition, noun phrases on identifying labels can be definite or preceded by *ko*.

19. English bare plurals also have a generic interpretation. So do Maori indefinites headed by *he*, as we pointed out in section 2.3.2.

20. In Matthewson's view (1999, 105), St'át'imcets has no definite determiners—only indefinite determiners. But she also shows (1999, 108–109) that the expressions she calls wide scope indefinites can be associated with discourse referents that are familiar or unique. It is not clear to us what empirical differences there are between her view and the hypothesis that so-called wide scope indefinites are ambiguous between a definite interpretation and a wide scope indefinite interpretation.

**Chapter 3**

1. But see Kratzer 1994 for an approach in which composition operations can target a predicate's argument without automatically saturating it. Kratzer's operation of Object Identification resembles our operation of Restrict in certain respects. A full comparison of her approach with ours is beyond the scope of this monograph.

2. Here is how Mithun (1984, 863) characterizes CNI: "A relatively general N stem is incorporated to narrow the scope of the V ... but the compound stem can be accompanied by a more specific external NP which identifies the argument implied by the N." We think that Chamorro incorporation is clearly an instance of the phenomenon that Mithun has termed CNI. But we are not committed to the details of her characterization, including her idea that the "external NP" is more specific than the incorporated "N stem." See section 3.7 for discussion.

3. Irrelevantly, these examples are grammatical under a different interpretation in which the extra object is associated with the verb on the right but not with the verb on the left. In this interpretation, for instance, (41b) means 'We have pets and are raising those dogs'.

4. Two points. (a) Though sentences of the type (46)–(47) are ungrammatical, their intended meaning can be expressed by grammatical clauses whose predicate is a possessed DP. Corresponding to (46a), for instance, is (i).

(i) Ti patgun Julia yu'.
    not child Julia I
    'I'm not Julia's child.'

(b) Some of the DPs identified as extra objects in (48) can also be analyzed as DP predicates of relative clauses modifying the incorporated object. (These relative clauses have the morphological form of so-called existential relatives; see Chung 1987.) It is important that not all extra objects of *tai-* are amenable to such an analysis. See the discussion immediately below in the text.

5. McNally's (1992) claim that the pivot of the existential construction must denote a property leads her to two predictions. First, both definite and indefinite common noun phrases should, in principle, be eligible to serve as pivots, because both are property-denoting. In her system, definite pivots are excluded by a different, discourse-based principle. Second, quantified noun phrases should be able to serve as pivots when the quantification is over properties.

The first prediction is evidently borne out for the existential verbs *guäha* 'exist' and *taya'* 'not exist'; see Chung 1987 for a few examples. As far as we can tell, though, neither prediction is borne out for *täi-* 'not have'. Further investigation is clearly warranted.

6. Notice that we are assuming that the affirmative polarity item *un* has a lexical entry distinct from the lexical entry of the complex determiner *ni un* 'no, not any', which is a negative polarity item.

7. It may be that English *have* exhibits a restriction similar to the Chamorro restriction described in the text. Consider pairs of examples like these:

(i) a. Do you have a key?
  b. Do you have your key?
(ii) a. I don't have a car.
  b. I don't have my car.

Notice that in the (a) examples, *have* can express temporary location (e.g., do you have a key with you at this time/place) or a more permanent relation of possession. But in the (b) examples, only the meaning of temporary location seems possible. Conceivably, the pragmatic considerations discussed in the text are responsible for the fact that the (b) examples seem not to be able to express any more permanent relation of possession.

8. Recall that the incorporated object never contains a possessor, given that it is NP but not DP, and given that possessors in Chamorro reside in the specifier of D.

9. Notice that we do not assume a meaning for *gäi-* like that proposed by Partee (1999) for relational *have*. There are two reasons for this. First, the subject and the incorporated object of *gäi-* can evidently be related in a wider range of ways than can the subject and the object of relational *have*. Second, the extra object of *gäi-* does not exhibit a definiteness effect (see section 3.5.1), whereas the object of relational *have* does. Notice that only the first reason would prevent us from assuming a relational meaning for *täi-* 'not have'. In order to simplify the exposition, we do not pursue this option in the text.

10. Among the aspects of Bittner's analysis that we do not deal with are its formalization, the notion of centering, and centering-related ambiguities.

11. Examples like (83) make the point that the incorporated object is not appropriately viewed as a "classifier" of the extra object.

Two further points. (a) Stenning (1978) takes a different approach to the corresponding examples of discourse anaphora. He suggests that noun phrases such as *the cat* and *Patrick's pet* can be anaphorically related if the context, or the text itself, reveals that they are coextensional.

(b) The observations made in the text do not extend to extra objects that are pronouns. Pronouns are, according to Stenning, essentially at the top of the hierarchy of class inclusion, so any incorporated object ought to be subordinate to them. Nonetheless, pronouns *can* serve as extra objects in Chamorro. See section 3.4 for extra objects that are definite pronouns and (i) for an indefinite pronoun that is a negative concord item.

(i) Täi-[lateria] esti na tenda *ni háfafa ha'*.
Agr.not.have-canned.goods this L store not anything Emp
'This store has no canned goods at all.'

One could view the contrast between this example and (81) in the text as a further indication that the relation between the incorporated object and the extra object is fundamentally not an anaphoric relation.

12. In (85a) and (85c), the donkey pronouns are null because all inanimate nonreflexive pronouns in Chamorro are null. Importantly, the agreement on the verbs *bendi* 'sell' and *na'bunitu* 'make pretty' is chosen from the transitive paradigm, a fact that reveals that a direct object is syntactically present, even though inaudible.

13. More radical approaches to languages of type (b) can be imagined. Baker (1996, 291) observes that in Mohawk, incorporated constituents "can have the full range of interpretations of any other nominal," an observation he connects to the fact that Mohawk lacks semantically significant determiners and, in this sense, does not distinguish semantically between NP and DP. He further suggests that the same is true of other languages with canonical versions of CNI.

One could exploit these connections by speculating that in languages with canonical CNI, all noun phrases—whether incorporated or not—would be property-denoting, and therefore equally eligible for composition via Restrict or via Specify. The result of composing the meaning of a noun phrase via Restrict would be a narrow scope indefinite, assuming that no further composition targeted the same argument and existential closure occurred. The result of composing the meaning of a noun phrase via Specify would be either a wide scope indefinite or a definite, depending on whether the choice function variable was existentially closed or had its value determined by the common ground. Whatever compositional route was chosen, a discourse referent would ultimately be introduced.

Such an analysis would attribute the discourse difference between incorporation in Chamorro and incorporation in Mohawk to a more wide-ranging difference in the way(s) that independent noun phrases were interpreted in these languages. We are very reluctant to pursue this possibility. For a different exploration of cross-linguistic differences in the interpretation of noun phrases, see Chierchia 1998.

14. Because the Chamorro verbs of possession are morphologically related to existential verbs, they could be viewed as asserting the introduction of a discourse referent corresponding to their internal argument. Chamorro could then be classified as a language of type (a) or type (d).

## Appendix A

1. Massam's (2001) analysis of the Niuean construction that resembles Maori incorporation is radically different from ours. She proposes that in the Niuean construction, which she calls pseudo noun incorporation, the entire VP consisting of V plus an NP complement raises to the specifier of IP.

2. The examples cited in the text involve nonpronominal subjects only. This is because the placement of weak pronouns is determined by prosodic considerations, not purely syntactic considerations.

# References

Abbott, Barbara Kenyon. 1976. A study of referential opacity. Ph.D. dissertation, University of California, Berkeley.

Abney, Steven P. 1987. The English noun phrase in its sentential aspect. Ph.D. dissertation, MIT.

Abusch, Dorit. 1993–4. The scope of indefinites. *Natural Language Semantics* 2, 83–135.

Anderson, Stephen R. 1992. *A-morphous morphology.* Cambridge: Cambridge University Press.

Anderson, Stephen R. 2000. Some lexicalist remarks on incorporation phenomena. *Studia Grammatica* 45, 123–142.

Bach, Emmon, Eloise Jelinek, Angelika Kratzer, and Barbara H. Partee, eds. 1995. *Quantification in natural languages.* 2 vols. Dordrecht: Kluwer.

Baker, Mark C. 1988. *Incorporation: A theory of grammatical function changing.* Chicago: University of Chicago Press.

Baker, Mark C. 1996. *The polysynthesis parameter.* Oxford: Oxford University Press.

Barker, Chris. 1991. Possessive descriptions. Ph.D. dissertation, University of California, Santa Cruz.

Bauer, Winifred. 1991. Maori *ko* again. *Te Reo* 24, 31–36.

Bauer, Winifred. 1993. *Maori,* with William Parker and Te Kareongawai Evans. London: Routledge.

Bauer, Winifred. 1997. *The Reed reference grammar of Māori,* with William Parker, Te Kareongawai Evans, and Te Aroha Noti Teepa. Auckland: Reed.

Benveniste, Emile. 1966. *Etre* et *avoir* dans leurs fonctions linguistiques. In *Problèmes de linguistique générale,* 187–207. Paris: Gallimard.

Biggs, Bruce. 1969. *Let's learn Maori: A guide to the study of the Maori language.* Wellington: Reed.

Biggs, Bruce, ed. 1997. *He* "indefinite" and subjects of sentences. *Te Paanui a Wai-wharariki* 2 11/09/97.

Bittner, Maria. 1998. Cross-linguistic semantics for questions. *Linguistics and Philosophy* 21, 1–82.

Bittner, Maria. 2001. Surface composition as bridging. *Journal of Semantics* 18, 127–177.

Bresnan, Joan W., ed. 1982. *The mental representation of grammatical relations*. Cambridge, Mass.: MIT Press.

Carlson, Gregory N. 1977. Reference to kinds in English. Ph.D. dissertation, University of Massachusetts, Amherst.

Chapin, Paul G. 1974. Proto-Polynesian *ai. *Journal of the Polynesian Society* 83, 259–307.

Chierchia, Gennaro. 1995a. *Dynamics of meaning: Anaphora, presupposition, and the theory of grammar*. Chicago: University of Chicago Press.

Chierchia, Gennaro. 1995b. Individual-level predicates as inherent generics. In *The generic book*, ed. by Gregory N. Carlson and Francis Jeffry Pelletier, 176–223. Chicago: University of Chicago Press.

Chierchia, Gennaro. 1998. Reference to kinds across languages. *Natural Language Semantics* 6, 339–405.

Chomsky, Noam. 1981. *Lectures on government and binding*. Dordrecht: Foris.

Chomsky, Noam. 1986. *Barriers*. Cambridge, Mass.: MIT Press.

Chomsky, Noam. 1995. *The Minimalist Program*. Cambridge, Mass.: MIT Press.

Chomsky, Noam, and Morris Halle. 1968. *The sound pattern of English*. New York: Harper and Row.

Chung, Sandra. 1978. *Case marking and grammatical relations in Polynesian*. Austin: University of Texas Press.

Chung, Sandra. 1987. The syntax of Chamorro existential sentences. In *The representation of (in)definiteness*, ed. by Eric J. Reuland and Alice G. B. ter Meulen, 191–225. Cambridge, Mass.: MIT Press.

Chung, Sandra. 1998. *The design of agreement: Evidence from Chamorro*. Chicago: University of Chicago Press.

Chung, Sandra, Te Haumihiata Mason, and J. W. Milroy. 1995. On Maori *he* and the uses of indefinites. *Journal of the Polynesian Society* 104, 429–459.

Cinque, Guglielmo. 1993. A null theory of phrase and compound stress. *Linguistic Inquiry* 24, 239–297.

Cook, Kenneth William. 1999. Hawaiian *he*, *'o* and *i*: Copular verbs, prepositions, or determiners? *Oceanic Linguistics* 38, 43–65.

Cooreman, Ann. 1982. Chamorro texts. Ms., University of Oregon, Eugene.

Cooreman, Ann. 1983. Chamorro texts. Ms., Saipan, Commonwealth of the Northern Mariana Islands.

Davidson, Donald. 1967. The logical form of action sentences. In *The logic of decision and action*, ed. by Nicholas Rescher, 81–95. Pittsburgh: University of Pennsylvania Press.

de Jong, Franciska. 1987. The compositional nature of (in)definiteness. In *The representation of (in)definiteness*, ed. by Eric J. Reuland and Alice G. B. ter Meulen, 270–285. Cambridge, Mass.: MIT Press.

de Swart, Henriëtte. 1999. Indefinites between predication and reference. In *Proceedings from Semantics and Linguistic Theory IX*, ed. by Tanya Matthews and Devon Strolovitch, 273–297. Ithaca, N.Y.: Cornell University, CLC Publications.

de Swart, Henriëtte. 2001. Weak readings of indefinites: Type-shifting and closure. *The Linguistic Review* 18, 69–96.

Diesing, Molly. 1992. *Indefinites*. Cambridge, Mass.: MIT Press.

Di Sciullo, Anna Maria, and Edwin Williams. 1987. *On the definition of word*. Cambridge, Mass.: MIT Press.

Dobrovie-Sorin, Carmen. 1997. Types of predicates and the representation of existential readings. In *Proceedings from Semantics and Linguistic Theory VII*, ed. by Aaron Lawson, 117–134. Ithaca, N.Y.: Cornell University, CLC Publications.

Enç, Mürvet. 1991. The semantics of specificity. *Linguistic Inquiry* 22, 1–25.

Fanselow, Gisbert. 1988. Aufspaltung von NPn und das Problem der "freien" Wortstellung. *Linguistische Berichte* 114, 91–113.

Farkas, Donka F. 1981. Quantifier scope and syntactic islands. In *Papers from the Seventeenth Regional Meeting of the Chicago Linguistic Society*, ed. by Roberta A. Hendrick, Carrie S. Masek, and Mary Frances Miller, 59–66. Chicago: University of Chicago, Chicago Linguistic Society.

Farkas, Donka F. 1995. Specificity and scope. In *Langues et grammaire 1*, ed. by Léa Nash and Georges Tsoulas, 119–137. Université de Paris VIII.

Farkas, Donka F. 1997. Toward a semantic typology of noun phrases. Paper presented at Colloque de Syntaxe et de Sémantique à Paris, 1997. [Published as Vers une typologie sémantique des syntagmes nominaux. In *Typologie des groupes nominaux*, ed. by Georges Kleiber, Brenda Laca, and Liliane Tasmowski, 17–46. Rennes: Les Presses Universitaires Rennes (2001).]

Fodor, Janet Dean, and Ivan A. Sag. 1982. Referential and quantificational indefinites. *Linguistics and Philosophy* 5, 355–398.

Freeze, Ray. 1992. Existentials and other locatives. *Language* 68, 553–595.

Frege, Gottlob. 1997[1862]. On concept and object. In *The Frege reader*, ed. by Michael Beaney, 181–193. Oxford: Blackwell.

Haïk, Isabelle. 1984. Indirect binding. *Linguistic Inquiry* 15, 185–223.

Heim, Irene. 1982. The semantics of definite and indefinite noun phrases. Ph.D. dissertation, University of Massachusetts, Amherst.

Heim, Irene. 1987. Where does the definiteness restriction apply? Evidence from the definiteness of variables. In *The representation of (in)definiteness*, ed. by Eric J. Reuland and Alice G. B. ter Meulen, 21–42. Cambridge, Mass.: MIT Press.

Heim, Irene. 1990. E-type pronouns and donkey anaphora. *Linguistics and Philosophy* 13, 137–177.

Hoeksema, Jack. 1985. *Categorial morphology*. New York: Garland.

Hohepa, Patrick W. 1967. *A profile generative grammar of Maori*. Indiana University Publications in Anthropology and Linguistics, Memoir 20. Bloomington: Indiana University.

Hohepa, Patrick W. 1969. Not in English and *kore* and *eehara* in Maori. *Te Reo* 12, 1–34.

Hooper, Robin. 1984. Neuter verbs, stative aspect, and the expression of agency in Polynesian. *Journal of the Polynesian Society* 93, 39–70.

Jackendoff, Ray. 1997. *The architecture of the language faculty*. Cambridge, Mass.: MIT Press.

Jones, Pei Te Hurinui, and Bruce Biggs. 1995. *Nga iwi o Tainui: The traditional history of the Tainui people*. Auckland: Auckland University Press.

Kadmon, Nirit, and Fred Landman. 1993. Any. *Linguistics and Philosophy* 16, 353–422.

Kamp, Hans. 1981. A theory of truth and discourse representation. In *Formal methods in the study of language*, ed. by Jeroen Groenendijk, Theo M. V. Janssen, and Martin Stokhof, 277–322. Amsterdam: Mathematical Centre.

Karetu, T. S. 1974. *Te reo rangatira: A course in Māori for sixth and seventh forms*. Wellington: GP Publications.

Karttunen, Lauri. 1976. Discourse referents. In *Syntax and semantics 7: Notes from the linguistic underground*, ed. by James D. McCawley, 363–385. New York: Academic Press.

Keenan, Edward L. 1987. A semantic definition of "indefinite NP." In *The representation of (in)definiteness*, ed. by Eric J. Reuland and Alice G. B. ter Meulen, 286–317. Cambridge, Mass.: MIT Press.

Kratzer, Angelika. 1994. The event argument and the semantics of voice. Ms., University of Massachusetts, Amherst.

Kratzer, Angelika. 1995. Stage-level and individual-level predicates. In *The generic book*, ed. by Gregory N. Carlson and Francis Jeffry Pelletier, 125–175. Chicago: University of Chicago Press. [Originally circulated in manuscript in 1988.]

Kratzer, Angelika. 1998. Scope or pseudoscope? Are there wide-scope indefinites? In *Events and grammar*, ed. by Susan Rothstein, 163–198. Dordrecht: Kluwer.

Kroeber, A. L. 1909. Noun incorporation in American languages. In *Verhandlungen der XIV. Internationaler Amerikanisten-Kongress*, 568–576. Vienna.

Kroeber, A. L. 1911. Incorporation as a linguistic process. *American Anthropologist* 13, 577–584.

Kuhn, Jonas. 2001. Resource sensitivity in the syntax-semantics interface: Evidence from the German split NP construction. In *Constraint-based approaches to Germanic syntax*, ed. by W. Detmar Meurers and Tibor Kiss, 177–215. Stanford, Calif.: CSLI Publications.

Ladusaw, William A. 1979. Polarity sensitivity as inherent scope relations. Ph.D. dissertation, University of Texas, Austin.

Ladusaw, William A. 1992. Expressing negation. In *SALT II: Proceedings from the Second Conference on Semantics and Linguistic Theory*, ed. by Chris Barker and David Dowty, 237–259. Columbus: Ohio State University, Department of Linguistics.

Ladusaw, William A. 1994. Thetic and categorical, stage and individual, weak and strong. In *Proceedings from Semantics and Linguistic Theory IV*, ed. by Mandy Harvey and Lynn Santelmann, 220–229. Ithaca, N.Y.: Cornell University, CLC Publications.

Levin, Beth, and Malka Rappaport Hovav. 1995. *Unaccusativity: At the syntax–lexical semantics interface*. Cambridge, Mass.: MIT Press.

Lewis, David. 1975. Adverbs of quantification. In *Formal semantics of natural language*, ed. by Edward L. Keenan, 3–15. Cambridge: Cambridge University Press.

Lieber, Rochelle. 1988. Phrasal compounds in English and the morphology-syntax interface. In *CLS 24*. Part 2, *Parasession on Agreement in Grammatical Theory*, ed. by Diane Brentari, Gary Larson, and Lynn MacLeod, 202–222. Chicago: University of Chicago, Chicago Linguistic Society.

Massam, Diane. 2001. Pseudo noun incorporation in Niuean. *Natural Language and Linguistic Theory* 19, 153–197.

Matthewson, Lisa. 1999. On the interpretation of wide-scope indefinites. *Natural Language Semantics* 7, 79–134.

May, Robert. 1985. *Logical Form: Its structure and derivation*. Cambridge, Mass.: MIT Press.

McCloskey, James. 1992. Adjunction, selection and embedded verb second. Working paper LRC-92-07. Santa Cruz: University of California, Santa Cruz, Linguistics Research Center.

McNally, Louise. 1992. An interpretation for the English existential construction. Ph.D. dissertation, University of California, Santa Cruz.

Mithun, Marianne. 1984. The evolution of noun incorporation. *Language* 60, 847–894.

Mithun, Marianne. 1986. On the nature of noun incorporation. *Language* 62, 32–37.

Montague, Richard. 1973. The proper treatment of quantification in ordinary English. In *Approaches to natural language: Proceedings of the 1970 Workshop on Grammar and Semantics*, ed. by K. J. J. Hintikka, J. M. E. Moravcsik, and P. Suppes, 221–242. Dordrecht: Reidel.

Musan, Renate. 1996. *There*-constructions revisited. In *Proceedings from Semantics and Linguistic Theory VI*, ed. by Teresa Galloway and Justin Spence, 167–184. Ithaca, N.Y.: Cornell University, CLC Publications.

Ngata, A. T. 1926. *Complete manual of Maori grammar and conversation with vocabulary*. 2nd ed. Auckland: Whitcombe and Tombs.

Ngata, H. M. 1994. *English-Maori dictionary*. Wellington: Learning Media.

*Ngā tāngata taumata rau, 1769–1869*. 1990. [Dictionary of New Zealand biography: Selections.] Wellington: Allen and Unwin.

Onedera, Peter R. 1994. *Fafa'ña'gue yan hinengge siha*. Tamuning, Guam: St. Anthony School.

Orbell, Margaret, transl. 1992. *Traditional Māori stories*. Auckland: Reed.

Parsons, Terence. 1990. *Events in the semantics of English*. Cambridge, Mass.: MIT Press.

Partee, Barbara H. 1984. Nominal and temporal anaphora. *Linguistics and Philosophy* 7, 243–286.

Partee, Barbara H. 1987. Noun phrase interpretation and type-shifting principles. In *Studies in Discourse Representation Theory and the theory of generalized quantifiers*, ed. by Jeroen Groenendijk, Dick de Jongh, and Martin Stokhof, 115–143. Dordrecht: Foris.

Partee, Barbara H. 1999. Weak NP's in HAVE sentences. In *JFAK: Essays dedicated to Johan van Bentham on the occasion of his 50th birthday*, ed. by Jelle Gerbrandy, Maarten Marx, Maarten de Rijke, and Yde Venema. URL: http://www.uva.nl/~j50/cdrom.

Pearce, Elizabeth. 2001. VP-raising versus V-raising in Māori. Paper presented at the 8th meeting of the Austronesian Formal Linguistics Association, MIT, Cambridge, Mass.

Perlmutter, David M., and Paul M. Postal. 1984. The 1-Advancement Exclusiveness Law. In *Studies in Relational Grammar 2*, ed. by David M. Perlmutter and Carol G. Rosen, 81–125. Chicago: University of Chicago Press.

Polinsky, Maria. 1992. Maori *he* revisited. *Oceanic Linguistics* 31, 229–250.

Postal, Paul M. 1969a. Anaphoric islands. In *Papers from the Fifth Regional Meeting of the Chicago Linguistic Society*, ed. by Robert I. Binnick, Alice Davison, Georgia M. Green, and Jerry L. Morgan, 205–239. Chicago: University of Chicago, Chicago Linguistic Society.

Postal, Paul M. 1969b. On so-called "pronouns" in English. In *Modern studies in English*, ed. by David A. Reibel and Sanford A. Schane, 201–224. Englewood Cliffs, N.J.: Prentice-Hall.

Reedy, Tamati M. 1979. Complex sentence formation in Maori. Ph.D. dissertation, University of Hawaii.

Reedy, Tamati M. 2000. Te reo Māori: The past 20 years and looking forward. *Oceanic Linguistics* 39, 157–169.

Reinhart, Tanya. 1987. Specifier and operator binding. In *The representation of (in)definiteness*, ed. by Eric J. Reuland and Alice G. B. ter Meulen, 130–167. Cambridge, Mass.: MIT Press.

Reinhart, Tanya. 1997. Quantifier scope: How labor is divided between QR and choice functions. *Linguistics and Philosophy* 20, 335–397.

Reuland, Eric. 1987. Indefinite subjects. In *Proceedings of NELS 18*, vol. 2, ed. by James Blevin and Juli Carter, 375–395. Amherst: University of Massachusetts, Graduate Linguistic Student Association.

Rogers, Robert E. 1995. *Destiny's landfall: A history of Guam*. Honolulu: University of Hawai'i Press.

Rosen, Carol G. 1984. The interface between semantic roles and initial grammatical relations. In *Studies in Relational Grammar 2*, ed. by David M. Perlmutter and Carol G. Rosen, 38–77. Chicago: University of Chicago Press.

Rosen, Sara Thomas. 1989. Two types of noun incorporation: A lexical analysis. *Language* 65, 294–317.

Sadock, Jerrold M. 1980. Noun incorporation in Greenlandic. *Language* 56, 300–319.

Sadock, Jerrold M. 1986. Some notes on noun incorporation. *Language* 62, 19–31.

Sadock, Jerrold M. 1991. *Autolexical syntax: A theory of parallel grammatical representations*. Chicago: University of Chicago Press.

Sapir, Edward. 1911. The problem of noun incorporation in American languages. *American Anthropologist* 13, 250–282.

Spaelti, Philip. 1995. Split topic in German. Ms., University of California, Santa Cruz.

Spencer, Andrew. 1991. *Morphological theory*. London: Blackwell.

Stenning, Keith. 1978. Anaphora as an approach to pragmatics. In *Linguistic theory and psychological reality*, ed. by Morris Halle, Joan Bresnan, and George A. Miller, 162–200. Cambridge, Mass.: MIT Press.

Strawson, P. F. 1959. *Individuals*. London: Routledge.

Szabolcsi, Anna. 1994. The noun phrase. In *Syntax and semantics 27: The syntactic structure of Hungarian*, ed. by Ferenc Kiefer and Katalin É. Kiss, 179–274. San Diego, Calif.: Academic Press.

van Geenhoven, Veerle. 1998. *Semantic incorporation and indefinite descriptions: Semantic and syntactic aspects of noun incorporation in West Greenlandic*. Stanford, Calif.: CSLI Publications.

van Riemsdijk, Henk. 1989. Movement and regeneration. In *Dialect variation and the theory of grammar*, ed. by Paola Benincà, 105–136. Dordrecht: Foris.

Waite, Jeffrey. 1994. Determiner phrases in Maori. *Te Reo* 37, 55–70.

Waititi, Hoani R. 1962. *Te rangatahi 1*. Wellington: R. E. Owen, Government Printer.

Waititi, Hoani R. 1974. *Te rangatahi, advanced 2: A Māori language course*. Wellington: GP Publications.

Williams, Herbert W. 1971[1844]. *A dictionary of the Maori language*. 7th ed. Wellington: A. R. Shearer, Government Printer.

Williams, W. L. 1923[1862]. *First lessons in Maori*. 7th ed. Auckland: Whitcombe and Tombs.

Winter, Yoad. 1997. Choice functions and the scopal semantics of indefinites. *Linguistics and Philosophy* 20, 399–467.

Woodbury, Hanni. 1975. Noun incorporation in Onondaga. Ph.D. dissertation, Yale University.

# Index

Abney, S., 25–26, 81
Abusch, D., 45
Anaphora
  class inclusion in, 119–121
  discourse, 16–17, 31–33, 65–68, 116–124
  donkey pronouns, 15, 17, 67–68, 121–124
  variable binding, 67–68, 121–124
Anderson, S., 121, 131–132
Argument
  event, 4, 9–10, 11–14, 16, 18–19, 47, 48–49, 50, 51, 52, 108, 125
  external, 56–60, 108
  internal, 53, 55, 58–59, 70, 77, 81–82, 88, 94, 98–99, 100–103, 106–112, 114–115, 116–117, 125, 136–137, 148

Bach, E., 25
Baker, M., 85, 94, 113–114, 125–127, 131–133
Barker, C., 33
Bauer, W., 22, 24–26, 27–28, 30, 36, 37, 42, 46, 56, 60, 62–64, 68, 69–70, 138–139
Benveniste, E., 98
Biggs, B., 22, 27–28, 31, 56, 62
Bittner, M., 107, 114, 116–118, 142
Bresnan, J., 75

Carlson, G., 70
Chamorro
  adjunct licensing in, 113–114
  adjuncts in, 79, 93, 94, 105–106, 134, 143, 146–147
  affirmative polarity item in, 100–103, 112
  anaphora constraint in, 103–106
  case marking in, 79–80, 81, 89, 105, 114
  coordination in, 87, 141–143, 146
  definiteness effects in, 81–82, 94–99, 117–118
  DP structure in, 80–81, 87–88

  existentials in, 81–82, 98–99, 102–103, 123
  islands in, 92–93, 146–147
  negative concord in, 97–98, 102, 112, 120–121
  NP structure in, 80, 85–87, 143, 144
  possessors in, 79, 81, 82, 88, 92, 103–107, 114
  quantifiers in, 80, 87, 95–97, 100–101, 104, 122
  subject-verb agreement in, 79, 83–84, 90
  verbs of possession in, 82–83, 144
  *wh*-movement in, 91–93, 134, 146–147
  word order in, 78–79, 80–81, 143–145
Chapin, P., 43
Chierchia, G., 108, 122, 127
Choice function, 5, 7, 9, 14–16, 18–19, 47–49, 51–52, 69–70, 71
Chomsky, N., 7, 75, 134, 135, 142
Chung, S., 22, 24, 30, 36, 56–59, 78, 80, 91, 92, 101, 103, 146
Cinque, G., 135
Cook, K., 29–30

Definiteness effect
  in existentials, 52–53, 81
  in incorporation, 94–99, 118
de Jong, F., 106
de Swart, H., 7, 23, 52–53, 75
Diesing, M., 12, 59, 125, 128–129
Di Sciullo, A., 131–132
Discourse referent, 16–17, 31–33, 67, 116–117, 118–124, 126–128, 137
Dobrovie-Sorin, C., 53, 98–99

Enc, M., 22
English
  bare plurals in, 70–71
Existential closure, 3–4, 5, 9, 10, 12–15, 16–17, 18–19, 48–52, 71–73, 108, 110, 116, 117, 124–125, 126

Existential construction, 41–44, 52–53, 54, 55, 56, 72, 81, 98–99, 101–103, 123, 127–128

Fanselow, G., 128
Farkas, D., 16–17, 45–46, 52–53, 75, 121
Fodor, J., 22, 45
Freeze, R., 98
Frege, G., 1, 3–4, 75

German
  split topics in, 128–130
Greenlandic
  incorporation in, 83, 113, 114–117, 126, 142, 146

Hale, K., 56
Halle, M., 135
Haik, I., 122
Heim, I., 12, 13–14, 32–33, 49, 54, 101, 122, 125, 126
Hoeksema, J., 135
Hohepa, P., 28, 36, 56, 57
Hooper, R., 56

Incorporation
  classificatory noun (CNI), 88–89, 131–134
  lexical approach to, 132, 133, 135–136, 141–143, 144–147
  semantic, 17, 70, 114–116, 129
  syntactic approach to, 131, 132–134, 135, 141–148
  typology of, 125–128
Indefinites
  interpreted as properties, 4–6, 8, 14–18, 21, 23, 47–48, 50, 52–53, 54–55, 60, 62, 65, 68, 69, 70, 71, 75, 99, 101, 112, 117, 121, 129
  as restricted free variables, 14, 49
  scope of, 13, 15–19, 30–39, 40–41, 45–46, 49–52, 54–55, 58, 70–72, 100–101, 112, 114, 116, 129, 137

Jackendoff, R., 135

Kadmon, N., 112
Kamp, H., 14, 49
Karttunen, L., 45
Keenan, E., 42, 82, 98
Kratzer, A., 4–5, 11–12, 16, 45, 49, 51–52, 71–72, 125, 127
Kroeber, A., 77, 131
Kuhn, J., 128–129

Ladusaw, W., 100, 108
Landman, F., 112

Lewis, D., 49
Lieber, R., 135

McCloskey, J., 148
McNally, L., 52–53, 55, 98–99, 101
Maori
  adjuncts in, 29, 137
  case marking in. See Maori, prepositions in
  conditionals in, 33–35
  DP structure in, 25–26, 42, 61, 63–64, 68, 138–141
  existentials in, 41–44, 54–55, 56
  generics in, 39
  habitual verbs in, 63–64
  identificational DP predicates in, 24, 60–62
  incorporation in, 113, 127, 136–141, 142, 146
  individual-level predicates in, 56, 57–58, 63–64
  modals in, 37–38
  negatives in, 36–37, 43–44, 60
  passive in, 24–25, 31, 58–59
  possessors in, 25–26, 42, 43, 44, 57–58, 64
  predicational DP predicates in, 24, 60, 62–65
  prepositions in, 22, 23–24, 25–26, 28–30, 37, 43, 57–58, 62, 64, 140
  quantifiers in, 25, 35–36, 60
  questions in, 38–39
  specificity constraint in, 56–60
  transitives in, 56–57, 136
  unaccusatives in, 31, 58–59
  unergatives in, 56, 57
  word order in, 23–24, 25–26, 36, 137–138, 139, 140
Mason, T., 56–59
Massam, D., 127–128, 136, 138
Matthewson, L., 16, 51–52, 70, 71–72
May, R., 13
Milroy, J., 56–59
Mithun, M., 85, 89, 121, 125–126, 131–132, 136, 137
Mohawk
  adjunct licensing in, 113–114
  incorporation in, 126–127, 132
Montague, R., 1, 8
Musan, R., 53, 98–99

Negation, scope of, 13–14, 18, 27–28, 33, 36–37, 40–41, 52, 100–103, 108–109, 112, 117–118
Negative concord, 97–98, 102, 112, 120–121
Ngata, A., 28, 62

# Index

Niuean
  incorporation in, 127–128
Novelty Condition, 32–33, 126

Parsons, T., 11
Partee, B., 7, 8, 23, 55, 98, 122
Pearce, E., 136, 138
Polinsky, M., 30, 40–41, 56, 60, 63, 69
Postal, P., 87, 127

Quantification, 33, 37–40, 41, 50, 122
  existential, 3, 5, 8, 45, 115
  tripartite structure of, 12, 49, 51
  universal, 35–36, 60, 87, 95, 96, 100–101, 104, 129
Quantifier
  adverbial, 13, 18, 35
  determiner, 13, 18, 25, 35, 80
  generalized, 7, 8, 13–14, 54–55, 77, 85
  raising, 13

Recomposition, 17, 115
Reedy, T., 63–64, 149
Reinhart, T., 5, 16, 45, 48, 51–52, 71, 72, 122
Reuland, E., 59
Rogers, R., 150
Rosen, S., 121, 131–132

Sadock, J., 83, 125–126, 131–132
Sag, I., 22, 45
Sapir, E., 77, 131
Spaelti, P., 129
Spencer, A., 135, 147
St'át'imcets (Lillooet Salish)
  indefinites in, 71–72
Stenning, K., 119
Strawson, P., 1–2
Szabolcsi, A., 98

Type shifting, 4, 6–9, 14–15, 17, 23, 46, 47–48, 50, 54–55, 71, 115

Unselective binding, 49, 50

van Geenhoven, V., 17, 52–53, 70, 75, 107, 114–116, 126, 128–129
van Riemsdijk, H., 128

Waite, J., 63
Williams, E., 131–132
Williams. H., 25, 42
Williams, W., 28, 42–43, 62
Winter, Y., 5, 16, 45, 47–48, 51–52, 71, 72
Woodbury, H., 121

[6] Edmond Missisen and Arthur L. Coffing, *Canada: Growth Potential of the Grain and Livestock Sectors,* USDA, Economic Research Service, Foreign Agricultural Economic Report No. 77, June 1972, p. 68.

[7] Dudley, Donald, and Barlowe, "Implications for U.S. Cotton," pp. 20-21.

[8] In 1966/67 the farm price of wheat per bushel was $1.63 and the export subsidy rate was $0.22. In 1967/68 the farm price declined to $1.39 and the export subsidy to $0.11. The price declined further to $1.24 in 1968/69 and there was no export subsidy. See Economic Research Service, *Foreign Agricultural Trade,* p. 81, and USDA, *Agricultural Statistics, 1972,* p. 2.

[9] If market prices should fall to or below the price support or loan levels, direct payments to make up the difference between the support level and the market price should be paid rather than resorting to export subsidies. The use of direct payments would minimize the real economic loss.

[10] USDA, *Agricultural Statistics, 1972,* p. 453.

[11] Obviously this conclusion is a personal judgment. It is based on the increase in participation, in payments and in the average payment made per acre diverted.

[12] Reinsel and Krenz, *Farm Programs,* p. 11.

[13] USDA, *Agricultural Statistics, 1972,* p. 635.

[14] See D. Gale Johnson, "Agricultural Trade and Foreign Economic Policy," in *Foreign Trade and Agricultural Policy,* National Advisory Commission on Food and Fiber, Technical Papers, vol. 6, August 1967, pp. 17-20.

## NOTE TO APPENDIX A

[1] This material is taken from USDA, Economic Research Service, *Cotton Situation,*         visions of 1973 Upla

Agricultural Organization of the United Nations, *Implications of the Possible Enlargement of the EEC for Agricultural Commodity Projections,* CCP 72/WP.6 (Rome, December 1971), pp. 11-12.

[6] Food and Agricultural Organization of the United Nations, *Agricultural Commodity Projections: 1970-1980,* CCP 71/20 (Rome, 1971), vol. 1, p. 69.

[7] David W. Culver, "A View of Food and Agriculture in 1980," *Agricultural Economics Research,* vol. 22, no. 3 (July 1970), p. 66.

[8] Johnson, "Impact of Freer Trade," forthcoming.

[9] The estimates of land and labor used in the production of sugar, peanuts and sheep have been derived from data on labor used on farms (USDA, *Agricultural Statistics, 1972,* pp. 541 and 568) and on total feed supplies and use by various types of livestock (Economic Research Service, USDA). Labor used on farms is classified as direct and farm maintenance (overhead). Only the direct is allocated by enterprise. It is assumed in the text that farm maintenance work (about 15 percent of the total) would not be affected by the changes in direct labor.

[10] Projected yields for 1980 have been taken from David W. Culver, "Food and Agriculture in 1980," p. 67.

[11] The EEC study referred to is available in *Note D'Information,* "*Objet:* Comparaison entre le soutien accordé à l'agriculture aux Etats-Unis et dans la Communauté (Informations internes sur l'Agriculture, n° 70. Commission des C.E.), Brussels, 30 October 1972. The gross domestic product of agriculture is for 1968 and has been derived from William P. Roenigls, *Agriculture in the European Community and the United States, 1958-68,* Economic Research Service, USDA, April 1971, p. 1968.

[12] Larry J. Wipf, "Tariffs, Nontariff Distortions and Effective Protection of U.S. Agriculture," *American Journal of Agricultural Economics,* vol. 53 (August 1970), p. 427.

[13] Such knowledge is essential if we are to know what adjustments farmers would be required to make under freer trade. An important source of opposition to freer trade is uncertainty—the lack of understanding of how much change would be required. This uncertainty has been generated, at least in part, by extravagant claims made for the effectiveness of farm programs in increasing farm incomes. Fortunately, in recent years official pronouncements in this area have been quite circumspect, but more positive indications of actual effects would be highly desirable.

## NOTES TO CHAPTER VII

[1] In addition to the shortness of the period, a factor that may have affected the elasticity measurement, was the rising trend in livestock prices over the period.

[2] Hermann Priebe, Denis Bergman and Jan Horring, *Fields of Conflict in European Farm Policy,* Agricultural Trade Papers, Trade Policy Research Centre (London, 1972), p. 44.

[3] Tweeten, *Foundations of Farm Policy,* pp. 244-45.

[4] For further discussion of the causes of poverty in agriculture and policy measures that have some chance of reducing poverty, see Johnson, *World Agriculture in Disarray,* pp. 205-25.

[5] Prior to the 1966 election, the price support for soybeans was increased from $2.25 to $2.50. In 1967 and 1968 the farm price went below the support price and, for the first time, the Commodity Credit Corporation acquired ownership of substantial quantities of soybeans. The CCC owned 9 million bushels on August 31, 1966 and 171 million bushels on August 31, 1969. See USDA, *Agricultural Statistics, 1971,* pp. 132, 477, 622-23.

[15] Willard Cochrane, *The City Man's Guide to the Farm Problem* (Minneapolis: University of Minnesota Press, 1965).
[16] Tweeten, *Foundations of Farm Policy*, p. 270.
[17] Earl O. Heady and Leo V. Mayer, "Opportunities and Alternatives in Program Modifications," in Center for Agricultural and Economic Development, *Farm Program Choices* (Ames, Iowa: Iowa State University Press, 1970), p. 99.
[18] Johnson, *World Agriculture in Disarray*, p. 243.
[19] USDA, Economic Research Service, *The Balance Sheet of the Farming Sector, 1969*, Agricultural Information Bulletin No. 340, January 1970, p. 29, and U.S. Bureau of the Census, *1964 United States Census of Agriculture*, vol. 2, chapter 8, p. 754. Data on land rented to others by farm operators is for 1954.
[20] U.S. Bureau of the Census, *Current Population Report, Consumer Income*, Series P-60, no. 80, October 4, 1971, p. 73.
[21] USDA, Economic Research Service, *The Hired Farm Work Force of 1971*, Agricultural Economic Report No. 222, p. 16.
[22] Economic Research Service, *Farm Income Situation*, pp. 68 and 72.
[23] *Economic Report of the President*, 1973, pp. 212-13, for real per capita in the United States, and Economic Research Service, *Farm Income Situation*, pp. 47 and 50 for farm population.
[24] The price index used to deflate current dollars was prices paid for family maintenance.
[25] Off-farm income includes some income earned from agricultural activities—wages earned from a farm job or rent on farm land. Farm income is income earned from a farm activity on a farm other than the one operated. Most of the off-farm income is from nonfarm jobs or nonfarm investments.
[26] USDA, *Agricultural Statistics, 1971*, p. 551.
[27] Tangible assets of nonfarm families estimated from data in *Statistical Abstract of the United States, 1972*, p. 337. The national wealth estimate includes public property valued at $6.8 million or approximately 20 percent of the national wealth. Such public property has been attributed to nonfarm families. If the public property were excluded, the average wealth per nonfarm family would be $50,000.
[28] USDA, *Agricultural Statistics, 1971*, p. 551.
[29] *Economic Report of the President*, 1969, p. 161.

## NOTES TO CHAPTER VI

[1] More than two decades ago I dealt with the inconsistency between farm programs and liberal trade policies in *Trade and Agriculture: A Study of Inconsistent Policies* (New York: John Wiley & Sons, Inc., 1950). The major difference between now and 1950 is that the inconsistent elements are now recognized to be a problem to a much greater extent than in the past.
[2] All direct export subsidies on farm products were eliminated in late 1972. However, some products may still be sold from Commodity Credit Corporation stock at less than domestic prices.
[3] USDA, Economic Research Service, *Foreign Agricultural Trade of the United States*, January 1973, p. 81.
[4] D. Gale Johnson, "Impact of Freer Trade on North American Agriculture," *American Journal of Agricultural Economics*, vol. 55, no. 2 (May 1973, forthcoming).
[5] See John Ferris et al., *The Impact on U.S. Agricultural Trade of the Accession of the United Kingdom, Ireland, Denmark and Norway to the European Economic Community*, Institute of International Agriculture (East Lansing, Mich.: University of Michigan, 1971), Research Report No. 11, p. 203, and Food and

²⁸ Luther Tweeten, *Foundations of Farm Policy* (Lincoln: University of Nebraska Press, 1970), p. 244.

²⁹ For summaries of the results of studies of supply response functions, see Johnson, *World Agriculture in Disarray*, pp. 112-13 and 114.

³⁰ Robert D. Reinsel and Ronald D. Krenz, *Farm Programs: Income Benefits and Capitalization into Land Values*, USDA, Economic Research Service, October 1972, p. 11.

# NOTES TO CHAPTER V

¹ For some evidence on the elasticities of demand for farm inputs, see Fred H. Tyner and Luther G. Tweeten, "Optimum Resource Allocation in U.S. Agriculture," *Journal of Farm Economics*, vol. 48, no. 3 (August 1966), p. 627.

² In a very different context, the classical economists investigated the effect of an increase in the demand for farm products upon the demand for land and labor. They were concerned that because of the inelasticity of supply of land, given their assumptions about the elasticity of the supply of labor, all the income gains from demand growth would accrue to land. In fact, some thought that the growth in food demand due to population growth would have a negative impact on the real wages of labor. It is somewhat curious that some of the main supporters of free trade in England did so in order to prevent most of the gains from economic progress going to the owners of land. Yet today there seems to be little or no concern in the major industrial countries that their farm policies have similar distributional effects within agriculture.

³ Edward W. Trychniewicz and G. Edward Schuh, "Econometric Analysis of Labor Market," *American Journal of Agricultural Economics*, vol. 51, no. 4 (November 1969), p. 779.

⁴ Elsewhere I have estimated the impact of a 10 percent increase in product price on the wage and employment of labor using the long-run elasticities of demand determined by Trychniewicz and Schuh. The wage rate would increase by 2.9 percent and employment by 4.4 percent. See my *World Agriculture in Disarray*, p. 189.

⁵ John E. Floyd, "The Effects of Farm Price Supports on the Returns to Land and Labor in Agriculture," *Journal of Political Economy*, vol. 73, no. 2 (April 1965), p. 156.

⁶ For development of the argument that the increase in the return to labor (or any other resource) due to an increase in the demand for that resource is a one-time only increase, see my *World Agriculture in Disarray*, pp. 198-203. Policy makers seem to assume that a high market price will solve farm income problems. This is simply not so. What would be required is a continuously increasing level of prices.

⁷ The discussion of the value of tobacco allotments relies on the excellent summary article by James A. Seagraves, "Capitalized Values of Tobacco Allotments and the Rate of Return to Allotment Owners," *American Journal of Agricultural Economics*, vol. 51, no. 2 (May 1969), pp. 320-34.

⁸ J. L. Hedrick, "Factor Returns Under the Tobacco Program," in George S. Tolley, ed., *Study of U.S. Agricultural Adjustments* (Raleigh: State University of North Carolina, 1970), pp. 219-74.

⁹ Seagraves, "Capitalized Values," p. 323.

¹⁰ Hedrick, "Factor Returns," p. 268.

¹¹ Ibid., pp. 264-66.

¹² Tweeten, *Foundations of Farm Policy*, pp. 260-61.

¹³ Reinsel and Krenz, *Farm Programs*, p. 14.

¹⁴ Ibid., p. 15.

[11] Ibid., pp. 2, 3, 34, 35, 44, 51, 52, 64, 65 and 637; USDA, Statistical Reporting Service, *Crop Production, 1972 Annual Summary,* January 15, 1973.

[12] There are a variety of reasons why farmers do not plant and cultivate every acre of land on their farms. Climatic conditions may be unfavorable at the planting time. Land may be fallowed to increase yields in the next year. And some land may have such low productivity that its use is profitable only when farm prices are high.

[13] Orville E. Krause, *Cropland Trends Since World War II,* USDA, Economic Research Service, Agricultural Economic Report No. 177, April 1970, p. 5.

[14] Cultivated summer fallow in which land is kept free of weeds increases yields in the following year. Depending on the amount of rainfall, wheat yields after fallow may be 30 to 100 percent greater than wheat yields after another crop.

[15] Hugh H. Wooten and James R. Anderson, *Major Use of Land in the United States: Summary for 1954,* USDA, Agricultural Research Service, Agricultural Information Bulletin No. 168, January 1957, p. 12, for 1951-53; for data for 1970 and 1972, see sources in note 11, this chapter. The year 1971 was excluded from the recent years because of the relaxation of the feed grain program features in that year following low yields due to corn blight in 1970.

[16] H. Thomas Frey, Orville E. Krause and Clifford Dicksson, *Major Uses of Land and Water in the United States,* USDA, Economic Research Service, Agricultural Economic Report No. 149, November 1968, p. 10 and sources indicated in note 11, this chapter. The decline in cropland is not due to any significant extent to expansion of urban areas or of transportation facilities. Between 1959 and 1964 urban areas expanded at an annual rate of 400,000 acres and transportation uses by 200,000 acres. Farmsteads and farm roads decreased by 225,000 acres annually (ibid., p. 28).

[17] The data for 1951 were used because there were no program controls on acreages and almost no difference between the state data for 1951 and for 1951-53. The 1969 data are representative of 1970 and 1972. Sources: USDA, *Agricultural Statistics, 1953* and *1971.*

[18] Diverted acreage by states from reports of Agricultural Stabilization and Conservation Service (USDA).

[19] Wooten and Anderson, *Use of Land in the United States,* p. 10, and Frey, Krause and Dicksson, *Uses of Land and Water,* pp. 53-54.

[20] Secretary of Agriculture Earl L. Butz, "Will We Overproduce Again?" address before the National Grain and Feed Association, Orlando, Florida, February 28, 1973.

[21] Leroy Quance and Luther Tweeten, "Excess Capacity and Adjustment Potential in U.S. Agriculture," *Agricultural Economics Research,* vol. 24, no. 36 (July 1972), pp. 59-60.

[22] Mayer, Heady, and Madsen, *Farm Programs for the 1970's,* pp. 31, 50 and 54.

[23] The acreage of all hay averaged 75 million acres in 1951-53 and 63 million acres in 1971. However, these totals include wild hay, which declined by at least 6 million acres between 1951-53 and 1971. Hay produced on cropland required 61 million acres in 1951-53 and approximately 55 million in 1971. See USDA, *Agricultural Statistics, 1972,* p. 319.

[24] Luther Tweeten, "The Demand for United States Farm Output," *Food Research Institute Studies,* vol. 7, no. 3 (1967).

[25] Mayer, Heady, and Madsen, *Farm Programs for the 1970's,* p. 30.

[26] Testimony before the Subcommittee of the Senate Appropriations Committee, June 4, 1969, and USDA, *Farm Income Situation,* July 1972, p. 64.

[27] Johnson, "Trade Policies," pp. 347-48.

# NOTES TO CHAPTER IV

[1] USDA, *Report from the United States Department of Agriculture on Farm Price and Income Projections, 1960-65*, Senate Document 77, 86th Congress, 2d session, January 20, 1960, p. III. The projection of the change in net farm income was made by an advisory committee established by the land grant colleges. Committee members were Harlow Halvorson, George Brandow, Willard Cochrane, Maurice Kelso, James Plaxico and John Schnittker. Their conclusions are given on pp. 27-30.

[2] U.S., Congress, Joint Economic Committee, *Economic Policies for Agriculture in the 1960's: Implications of Four Selected Alternatives*, Joint Committee Print (no number), 86th Congress, 2d session, November 26, 1960, p. 18. Studies by Walter W. Wilcox, John A. Schnittker, Dale E. Hathaway and George Brandow are included.

[3] Dale Hathaway makes this point regarding the two studies: "An observation is needed regarding these market price estimates. Most of them implicitly assumed that the productive resources in agriculture were fixed for the time period involved.... Thus, the prices that were projected were market-clearing prices, assuming that all of the resources in agriculture in the late 1950's had no salvage value elsewhere and there would be no outmovement. This probably was a reasonable assumption for the short-run periods involved, but it does not follow that these projected price levels would persist indefinitely in a full-employment economy." See Dale E. Hathaway, *Government and Agriculture* (New York: Macmillan, 1963), pp. 243-44.

[4] Leo V. Mayer, Earl O. Heady and Howard C. Madsen, *Farm Programs for the 1970's*, Center for Agricultural and Economic Development, Report No. 32, Iowa State University, October 1968, pp. 34 and 51.

[5] See below, p. 48.

[6] This point is developed more fully in my paper, "Trade Policies and U.S. Agriculture," *Journal of Farm Economics*, vol. 48, no. 2 (May 1966), pp. 346-48. It is argued there that projected yield would have to be fixed for the life of the program to eliminate the effects of payments on crop yields. The use of a projected yield rather than a fixed yield in determining payments has a mixed motivation: (1) when programs are voluntary, decisions to participate are influenced by payments that can be earned, and (2) it is accepted as "fair" that transfer payments are closely related to productivity of land rather than to income or some other criteria.

[7] USDA, *Agricultural Statistics, 1972*, p. 637.

[8] George E. Dudley, James R. Donald and Russell G. Barlowe, "Yield and Acreage Implications for U.S. Cotton," *Cotton Situation*, August 1970, pp. 17-23.

[9] No land diversion was required by the cotton program in 1969 and 1970, with rather significant diversion in 1966 and 1967 and a smaller amount in 1968. In Mississippi when diversion under the cotton program was 496,000 acres in 1967, planted area of 17 major crops averaged 5.1 million; in 1969 when there was no diversion in the cotton program, planted acreage was 5.0 million. In Texas diversion under the cotton program was 2.1 million acres in 1967 and planted area was 23.2 million acres. In 1969, with no diversion under the cotton program, planted acreage was 23.9 million acres. It should be noted that in 1967 there was no wheat program diversion and such diversion was 1.1 million acres in 1969. In Alabama where diversion in the cotton program was 294,000 acres in 1967, planted acreage declined between 1967 and 1969. Data on planted area from *Agricultural Statistics*, various years. Acreage diversion from reports of the Agricultural Stabilization and Conservation Service, U.S. Department of Agriculture.

[10] USDA, *Agricultural Statistics, 1972*, p. 637.

³ George W. Coffman, *Corporations with Farming Operations,* USDA, Economic Research Service, Agricultural Economic Report No. 209, June 1971, p. 9.
⁴ Calculated from USDA, *Agricultural Statistics, 1972,* pp. 504-05. Land in farms in 1971 assumed same as in 1969.
⁵ USDA, Economic Research Service, *Farm Income Situation,* July 1972, pp. 68 and 72.
⁶ McElveen, *Family Farms in a Changing Economy,* p. 19; Nathan M. Koffsky and Ernest W. Grove, "The Current Income Position of Commercial Farms," in Joint Economic Committee, *Policy for Commercial Agriculture,* 85th Congress, 1st session, Joint Committee Print, 1957, p. 86; and Economic Research Service, *Farm Income Situation,* p. 72.
⁷ Organization for Economic Cooperation and Development (OECD), *The Growth of Output, 1960-1980* (Paris, December 1970), p. 35.
⁸ USDA, Economic Research Service, *Changes in Farm Production and Efficiency, A Summary Report, 1972,* Statistical Bulletin No. 233, Revised June 1972, pp. 12 and 21, and USDA, *Agricultural Statistics, 1962,* p. 41. In 1960, 95.9 percent of all corn was planted with hybrids; the series was discontinued after that year.
⁹ USDA, *Agricultural Statistics, 1972,* pp. 1, 2, 34, 35, 64, 65, 74 and 75.
¹⁰ The analyses in this section are developed more fully in D. Gale Johnson, *World Agriculture in Disarray,* Fontana World Economic Issues (London: Macmillan and Fontana; New York: St. Martin's Press and New Viewpoints, 1973), pp. 82-99.
¹¹ Economic Research Service, *Changes in Farm Production and Efficiency,* p. 31.
¹² Calculated from USDA, *Agricultural Statistics, 1972,* pp. 502 and 555. Wage rates and net farm operator income per farm were deflated by prices farmers paid for family maintenance. Real weekly earnings are calculated from *Statistical Abstract of the United States, 1972* (Washington, D. C.: U.S. Government Printing Office, 1972), p. 233. Weekly earnings were deflated by consumer price index; earners included private nonagriculture.
¹³ Don Paarlberg, "Efficiency—Its Economic Impact on Farmers," speech at 21st Annual Meeting of the Agricultural Research Institute, Washington, D. C., October 10, 1972.
¹⁴ Ibid.; also, Glen T. Boston and Donald D. Durost, "The New USDA Index of Inputs," *Journal of Farm Economics,* vol. 42, no. 5 (December 1960), p. 1402.
¹⁵ Economic Research Service, *Changes in Farm Production and Efficiency,* p. 30. Nonpurchased inputs include labor, as well as operator-owned land and other capital inputs.

## NOTES TO CHAPTER III

¹ *Economic Report of the President* (Washington, D. C.: U.S. Government Printing Office, 1973), p. 220.
² Economic Research Service, *Farm Income Situation,* p. 72.
³ USDA, *Agricultural Statistics, 1972,* pp. 566 and 698. Calculated from cash receipts from marketings.
⁴ USDA, *Possible Methods of Improving the Parity Formula,* Report of the Secretary of Agriculture pursuant to Section 602 of the Agricultural Act of 1956, Senate Document 18, 85th Congress, 1st session, 1957, pp. 34-35, for data from 1940 through 1956. Extended by author from data in Economic Research Service, *Farm Income Situation,* pp. 45, 46, 50 and 51.
⁵ USDA, *Parity Returns Position of Farmers,* Report to the Congress of the United States by the Department of Agriculture, Senate Document 44, 90th Congress, 1st session, 1967, pp. 9-19. For discussion of the parity income concept and its history, see pp. 5-7.

# NOTES

## NOTES TO CHAPTER I

[1] The two terms—diverted and set-aside—refer to cropland that farmers have not used for current crop production in compliance with program provisions. Prior to the Agricultural Act of 1970, such land was called diverted land. For 1971 and after, such land is referred to as set-aside. The major difference between the Agricultural Act of 1970 and the legislation that preceded it relates to the uses that could be made of the land that was cultivated since acreage allotments for the individual crop did not act as a restraint on production decisions. Under the 1970 act, once a farmer meets the set-aside requirement, he may use the remainder of his land as he sees fit except for the need to plan a minimum amount of cotton and some less stringent requirements for utilizing land that serves as the basis for receiving payments under the wheat and feed grain programs. In this essay, when the time reference is 1970 or earlier, the term diverted is used; where the time reference is 1971 or later, set-aside is used. However, where the reference covers both time periods, either term may be used.

[2] The report on prospective plantings issued January 19, 1973, indicated the following increases in plantings of spring planted or sown crops over 1972: corn—up 7 percent, cotton—down 7 percent, soybeans—up 5 percent, oats—up 1 percent, spring wheat—up 15 percent, and sorghum—up 10 percent. The planting intentions for the major spring crops indicated an increase of only 6 percent and about 11 million acres. See U.S. Department of Agriculture (USDA), *Crop Production*, January 19, 1973.

[3] In the 1973 program as announced on December 11, 1972, a farmer who met the minimum set-aside requirement of 30 percent and had a program yield of 87 bushels per acre (the national average) would have received $50 per acre for each acre set aside. In 1969 cash rent paid for cropland in Iowa and Illinois was about $36.00. See U.S. Department of Agriculture, *News*, December 11, 1972, and Robert D. Reinsel and Bruce Johnson, *Farm Tenure and Cash Rents in the United States*, USDA, Economic Research Service, Agricultural Economic Report No. 190, p. 25.

[4] USDA, Economic Research Service, *Cotton Situation*, February 1973, p. 5.

[5] Testimony before Subcommittee of the Senate Appropriations Committee, June 4, 1969.

[6] In 1970 total payments under the feed grain program were $1.5 billion and acreage diverted was 37.4 million acres. In 1972 a similar acreage set-aside earned payments of $1.9 billion. The percentage of feed grain acreage in the program increased from approximately 44 percent in 1970 to 75 percent in 1972. See USDA, Economic Research Service, *Feed Situation*, February issues, 1971 and 1973.

## NOTES TO CHAPTER II

[1] Jackson V. McElveen, *Family Farms in a Changing Economy*, USDA, Agricultural Research Service, Agricultural Information Bulletin No. 171, March 1957, p. 54.

[2] Radoje Nikolitch, *Family-Size Farms in U.S. Agriculture*, USDA, Economic Research Service, February 1972, p. 4.

**Table A-3** *(Continued)*

| State [a] | Annual Average Per Farm | |
|---|---|---|
| | Government payments | Net income |
| South Dakota | 1,892 | 8,246 |
| Wyoming | 1,765 | 6,911 |
| Iowa | 1,656 | 8,574 |
| Idaho | 1,627 | 8,797 |
| Illinois | 1,425 | 6,600 |
| Mississippi | 1,419 | 4,895 |
| Oklahoma | 1,265 | 3,801 |
| Washington | 1,238 | 6,323 |
| Minnesota | 1,161 | 5,874 |
| Indiana | 1,141 | 5,753 |
| Arkansas | 1,127 | 6,293 |
| Georgia | 1,011 | 6,307 |
| Louisiana | 1,007 | 5,811 |
| South Carolina | 992 | 3,573 |
| Missouri | 983 | 4,112 |
| Alabama | 862 | 3,583 |
| Nevada | 861 | 10,876 |
| Ohio | 786 | 3,696 |
| Utah | 764 | 4,414 |
| Michigan | 743 | 3,092 |
| Oregon | 571 | 3,838 |
| Florida | 517 | 15,544 |
| Tennessee | 510 | 2,250 |
| Delaware | 463 | 13,322 |
| Pennsylvania | 459 | 4,382 |
| Wisconsin | 431 | 4,996 |
| Maryland | 417 | 6,812 |
| New York | 368 | 5,790 |
| North Carolina | 360 | 4,318 |
| Alaska | 348 | 2,089 |
| Kentucky | 332 | 3,598 |
| New Jersey | 320 | 5,370 |
| Virginia | 250 | 2,756 |
| Vermont | 169 | 7,404 |
| Maine | 154 | 7,236 |
| Connecticut | 147 | 10,528 |
| New Hampshire | 141 | 2,793 |
| West Virginia | 116 | 634 |
| Massachusetts | 93 | 7,180 |
| Rhode Island | 73 | 4,502 |
| *Summary* | | |
| Top 10 states [a,b] | 3,088 | 13,062 |
| Next 15 states [a,b] | 1,314 | 5,703 |
| Next 15 states [a,b] | 564 | 6,600 |
| Lowest 10 states [a,b] | 180 | 5,200 |

[a] Ranked by government payments per farm.
[b] Simple or unweighted average of the state data.
**Source:** USDA, *Farm Income: State Estimates, 1959–1971*, a supplement to the July 1972 *Farm Income Situation*, August 1972.

increase varies by different qualities of beef, and beef qualities vary substantially from state to state. Furthermore, there are substantial sales of beef from farmer to farmer across state lines. Thus it does not seem appropriate to present the estimates by states. However, the state estimates for the four groups of states are averaged in the summary of Table A-3. This was done to determine if there had been any significant effort to concentrate direct governmental payments to those states that received little or no transfer through higher product prices. The results indicate that if such an effort had been made, it was relatively unsuccessful. On a per farm basis, it was estimated that the income transfer through higher prices averaged approximately $3,700 per year for the 10 states with the highest level of direct payments. The 10 states with the lowest level of direct payments had a gross transfer per farm of approximately $1,400. The other two groups of states were in the approximate range of $1,200 to $1,300.

As noted earlier, it should not be concluded that net farm incomes would decline by the amount of the direct payments or the gross transfers through higher prices. In part, the size of the gross transfers through higher prices reflects the effects of U.S. trade restrictions in international prices. If all industrial countries removed their trade interferences on farm products, the size of the gross transfer would be reduced even further. And some considerable part of the direct payments reflects earnings foregone as well as expenses incurred in order to increase the future level of payments.

### Table A-3
### GOVERNMENT PAYMENTS AND NET REALIZED INCOME PER FARM, ANNUAL AVERAGES, 1969–71

| State [a] | Annual Average Per Farm ||
|---|---|---|
| | Government payments | Net income |
| Arizona | $8,226 | $32,233 |
| Montana | 3,071 | 9,094 |
| New Mexico | 2,912 | 10,876 |
| Texas | 2,689 | 10,229 |
| Nebraska | 2,624 | 8,667 |
| Kansas | 2,607 | 7,600 |
| Hawaii | 2,406 | 18,002 |
| North Dakota | 2,179 | 7,134 |
| California | 2,115 | 18,852 |
| Colorado | 2,051 | 7,928 |

## APPENDIX B: DISTRIBUTION OF GROSS BENEFITS OF ALL FARM PROGRAMS, BY STATE

There are a variety of ways of considering the distribution of payments and benefits of the farm programs. Some of them were presented in Chapter V. In this appendix the direct payments from all governmental programs are given by states for the annual average per farm for the three years, 1969 through 1971. For comparison, the average realized net incomes per farm operator are also given in Table A-3. The average amount of direct payments per farm ranges from a low of $73 per farm in Rhode Island to a high of $8,226 in Arizona. West Virginia, whose lowest average annual income per farm of $634 is the nation's lowest, received only $116 per farm from direct government payments. Arizona had the largest average farm income per farm and the highest level of payments per farm.

At the bottom of Table A-3 the 50 states are classified into four groups—the 10 states with the highest level of payments per farm, the 10 states with the lowest level of payments per farm, and two groups of 15 for the remaining states. Average farm incomes of the 10 states with the highest level of payments were 2.5 times greater than those of the 10 states with the lowest level of payments, and payments received by the former were 17 times that of the latter. For the middle two groups, there was not much relationship between the level of payments and the level of net farm income.

Estimates were also made of the gross transfers to farmers because of the higher prices received by farmers as a result of price supports, export subsidies and import restrictions. The farm products analyzed included wheat, rice, peanuts, tobacco, sugar, beef and veal, and dairy products. The results are admittedly very rough since the effects of the trade interferences have been based on the assumption that, if these interferences were removed, international prices would remain unchanged. This is an incorrect assumption for a number of important farm products, especially manufactured dairy products. In addition, it is difficult to allocate the effects of price increases for beef and veal among the various states since the price

| Acreage diversion or set-aside | | | |
|---|---|---|---|
| Grains included<br>Base period | Corn, grain sorghum and barley<br>1959 and 1960 | Corn, grain sorghum and barley<br>1959 and 1960 | Corn and grain sorghum<br>1959 and 1960 |
| Acreage to be diverted | | | |
| Minimum [b]<br>Maximum | 20% of base<br>50% of base<br>(or 25 acres if larger) [c,d] | 20% of base<br>50% of base<br>(or 25 acres if larger) [c,d] | Set-aside 20% of base<br>No additional diversion for payment [e] |
| Limitation on acreage planted | Not more than 80% of base plus eligible substitution | Not more than 80% of base plus eligible substitution | No limitation after meeting set-aside requirement and maintaining conserving base. |
| Payment rates for acreage diversion | County total support rate times: | County total support rate times: | |
| First 20% diverted | No payment (except small farms) | No payment (except small farms) | No direct payment—set-aside payment considered payment for required set-aside |
| Diversion of 20 to 50% | 45% of projected production | 40% of projected production | No additional diversion for payment |
| Small producer—25 acres of feed grains or less | May divert entire acreage. Payment on first 20% based on 20% of projected production; additional diversion based on 45% of projected production [f] | May divert entire acreage. Payment on first 20% based on 20% of projected production; additional diversion based on 40% of projected production [f] | No special provision. Unlike 1970, producers receive set-aside payment even if no feed grains are planted. |

[a] If final set-aside payment is less than preliminary payment, producers not asked for a refund. If set-aside percentage is less than 20%, preliminary payment reduced proportionately. [b] Minimum diversion to be eligible for diversion payments and price support. [c] Maximum acreage that can be diverted; no payment for minimum (required) diversion except on "small farms." [d] Producers could divert for payment up to 25 acres if no feed grains planted. [e] Set-aside tentatively 20%. Final determination announced prior to sign-up. [f] Producers with bases of 26-125 acres may elect to have base temporarily reduced to 25 acres and be paid as a small producer, provided no corn, grain, sorghum or barley is planted.

Source: USDA, Feed Statistics, 1972, Table 35.

## Table A-2
## FEED GRAINS: COMPARISON OF THE 1969, 1970 AND 1971 PROGRAMS

| Item | 1969 Program | | | 1970 Program | | | 1971 Program | | |
|---|---|---|---|---|---|---|---|---|---|
| | Price support loan | Price support payment | Total support | Price support loan | Price support payment | Total support | Price support loan | Set-aside payment | Guarantee support |
| **Price support** | | | | | | | | | |
| Corn, per bu. | $1.05 | $0.30 | $1.35 | $1.05 | $0.30 | $1.35 | $1.05 | Corn and sorghums; difference between Oct.-Feb. average price received and price guarantee | $1.35 |
| Grain sorghum, per cwt. | 1.61 | .53 | 2.14 | 1.61 | .53 | 2.14 | 1.73 | | 2.21 |
| Oats, per bu. | .63 | .00 | .63 | .63 | .00 | .63 | .54 | | ..... |
| Barley, per bu. | .83 | .20 | 1.03 | .83 | .20 | 1.03 | .81 | | ..... |
| Production eligible for price support | Price support loan on total production | Price support payment on projected production of the smaller of the acreage planted to feed grains or 50% of base | | Price support loan on total production | Price support payment on projected production of the smaller of the acreage planted to feed grains or 50% of base | | Price support loan on total production | Set-aside payment on production from 50% of base. Payment made if planted to feed grains, other crops or left idle. | |
| Preliminary or advance payment | 50% of payment for additional diversion only (no advance on price support payment) | | | | | | Preliminary set-aside payment made soon after July 1 depending on set-aside percentage: a | | |
| Corn | | | | None | | | 20% $0.32 per bu. | | |
| Grain sorghum | | | | None | | | 0.29 per bu. | | |
| Yield used for determination of payments | Projected for 1969 (based on 1963-67 average adjusted for trend) | | | Projected for 1970 (based on 1964-68 average adjusted for trend) | | | Based on yield established for farm for preceding year with adjustments needed to be fair. | | |

| Item | 1970 Program | 1971 Set-aside Program |
|---|---|---|
| Marketing quotas | None | None |
| Conserving base | Acreage diverted must be in addition to the conserving base, i.e., acreage devoted to conserving uses in recent years. | Same as 1970 |
| Planting requirement to prevent loss of allotment | Farm allotment was reduced if producer failed to plant at least 75 percent of the farm allotment in one out of three years. | Producer who fails to plant 90 percent of his domestic allotment to wheat, corn or sorghum in 1971 will have his 1972 allotment reduced by the underplanting—up to 20 percent. Acreage not planted due to natural disaster or conditions beyond producers control will be considered planted and producer who makes a set-aside but elects to receive no payment will not suffer an allotment loss. |
| Substitution | Producer with a wheat allotment and a feed grain base who made the required diversion and maintained his conserving base could plant the total of his wheat allotment and 80 percent of his feed grain base to wheat or feed grains without loss of base or allotment. However, he could only receive feed grain payments and wheat certificates by planting 90 percent of his certificated acreage to wheat and 45 percent of his feed grain base to corn, sorghum or barley. | Any producer who sets aside cropland equal to the required percentages of his base and allotment can plant his entire acreage to wheat, corn or sorghum without loss of payments, certificates, base acreage or allotment. A producer with only a base or only an allotment can participate in one program and plant all wheat or all feed grains without loss of benefits, base or allotment. |

**Source:** USDA, Wheat Situation, February 1971, Table 21.

**Table A-1** *(Continued)*

| Item | 1970 Program | 1971 Set-aside Program |
|---|---|---|
| Export certificates | None | None |
| Preliminary payments | None | 75 percent of estimated value of certificates soon after July 1, 1971. (Final payments made the following December and January). If preliminary payment larger than value of certificates finally determined, no refund will be required. |
| Payment limitation | None | Maximum value of 1971 wheat certificates to any person $55,000 |
| Production eligible for loan | Total production on participating farms | Total production on participating farms |
| Required diversion or set-aside | 30.3 percent of farm wheat allotment | 60 to 75 percent of farm domestic wheat allotment (exact percentage will be specified prior to signup). |
| Compensation for required diversion or set-aside | Value of wheat certificates | Value of wheat certificates |
| Additional diversion for payment | Larger of 25 acres or 50 percent of the farm wheat allotment | None |
| Payment for additional diversion | 50 percent of loan times farm yield times additional acres diverted | None |
| Farm program yield (used to calculate benefits) | Projected from 1966–68 average | Projected from 1967–69 average |

## Table A-1
## WHEAT: COMPARISON OF 1970 AND 1971 PROGRAMS

| Item | 1970 Program | 1971 Set-aside Program |
|---|---|---|
| National wheat allotment | 45.5 million acres | Not applicable |
| National domestic wheat allotment | Not applicable | 19.7 million acres |
| Production eligible for domestic certificates | Production on 48 percent of farm wheat allotment | Production on 100 percent of farm domestic wheat allotment |
| Certificated production on participating farms—estimated | 530 million bushels | 535 million bushels |
| Limitation on acreage planted to wheat | Maximum permitted 100 percent of farm wheat allotment plus eligible substitution | No limit. Participant who sets aside cropland equal to the required percentage of his domestic wheat allotment and maintains his conserving base may plant all the remaining cropland on the farm to wheat—or any other crop he wishes—without loss of certificates (planting of quota crops limited by other programs). |
| Loan | $1.25 per bushel | $1.25 per bushel |
| Domestic certificate | Difference between loan and 100 percent of wheat parity as of July 1, 1970 ($1.57 per bu.) | Difference between price received by farmers in the first 5 months (July-Nov. 1971) of the marketing year and 100 percent of wheat parity on July 1, 1971. |
| Total support or guarantee to program participants for certificated production | 100 percent of parity ($2.82) | 100 percent of parity |

As in the past, any cotton farmer may participate in the 1973 cotton program by signing up and complying with his conserving base requirements. He may participate on any farm or all farms in which he has an interest. Also, as in the past a producer's cotton allotment will be used to determine his program payment, but he will be free to plant the acreage that he decides upon after studying the outlook for supply, demand, price, and other factors, including profitability of other crops.

The 1973 national average loan, announced earlier, is 19.50 cents per pound (Middling 1-inch basis, micronaire 3.5 through 4.9) net weight at average location. This is the same as for 1972.

Cotton farmers have been shifting toward greater reliance on markets as their source of income for the past two years by transferring allotments through the leasing process to areas where cotton can best be produced, Secretary Butz said. This enables producers in areas where the crop is not profitable to diversify, obtaining additional income from alternate land uses. The 1973 program will continue to allow such transfers.

Failure to plant at least 90 percent of the farm's base acreage allotment will result in a reduction in payment. If no cotton has been planted for three consecutive years, the entire allotment can be lost. Allotments removed from farms are reallocated to other cotton farmers.

The same skip-row planting rules which were in effect for the 1971 and 1972 crops will be applicable to the 1973 crop. Skips of one or more rows will count toward the conserving base requirement for the farm.

The final payment, together with the national average market price for Middling 1-inch upland cotton, micronaire 3.5 through 4.9, in the designated sport markets during the August-September 1973 period must equal the higher of (1) 35 cents, or (2) 65 percent of parity as of the beginning of the marketing year, August 1, 1973. However, the payment will not be reduced if the rate as finally determined is less than the 15-cent preliminary rate. The payment is made on a quantity of cotton determined by multiplying the acreage planted within the farm base acreage allotment by the payment yield established for the farm.

**Wheat and Feed Grains.** The major provisions of the 1970 and 1971 wheat programs are set forth in Table A-1. The feed grain programs for the three years 1969 through 1971 are summarized in Table A-2.

# APPENDIX

## APPENDIX A: MAJOR PROVISIONS OF COTTON, WHEAT AND FEED GRAIN PROGRAMS

**Cotton.**[1] The major provisions of the 1973 upland cotton program, announced in November, include:

> A national base acreage allotment of 10 million acres, down from 11½ million in 1972.
>
> No cropland set-aside requirement as a condition of program eligibility compared with a 20 percent requirement in 1972.
>
> A national production goal of 12.1 million 480-pound net weight bales, nearly a million below the year-earlier goal.
>
> A preliminary payment of 15 cents per pound, same as 1972.

In making the announcement, Secretary Butz stated in part:

> The program designed for 1973 takes into account today's cotton situation, and aims at providing a stable supply and maintaining adequate carryover stocks. The program should provide farmers with broad opportunities to diversify their operations by raising other crops, such as soybeans or grain sorghum, on formerly what would have been set-aside land or land in cotton. Thus, they can capitalize on their individual farming skills and special resources.
>
> Adjustment of the national base acreage allotment to 10 million acres will improve cotton's position in the marketplace. At the same time, individual producers can increase their overall income by putting lands formerly in set-aside or in cotton into other crops that are currently in short supply.
>
> Elimination of the set-aside requirement will free about 2 million additional acres of cropland on cotton farms for any crops that producers choose. This step is important for our cotton producers. A larger acreage of soybeans is needed in 1973, and this important crop is considered a good alternative in many areas of the Cotton Belt. Further, selective increases in the acreages of some grain crops are also needed.

determined as indicated above. Such payments might be made for several years, perhaps as many as ten. During the last five years of the total period, one might hope that trade negotiations would have reduced import duties to more reasonable levels.

In the case of manufactured dairy products resource adjustments would also be required of the processors of such products. Some processing plants would have to close. There would be a loss of jobs and of capital asset values. It seems reasonable that if dairy producers are to be compensated for their losses, the owners of processing plants and workers in those plants should also be compensated.

## An Opportunity That Should Not Be Missed

It is incorrect, in my opinion, to assume that the 1972-73 levels of farm prices and incomes are likely to continue for long. The present situation is a temporary one, caused by poor crops in some countries and by inflation and rapid improvement in real incomes in the United States. A more reasonable assumption is that farm prices and incomes will return to the levels of 1969-71, adjusted for changes in the general price level, within two or three years.

Current supply management and price support programs should not be abandoned on the grounds that a new era of prosperity for American agriculture has arrived. Rather, the move is indicated because existing programs are costly to consumers and taxpayers and of little benefit to farmers. The amount of supply management achieved is small. Most of the direct payments have gone for loss of income foregone, for maintaining production in order to receive payments, and into higher land values; farm labor has received no benefit. A new approach is needed because outmoded programs have imposed higher and higher costs and provided fewer and fewer benefits.

In 1973, because of the coincidence of the expiration of major farm legislation and the beginnings of trade negotiations, an opportunity exists to make changes that will benefit consumers and taxpayers and will have only limited adverse consequences to farm operators and hired farm workers. Most of the adverse consequences can be fairly fully compensated as a part of a transition program.

This opportunity should not be missed. There is unlikely to be another equally propitious time during the present decade.

cent for 100 to 250 acres, and 20 percent for allotments in excess of 250 acres. Thus a farm allotment of 75 acres would receive about 68 percent of the full value of the allotment over a three-year period. In 1971 approximately 80 percent of all cotton allotments were smaller than 50 acres. However, 65 percent of total allotment acreage was in allotments of 50 acres or more.[13] If a schedule such as indicated here were used, payments at the recent level of $800 million annually for three years would be sufficient to cover the cost.

*Wheat and feed grains.* Because of the lesser importance of payments as a share of gross income from the production of wheat and feed grains and because of the difficulty in estimating the net value of the payments over and above what has been required for supply management, a transition approach might be to relate such payments to the average amounts received by each farmer for 1971 through 1973. In 1974 the payment would be the average of the three years, in 1975 two-thirds of the average and in 1976, the last year in which a payment would be made, one-third of the average. Based on a rough estimate of the 1973 payments under the wheat and feed grain programs, the average payments for 1971-73 would be approximately $2.1 billion. This schedule of payments would provide for a total payment of $4.2 billion spread over a three-year period.

*Manufactured dairy products.* As noted earlier, a market-oriented policy for dairy products would require substantial resource adjustments. Over a period of time, total milk output might fall by as much as 25 percent under free or nearly free trade in manufactured dairy products. It is not unreasonable to assume that the real price of butter would fall by 20 percent and that of other manufactured milk products by a similar percentage. If it is assumed that the reduction in trade barriers would occur gradually, price support could also be lowered gradually. There would be some loss in asset values—cows and land—and this could be compensated by making payments based on actual sales of milk used for manufactured purposes for the past three to five years. With payments based on past production, output decisions would be guided solely by current or expected market prices. Thus the payments would continue for the specified period if a farmer gave up dairy production in favor of other farm products or gave up farming entirely.

The transition might be made by removing all import quotas immediately but retaining the relatively high tariffs for a number of years.[14] Under this approach, payments would be made to equal the difference between the support price for manufactured milk and the actual market price in a given year, with the quantities involved

by 2 percent annually since 1964, approximately half of the needed adjustment to free trade would already have been made. If farm prices had been stabilized near the 1965 level, perhaps all of the adjustment would have been completed.

With the rapidly growing demand for beef and the increase in off-farm work by farm operators and members of their families, the adjustment problems facing farmers who produce manufactured milk are real but are also manageable. What is required is the political will to assist the adjustment process instead of impeding it.

As has been noted, the cotton programs have had little effect on cotton output in recent years. However, since 1969 direct payments have equaled approximately 62 percent of the cash receipts from the production and marketing of cotton lint and seed. Thus the immediate elimination of the payments would result in a loss of about 40 percent of the total cash income, including government payments, received by cotton producers.

The payments under the wheat and feed grain programs have been a mixture of transfer payments and payments for alternatives foregone. It is probably a reasonable assumption that approximately half of the payments under the feed grain and wheat programs in 1971 and 1972 were transfer payments—payments over and above what would have been required to induce the farmers to withhold the amount of land diverted from current production.[11]

If the above assumptions are accepted, and it is clearly possible to refine them, it is possible to outline transition programs that would prevent most of the capital losses that would result from eliminating the income transfer component of the direct payments.

*Cotton.* The Economic Research Service of the U.S. Department of Agriculture estimates the annual rental value of cotton allotments in 1970 at a third of the direct payments made in that year.[12] If a 7 percent interest rate is used to capitalize the annual allotment values, this would mean that a certain payment for five years at the recent level of about $850 million would almost fully compensate for the allotments. If farm operators were relieved of the need to produce cotton in order to receive the payments, as they would be under the reform discussed here, a smaller amount would compensate for the value of the allotments.

Because of the very great differences in the income and wealth position of the farm operators who "own" cotton allotments, there are equity grounds for varying the size of the payments per acre of allotment inversely by total allotment size. For example, full compensation could be paid for allotments of, say, 30 acres or less, 80 percent for 30 to 50 acres, 60 percent for 50 to 100 acres, 40 per-may be made during the transition period if this is required to induce other nations to reduce their barriers to agricultural imports or their inducements to expand exports.

The above long-term farm program is presented for all of U.S. agriculture. However, the following discussion of transition problems covers only cotton, feed grains, wheat and dairy products. A later monograph will analyze the transition and adjustment problems for sugar, peanuts and rice.

**The Transition.** The necessary resource adjustments have already occurred for cotton and only limited adjustments would have to be made for feed grains and wheat. With the removal of the wheat and feed grain programs, output of these two products would not increase by more than 5 percent assuming the farm price of corn at about $1.10 and wheat at $1.20 (or its feed value relative to corn). If demand pushed prices higher than these levels, output would increase by more than 5 percent. Over time output would continue to grow as it has in the past. The projected increase in output assumes long-run adjustment but with technological conditions as of the present.

The major resource adjustment problem would be in dairying. Under free trade, milk production could decline by as much as a fourth. Total milk production is now less than it was fifteen years ago. Had it not been for the rapid increase in price support levels since 1965, much of the needed adjustment could have been completed by now.

The average price of milk received by farmers was nearly constant from 1956 through 1965. Production increased slightly, reaching a peak in 1964. For a variety of reasons, of which the rising price of beef was an important one, dairy cow numbers and milk production declined significantly between 1965 and 1966. The downward trend would surely have continued at the rate of 3 or 4 percent annually except for an increase in milk prices of about 15 percent, caused in part by higher support prices and in part by an unwillingness to permit increased imports of dairy products. Milk prices have increased annually since 1966.[10] Considerable attention has been given to the increase in the price support level in 1971. But little attention has been given to the restrictive import quota on manufactured dairy products that made the higher price support feasible without a significant increase in governmental costs. Because of the higher milk prices, the downward trend in milk production that started in the mid-1960s was interrupted, and milk production has been increasing since 1969. Had milk output declined

prices have been directly related to export prices and both have been above support levels). Yet the import quota remains. Nor has the functioning of the wheat program required import quotas, but those quotas remain also.

Wheat export subsidies have also been continued even when market prices have been significantly above the support level, as in the summer of 1972. However, wheat price supports have been at a level that has at times been too high. In 1968 and 1969 wheat exports would have been adversely affected if export subsidies had not been paid. A rather surprising and disconcerting feature of the U.S. export subsidy program in the past several years is that the size of wheat export subsidies have tended to be highest when market prices exceeded the support level the most.[8]

**The Long Term.** The program toward which the United States should gradually move—over a period long enough to allow the required adjustments—should have the following features:

    1. Price supports should be established at some margin below the market prices expected to prevail under normal supply and demand conditions. In the case of wheat, the price support should be based upon the feeding value of wheat and related to the price support for corn and other feed grains.

    2. A standby program for acreage diversion to be utilized when unusual demand or supply conditions have prevailed and stocks have accumulated. Payments under the program should be only those necessary to induce farmers, on a voluntary basis, to reduce output to the desired level. The program should not be used to transfer income to farmers except insofar as higher market prices have that effect. Moreover, the program should be designed so that acreage diverted or set aside is "real acreage"—acreage that in the absence of the program would otherwise be devoted to current production. A major loophole in the acreage diversion programs of the past decade has been permitting cultivated summer fallow to count as diverted land. This should and can be prevented by requiring that the average amount of summer fallow land of the past two or three years be counted as land devoted to wheat and by making diversion payments only for land actually withdrawn from wheat and other grain production.

    3. Import quotas and export subsidies should be eliminated. All legislative authorization for them should be repealed.[9]

    4. The President should be given authority to negotiate reductions in tariffs and other barriers to trade in agricultural products as a part of general trade negotiations. He should also have the authority to negotiate a scheduled reduction in any payments that

Relatively full market orientation is interpreted here to mean continuing price supports at levels somewhat below the market price that would prevail with normal growing conditions and stable demand conditions. This would in effect continue the apparently rather effective use of price supports that we have had for some major farm commodities in recent years, especially cotton and corn —and, with the exception of one politically induced aberration, also soybeans.[5] By the criterion indicated, wheat price supports have been too high, though by no more than 10 percent. Obviously price supports for dairy products, peanuts and rice have been too high to meet the criterion.

Price supports, if set at appropriate levels, can serve useful purposes. As administered through nonrecourse loans, price supports provide a ready source of credit to facilitate both the seasonal and year-to-year carrying of stocks of farm products. The procedure does not place a fixed floor under prices at all times and in all places. It permits a reasonable degree of flexibility for the market even when farm prices are at or somewhat below the loan levels.

Nor should standby acreage diversion programs be ruled out. Climatic conditions can be favorable for a number of years in a row, and important export markets can be restricted by political, economic or natural phenomena. Moreover, even if price supports are established without political intervention, some may be set too high with a consequent accumulation of stocks. U.S. acreage diversion programs have not been very effective in influencing crop output in recent years, but such diversion can be effective in the short run. This was clearly demonstrated by the LIFT program in Canada in 1970. That program reduced wheat acreage and production by half and did so without increasing the acreages devoted to other major crops.[6] In the U.S., the imposition of acreage allotments and marketing quotas for wheat in 1954 was apparently reasonably successful in reducing wheat acreage and production in the short run. And cotton programs in 1966 and 1967, while assisted by significantly lower market prices, had a significant impact on output.[7]

If the United States moves to a market-oriented agricultural policy, two instruments that violate liberal trade policy can and should be eliminated—export subsidies and import quotas. Such trade-disruptive devices are not necessary if interferences with market prices are nil or minimal. But deliberate action is needed to eliminate them even when they have been made unnecessary. They do not automatically go away. Since 1965 the U.S. cotton program has not required import quotas (because domestic market

over the two years 1971 and 1972, and may well increase by an additional 10 percent in 1973. Some of the 1971-72 increase in land values was a response to general inflationary factors, but not all of it: the land price increase was almost three times the increase in the consumer price index.

Thus the transition to freer markets, both domestically and internationally, may pose much smaller problems now than would have been the case at any other time in the last two decades. A gradual and fairly short-term elimination of the part of the payments that are now being capitalized into land prices may prevent further land price increases. This prospect results, of course, from the rather strong market situation in which agriculture finds itself—a situation that it is likely to enjoy for at least two more years. Stocks of farm commodities are low throughout the world. The demand for livestock products, especially beef, appears to be increasing more rapidly than supply. The Soviet Union is likely to be a large purchaser of feed supplies for at least two more years and perhaps for as many as five.

### Outlines of a New Commodity Program

**Relatively Full Market Orientation.** New farm legislation should have as its long-run objective a relatively full market orientation for American agriculture in both domestic and international markets. But for several reasons complete market orientation, either in the short or long run, does not appear advisable. First, the outcome of efforts to gradually eliminate barriers to trade in farm products is uncertain. Second, even with some success in reducing trade barriers, periods of one to three years may occur in which favorable climatic conditions in major producing areas or coincidental depressions of demand could cause substantial, though temporary, declines in farm product prices.

Moreover, in a time when most segments of the economy are insulated against the severest impacts of adverse circumstances—through such means as unemployment compensation, public welfare, income tax averaging, and compensatory governmental spending—it is unreasonable to expect agriculture to operate without some degree of protection against general adversity. One can argue that general income maintenance, such as some form of family assistance program, would be preferable to the discrete and separate programs. But until such a general national program replaces the current batch of special programs, farm people can legitimately expect some degree of income security.

of American agriculture. Freer trade would have a major impact on U.S. farm income. It would make it possible for farmers to reduce their dependence upon governmental programs. The potential expansion of net exports could result in an increase in net farm income substantially greater than the amount of payments now received from the government.

It may be argued that the potential expansion of net exports may not be realized and that therefore it would be safer and better to stay with the known, namely, a continuation of present programs. But this position ignores the high probability that unless the new round of trade negotiations is successful in reducing barriers to trade in farm products, the value of U.S. farm exports will be no higher by 1980 than they were in 1970. If that should be the case, the current farm programs may well be inadequate to hold farm incomes at the 1970 level. With population growth slowing in the United States, domestic demand growth for farm products will be slower in the 1970s than in the 1960s, assuming approximately the same rate of growth of per-capita income.

A continuation of present farm programs in the United States and other industrial countries poses very great risks for American farmers. The choice is not between two situations in which one is highly uncertain and the other is quite certain. The choice is, rather, between two somewhat uncertain situations—one with the potential for a very favorable outcome, and the other with a potential for a quite unfavorable outcome, both for farmers and for taxpayers and consumers.

The impact of supply management programs on farm output has been small in recent years. This was true even prior to the very favorable demand conditions that emerged in 1972 as a result of large-scale exports to the Soviet Union and more limited exports to China. The increase in the output of farm products that would result from eliminating the supply management programs would be no more than 2 percent, assuming farm price levels of 1969-71.

Supply management and direct payments have not increased the returns to farm labor, whether hired or operator or unpaid family workers. The elimination of direct payments would have almost no effect on the return to labor. Its only important effect would be upon the return to land. In the past, most agricultural economists and public officials have been deeply concerned about the effect upon asset values in agriculture of eliminating the farm programs and the income transfers other than those required for supply management. Even on this score it appears that 1973 is a propitious time for major reform. Farm land values increased by 18 percent

operator families with farm sales between $2,500 and $9,999 and nearly as high as families with farm sales of $10,000 to $19,999.

The causes of permanently low incomes among farm families are limited resources, not low farm prices. And generally the limited resources are human resources, not limited land and physical capital, though the two tend to be closely associated. Low levels of education (in terms of both quality and quantity), physical and mental disabilities, and age are the major causes of poverty in farm areas.

Programs to minimize poverty in rural areas should emphasize improving education and access to it, facilitating migration and job mobility as necessary and, where justified on the basis of benefits and costs, influencing the location of new job opportunities. The poverty that would then remain should be ameliorated by direct assistance in a form that would involve dignified supplementation to the income of the working poor. The vast majority of the poor on farms are engaged in productive activity, limited as the income earned from that activity may be. The negative income tax would be an appropriate means of transferring income to the rural poor.

### The Basis for a New Approach

The Agricultural Act of 1970, which provides the framework for cotton, wheat and feed grain programs and dairy price supports, expires at the end of 1973. Also a new round of trade negotiations is planned in 1973. The fact that the expiration of the 1970 act occurs in the same year as new trade negotiations are to begin offers an important opportunity to American agriculture. If the United States is to achieve a reduction in barriers to trade in farm products, it must make changes in its own farm programs. It is unlikely that there will be another time soon that is as favorable for a major overhaul of commodity programs as the nation has at the present.

In the past the United States has argued that at least some of its farm programs are justified because the programs reduce output levels and thus enhance international market prices. But this is not a view that is generally accepted outside the United States, partly because the United States has never made a convincing case that it has, in fact, significantly reduced its output. The various estimates that have been presented indicate that the restriction of output has been small. The best the United States can claim is that it has not done much to encourage uneconomic production.

The position that farm legislation and the trade negotiations should be related to each other is one that is in the clear interest

changes in output and farm prices in Denmark and the Netherlands during the 1960s:

> These are countries whose agricultures are about equal in size, quality of soil and climate, are of equally high technical standing and are both business-like in managerial attitude. The average yearly production [of farm products] in the three years 1967-69, compared with the five years 1960-64, was 24 percent larger in the Netherlands but only 2 percent in Denmark. However, the average prices farmers received in the Netherlands during 1960-61 were 18 percent higher, during 1964-65 already 31 percent higher and in 1968-69 even 48 percent higher than in Denmark.[2]

This comparison is a useful one because the difference in response to incentives can hardly be attributed to rapid changes in technology or to other factors that are difficult to hold constant over time. Although the time period was very short, the response in the Netherlands was very great.

3. *Elasticity of supply for farm output is very low.* When farms used relatively few purchased inputs, the price elasticity of supply was low. But given the organization of modern agriculture, land and labor together may make up only about two-fifths of total farm inputs today. The majority of the purchased inputs, except for farm machinery, are acquired anew each year. As a result, recent estimates of the long-run elasticity of supply of farm products in the United States have been approximately 1.5 to 1.8.[3] Understanding of the elasticity of supply of total farm output is still rather weak and much further work is required. Yet evidence is accumulating that with the increased importance of purchased inputs the supply response to price changes can be quite substantial over a period of three to five years.

### Poor Farm Families [4]

Existing programs have been of little or no benefit to low-income farm families, and the farm program outlined below does nothing to improve the income levels of the farm poor. Put quite simply there is nothing that the commodity programs can do to make any particular or important difference in the economic status of low-income farm families. Special provisions for small farms do not distribute benefits according to income. As was shown in Chapter V, farm operators living on very small farms—those with annual sales of less than $2,500—have average incomes higher than those of farm

much that a basic reexamination is required. First, let us briefly review these assumptions.

1. *Elasticity of demand for farm output is very low.* It has long been an article of faith of farm program supporters that small changes in farm output result in large opposite changes in farm prices and incomes. It is true that the price elasticities of demand for most farm products, especially the major crops, are below unity. Long-run price elasticities of demand of unity or greater are consistent with short-run price elasticities of demand that result in significantly larger and opposite fluctuations in prices than in quantities. However, some quite tentative analyses of demand elasticities for corn and the feed grains for the period since price supports were established at or somewhat below market prices indicate that the short-run (one year) price elasticity of demand for feed grains (including wheat fed) may be $-0.65$ and for corn alone $-0.70$ or larger.[1] Admittedly the time period (1963 through 1971) is very short. The results must be interpreted with caution. Yet the results for the recent years clearly caution against the continuation of a program that is assumed to transmit important income gains to producers, even in the short run, through supply management and restriction.

2. *Farm output has an inherent tendency to increase faster than demand.* There can be little doubt that for the past two decades there has been excess capacity in agriculture, not only in the United States but in most other industrial countries as well. But it does not follow that this excess capacity has been the result of "an inherent tendency" for output to grow more rapidly than demand. Much, if not all, of the excess capacity has been the result of actions taken by government—through price supports, direct payments and trade barriers that have attracted or held resources in farm production. Undoubtedly there was fairly significant excess capacity in American agriculture in the late 1950s and early 1960s, but this was due to a price policy that gave farmers the wrong signals—signals that significantly overestimated the real value of farm output. With the lowering of prices for major farm products that had occurred by the mid-1960s, there apparently was little excess capacity by the end of the decade. The output restraint imposed by the major commodity programs was small, representing at most 2 percent of total farm output. And this restraint is estimated by assuming that the payments did not increase farm yields.

The very large impact of governmental policies on the growth of farm output is illustrated by a striking comparison made by the Dutch agricultural economist, Jan Horring. He has compared the

CHAPTER VII

# FARM PROGRAMS OF THE FUTURE

If one accepts the previous analysis, U.S. farm policies need major overhaul. Current programs involve substantial expenditures of governmental funds. A large fraction of the direct payments go to farm producers whose family incomes are higher than the national average. Low-income farm families obtain little benefit, and there is no evidence of a positive effect on the return to farm labor. The income gains go primarily to land and become imbedded in higher land values. A large fraction of the gains to land go to others than those who operate the land, and only a portion of the cost of farm programs becomes an income gain to anyone. The income gain of those who benefit is much less than the income loss of taxpayers and consumers.

Further, the effectiveness of supply management in restraining output has been much smaller than is generally thought. It appears that if 60 million acres of cropland are set aside, no more than 20 million acres would be returned to cultivation with farm prices at the level of recent years. Thus far output has been reduced to a very modest degree—perhaps 2 percent rather than the 6 or 7 percent often assumed.

The relative lack of success of the farm programs in limiting farm production is, of course, now an asset. A rather modest expansion of demand relative to the growth in supply would mean that the limited quantity of resources withdrawn from production could be returned to use without putting significant downward pressure on farm prices.

It is now clear that supply management policies have rested on several important assumptions that may have had some validity in the past, but have very little today. Circumstances have changed so

Even with the adjustments made here, the EEC study overestimates the effective rate of protection of U.S. agriculture in 1967. A more detailed study of the subject has been made by Larry J. Wipf.[12] In figuring elements of protection, he excluded the portion of direct payments made for acreage diversion (about a third of the total payments from the cotton, wheat and feed grain programs) but included the remainder. His estimate of the average rate of effective protection for all U.S. agriculture was 19 percent. But the variation by individual sectors was enormous, ranging from a negative rate of 10 percent for tree nuts to 102 percent for cotton, 146 percent for dairy products and 590 percent for sugar.

In preparing for the 1973 trade negotiations, the United States should learn much more about the effects of its farm programs and its trade interferences than it now knows.[13] It also needs a detailed analysis of the effective protection provided to agriculture by other countries and of the ouput, consumption and trade effects of price supports and trade barriers. Third, it should have a rather clear conception of how U.S. domestic programs could be changed to be consistent with trade liberalization.

## Conclusion

There is a very close relationship between the future of agricultural trade and U.S. farm programs. If the current farm and trade programs of the major industrial nations are unchanged during the 1970s, the United States is likely to be faced with the need to reduce the resources engaged in agriculture. While such a reduction could no doubt be achieved by permitting market forces to function, it is not at all certain that the political process would allow adjustment through lower short-run returns to farm land and capital. Certainly past experience indicates that the political response would be to turn to supply management, import restrictions, and direct payments in order to slow the necessary adjustments.

Unless the United States stands ready to modify its farm programs and to reduce its major barriers to imports, there is little prospect that trade negotiations will have any success in reducing the numerous and highly protective devices that significantly restrict agricultural trade. Americans cannot have it both ways: freer access to markets in other countries will require change in U.S. domestic farm programs and trade measures.

the protection provided to agriculture. The estimates indicate that if all forms of protection were eliminated (including import restrictions, export subsidies and governmental payments), net farm operator income in the United States would have been 44 percent less than it was in 1967—$8.2 billion compared to $14.6 billion.

A comparable calculation for the EEC indicates that the removal of protection would reduce net farm operator income from $19.1 billion to $9.5 billion, or by 50.4 percent. The difference between the relative importance of the income attributed to protection in the two cases is clearly small. If the underlying analysis is accepted, it is understandable that spokesmen for the EEC are more than a little irritated by Americans who emphasize the high rates of protection provided for EEC agriculture and ignore that provided in the United States.

Fortunately for the American view that the U.S. is the offended party, there is an important conceptual error in the calculations made for the EEC. The difficulty with the analysis is the use of an inappropriate income concept. Presumably what was to be measured was the effective protection afforded to agriculture. The effective rate of protection of an industry is defined as the percentage difference between the industry's value added per unit of output with protection and the value added per unit of output in the absence of protection (in the absence of tariffs, quantitative restrictions and input or output subsidies). If output at domestic prices is valued at $20 billion and value added at $10 billion and if output (and all purchased inputs) at international prices is valued at $16 billion and value added at $7 billion, then the effective rate of protection is 43 percent.

The EEC study did not base its calculations of the rate of effective protection on value added (gross domestic product) of agriculture. Instead, for reasons that are unclear, it used net farm operator income. For the United States this meant that the level of farm operator income declined from $14.6 billion at domestic prices with subsidies added to $8.2 billion at international prices and with no subsidies. This implied an effective rate of protection of 78 percent. The same approach for the EEC indicated a rate of effective protection of 102 percent. Net farm operator income is an inappropriate base; because it excludes wages paid to farm workers, rent to landlords and most of the gross return to farm capital. If the gross domestic product of agriculture is used, the effective rates of protection were approximately 35 percent for the United States and 70 percent for the EEC. Clearly the latter is much higher than the former—but an effective protection rate of 35 percent is substantial.

The expansion in demand for labor due to free trade is more conjectural than it is for land. The farm products with a clear comparative advantage used 35 percent of all direct farm labor in 1970. Included in the total were feed grains, food grains, hay and forage, tobacco, poultry and soybeans. If one adds beef, cotton and fruits and nuts, an additional 26 percent of the direct labor is involved. If the increase in exports due to free trade is the lower of the projections—$4 billion—the increased labor requirements would be about 7 percent. This is roughly the same as the decline in labor use as a result of imports replacing domestic production. If the increase in exports is the higher of the projections—$6 billion—the added demand for farm labor would be another 4 or 5 percent. The somewhat higher proportionate increase in demand for labor would occur because it was assumed in the lower projection that all of the increase in exports consisted of grains and soybeans. These are relatively labor-extensive products. Most of the additional exports are relatively labor-intensive, especially fruit and tree nuts and beef.

At a minimum, free trade would increase the demands for cropland and leave the demand for labor unchanged. Under favorable circumstances, it would increase the demand for both.

### Preparations for Trade Negotiations

There is a tendency, both in some governmental circles and in farm organizations, to assume that the United States needs to make few changes in either its farm programs or in its trade restrictions as a part of general trade negotiations. Part of the argument for this position is that the other major industrial nations have little or no direct interest in the farm products that we protect. This is true for peanuts, rice, sugar and wool. It is certainly not true with respect to Europe's interest in manufactured dairy products. And Europeans are not all that sympathetic about U.S. complaints against variable levies since they know that American producers of wheat, feed grains and cotton receive substantial direct payments from the government. Moreover, the United States has used variable export subsidies, which are the direct counterpart of variable levies.

It apparently comes as something of a shock to many Americans to learn that West Europeans believe U.S. agriculture is nearly as heavily protected as is the agriculture of the European Economic Community. Not only do officials, both public and private, in the EEC believe this, but their conclusion is drawn from a study of the degrees of protection in the United States and the EEC.[11] This study shows that the United States and the EEC differ only marginally in

other uses. The loss in employment would be twofold—that used to produce milk (3.5 percent of all direct farm labor) and that used to produce the feed (about 15 percent of such farm labor). The reduced use of feed would cause a displacement of less than 1 percent of farm work, and the total displacement due to increased dairy imports would amount to about 4.5 percent of all direct farm labor under my extreme assumptions.

The total loss in employment and resource use for the four commodity groups would be about 7 percent of farm labor and 8 percent of farm land. These losses should be compared to the gains in employment and resource use from expanded exports resulting from freer trade.

**Gains from Free Trade.** Including summer fallow as a part of cropland utilized, approximately 85 percent of the cropland is utilized for wheat, feed grains, oilseeds and forage crops. Except for the feed grains and forage crops used for dairy production, the area devoted to the specified crops either has a comparative advantage or is used for further processing by farm products having a comparative advantage or where there would be no significant increase in imports under free trade. Based on the estimates of the effect of free trade on the use of land resources for dairying, the reduced output of dairy products would result in a loss of an outlet for about 5 percent of total land resources. Thus the expansion of output due to increased export would apply to approximately 80 percent of total cropland and a somewhat smaller fraction of total pasture.

Based on projected yields in 1980, the projected expansion of wheat, feed grains and soybean exports due to free trade would require approximately 35 million acres of cropland.[10] If the reduction in total feed lost due to larger dairy imports were converted into the cropland used for feed grain production, the loss in demand for such land would be 8.5 million acres, based on projected 1980 feed grain yields. To this should be added approximately 6.5 million acres for the loss of land employment due to the total elimination of sugar and peanuts—an exaggerated assumption. The total loss comes to 15 million acres. The combined effect of free trade would result in expanded use of cropland (or its equivalent) of 20 million acres. And this is based on the assumption that there would be export increases for only wheat, feed grains and soybeans. If fed beef exports become significant, there would be a further and important increase in demand for land resources. In this situation, more cropland would be required and improvements in pasture would become profitable.

sectors that would gain from increased exports employ approximately half of all direct farm labor and 80 to 85 percent of all cropland and pasture.

How much resource employment would be lost due to increased imports? Let us assume that imports would completely displace domestic production of sugar, peanuts, and sheep (including wool). This is an extreme assumption, especially for peanuts. If the land used for sugar beets, most of which is irrigated, is assumed to be three times as valuable as average cropland, these two crops utilize 2 percent of all cropland. They also utilize approximately the same percentage of all direct farm labor. Based on animal unit conversions, sheep and lamb utilize approximately 2.5 percent of all feed, including pasture, in the United States. The amount of labor used on sheep is not known. But a reasonable estimate may be derived by using the ratio of the cash receipts from sheep, lamb and wool to total cash receipts from livestock products (less purchases of livestock) and by assuming that this ratio is equal to the percentage of the total labor used to produce meat animals. Sheep, lamb and wool account for slightly less than 2 percent of the value of livestock sales. Labor used to produce meat animals was 17 percent of all direct farm labor in 1970, so the labor used for the sheep enterprise was probably about 0.4 percent of all direct farm labor.[9]

The dairy sector is much the largest of the four sectors that would be adversely affected by free trade. In 1970 dairy cows required 14 percent of all direct farm labor and 18 percent of all feed, including pasture, consumed by livestock.

However, it should be noted that the milk produced is divided into two roughly equal parts—that used for fluid purposes and that used for manufacturing. A large fraction of the manufactured milk supply is a by-product of fluid milk use because of the need to ensure adequate supplies of fluid milk. As a rough estimate, it appears that with free trade the amount of manufactured milk that would result from the provision of fluid milk would be equal to half the milk used for fluid purposes. Thus the output of manufactured milk would decline by about half and total milk by about a quarter. This is probably an extreme assumption since free trade in manufactured milk products would increase international market prices significantly. While international prices would not move to the high U.S. level (our prices for manufactured milk are among the highest in the world), the price increase might well be enough so that low-cost producers in the United States could produce profitably.

If total milk production in the United States dropped 25 percent, approximately 4 percent of farm land would have to be shifted to

Unless trade negotiations reduce the barriers to agricultural trade, there is a significant probability that U.S. farm exports will be no larger (after adjustment for inflation) in 1980 than they were in 1970. Some economists disagree with this projection, arguing that farm exports will increase significantly during the decade—perhaps by 30 to 40 percent—even if there are no changes in farm and trade policies.[7] This more optimistic projection appears to rest on the presumption that the Soviet Union will be a net importer of feed over the long run and a substantial importer at that. It also assumes a further and significant increase in Japanese food imports as a result of trade liberalization. Except for Japan's liberalization in food imports, the projected expansion of exports due to free trade should be additive to the more optimistic projection.

### Agricultural Resource Demands under Free Trade

The available evidence indicates that the United States has a clear comparative advantage in the production of corn, barley, grain sorghums, soybeans, wheat, tobacco and poultry. It has a clear comparative disadvantage in manufactured dairy products, sugar, wool, lamb and mutton.[8] The comparative advantage position of U.S. rice, cotton, flaxseed, pork, beef, fruits, vegetables and oats is uncertain. For the latter group, the net trade position of the United States depends upon relative prices. If the farm price of cotton were to remain in the 25 to 30 cent range, the U.S. would probably be a significant exporter; if the price were at or near 20 cents and there were no program subsidies, U.S. production would probably just about equal domestic consumption needs. With respect to beef, as already discussed, free trade would probably result in higher prices for beef and the export of significant quantities of fed beef. Although continuing to import lower quality (manufacturing) beef, the United States would be on balance an important net exporter in value terms.

**Losses from Free Trade.** Free trade would increase U.S. imports of farm products. On this point there can be no question. Comparing the efforts that have been devoted to keeping out imports and to expanding exports, one might conclude that the losses in resource employment and use from increased imports would significantly exceed the gains in resource employment and use from increased exports. Nothing could be further from the truth.

The producing sectors of U.S. agriculture that would suffer a loss from free trade employ a minor fraction of total U.S. resources. The

present farm and trade policies continue unchanged throughout the present decade, U.S. farm exports could decline (comparing 1970). Admittedly the value of farm exports—$11 billion in 1972-73—is now very high. But we should not be misled about the longer run prospects. The increase from the 1970-71 level of $7 billion or the 1971-72 level of $8 billion is due primarily to adverse weather conditions in the Soviet Union, China and Australia and the effects of increased demand upon prices.

One of the adverse circumstances facing U.S. farm exports, if present farm and trade policies continue, is the enlargement of the European Economic Community to include the United Kingdom, Denmark and Ireland. One study projects that the enlarged EEC will import less than a million tons of grain in 1980 compared to 10.5 million tons in 1968. Half of this estimated decline is attributed to the impact of higher grain and livestock prices on grain production and use in the three new member countries. A projection by the Food and Agricultural Organization (FAO) of the U.N. indicates that the EEC's enlargement will result in a decline of grain imports by 5 million tons.[5]

Of even greater impact would be the continuation of high grain prices throughout Western Europe and high livestock prices in Western Europe and Japan. The price policies of many industrial countries limit imports by encouraging domestic output expansion on the one hand, and by discouraging consumption on the other hand. In some cases these combined effects turn an import surplus into an export surplus.

While projections of exports and imports are subject to substantial error, since trade is a residual for both exporters and importers, the several projections that have been made for the 1970s present a gloomy picture for temperate zone products if current farm and trade policies continue throughout the decade. For each of the current major farm export products of the United States, the FAO projects that export availabilities will increase substantially more than import requirements or demand during the 1970s.[6] The excess of export availability for wheat and feed grains is an enormous 66 million tons (excluding the trade of Asian centrally planned countries). This compares to total world exports in 1970 of about 90 million. Smaller imbalances are projected for rice, oilcakes, fats and oils, and cotton. Obviously the enormous excess supply of wheat and feed grains will not materialize, but if the projections of production and consumption with existing policies are at all reasonable, it means that there will be an enormous downward pressure on export prices until policies are modified.

between the requirements of a liberal trade policy and the features of its wheat, cotton and feed grain programs. But there are other farm programs and trade barriers that would require substantial modification if this country is to expect other nations to significantly reduce the protection they provide for agriculture. While it is beyond the scope of this essay to consider such changes in detail, a liberal trade policy would require reductions in dairy price supports and the gradual elimination of import quotas. Major changes in our sugar and peanut programs and associated import restrictions, the elimination of beef import quotas (now suspended), the lowering of price supports for rice and the elimination of export subsidies (now suspended), and the lowering of some rather high tariffs (such as on wool) would also be required.

### Free Trade Benefits for Agriculture

It would be very much in the economic interest of U.S. agriculture if free trade in farm products could be established by the major industrial nations. Some sectors of U.S. agriculture would be faced with adjustment problems. But on balance there would be a significant increase in the demand for America's agricultural resources.

A detailed set of projections indicates that free trade in agricultural products would increase the value of U.S. exports of grains and soybeans by $4 billion over the level of the late 1960s.[4] This assumes a gradual transition to free trade by 1980. In my view, this is a minimum estimate of the expansion of exports. There is a potential for a substantial expansion of exports for fed beef if consumer prices were lowered in Western Europe and Japan. There is a smaller, but still significant, potential for increased poultry exports. The agricultural expansion in exports might well expand to a level that is $6 billion higher than that of the late 1960s.

These projections do not include increased exports to the Soviet Union and China. While it is possible that the Soviet Union might become a substantial importer of high protein feeds such as soybeans, wheat imports will not occur except as dictated by adverse weather. Moderate levels of feed grain imports—perhaps as much as 10 million tons—might occur for the next several years, but probably not on a long-run basis. If these expectations turn out to be too pessimistic, then the growth of U.S. farm exports would be greater than indicated by at least $1 billion annually.

But there is more to be said about the expansion of farm exports that would result from free trade. Available evidence indicates that if

farmers. The U.S. sugar program has maintained a much higher level of domestic output than would have been the case under free trade or with a tariff rate of 50 to 100 percent.

## Farm Programs and Trade Policy

With respect to the three main farm products under consideration, a change in farm policy in the mid-1960s ended the use of export subsidies on cotton and nearly did so for the feed grains. Since 1962, no export subsidies have been paid on corn, the major feed grain, and such subsidies have been used for barley only occasionally. For the decade ending with 1971-72, export subsidies on feed grains averaged less than 1 percent of the value of such exports.[3] However, subsidies were paid on most wheat exports after 1963 until the suspension of the program in September 1972.

The farm program changes that permitted the elimination of export subsidies on cotton and the feed grains, and could have done so for wheat, were the lowering of price support levels to the anticipated export price and the shift to direct payments for acreage diversion. Even though there was no legislative requirement that export subsidies be continued for wheat, the subsidies were maintained by two national administrations.

It would not require major changes in the wheat, cotton and feed grain programs to make them consistent with a liberal trade policy. If price support loans were set at levels that permit exportation without subsidies, import quotas for wheat and cotton could be eliminated. The feed grain program has been operated without import quotas. So could the other two. To prevent the need to resort to export subsidies on wheat, it would be necessary to reduce the price support level to the feeding value of wheat relative to corn. Then if the export demand for wheat were low, the price of wheat would fall, and wheat would be an economical feed grain.

The other change would be to eliminate the direct income transfer portion of the payments. There would be no significant objection from our major trading partners if farm program payments were set solely on the basis of the amount needed to induce farmers to divert the amount of land deemed necessary. As noted in Chater IV, if payments had been set according to this criterion in recent years, the total would have been less than half the amount actually paid. In Chapter VII the implications of modifying farm programs in this way is explored in detail.

With these changes, the United States could enter the trade negotiations scheduled to start in 1973 without any significant conflict

CHAPTER VI

# FARM PROGRAMS AND AGRICULTURAL TRADE

For three decades there has been a major inconsistency between our domestic farm programs and our efforts to liberalize international trade.[1] A policy of freer trade emphasizes lowering barriers to trade generally, accepting tariffs as the only legitimate barrier at the border, and avoiding the use of export subsidies. Further, liberal trade carries with it the presumption that domestic subsidies will not be used to achieve an "unfair" advantage in increasing exports or reducing imports.

Efforts to increase domestic prices above international prices inevitably require interferences with imports and exports. If the commodity involved is normally exported, increasing domestic prices by price supports and output restrictions soon results in a loss of exports as other countries fill a larger fraction of the world's import demand. The alternatives are to accept a declining export market or to engage in export subsidies. The United States has employed export subsidies for a wide range of farm products—cotton, wheat, tobacco, manufactured dairy products, feed grains, rice and peanuts.[2] Then, to prevent the reentry of the subsidized exports, it has been necessary to resort to import quotas, principally for cotton, wheat, peanuts and manufactured dairy products.

The rationale for the use of export subsidies and import quotas was that the United States was attempting to limit domestic production, whereas other nations were not accepting this responsibility. While this was true in some cases (cotton, wheat and feed grains), it was clearly not true in others. For dairy products, relatively high support prices have been coupled with no workable production adjustment program. For peanuts and rice, acreage limitations exist, but output has expanded due to profitable prices guaranteed to

73

federal taxes are distributed by income level. Based on a distribution of federal taxes by family income level estimated by the Council of Economic Advisers for 1965,[29] I have estimated that 55 percent of all federal taxes are paid by the top fifth of the income distribution. In 1970, 21.5 percent of all farm operators received 59.3 percent of all direct government payments. Not all of the farm operators operating farms with sales of $20,000 or more actually received government payments—but what this means is that the payments were more unequally distributed than indicated by the comparison given. The farm operator families who were in the farm sales group that received almost 60 percent of the payments had net incomes somewhat below the families in the top fifth of the income distribution nationally. However, it is quite clear that a major fraction of the direct payments went to families with relatively high incomes, averaging nearly $20,000. Thus it cannot be claimed that the payments under the programs made much, if any, contribution to reducing the degree of inequality in the distribution of income.

It may be of interest to compare the average tangible assets (total assets minus financial assets) of the farms that received 60 percent of the direct payments with the national average assets per nonfarm family. In 1968 it is estimated that nonfarm tangible assets had a total value for the nation of $2,847 billion; this included public as well as private property.[27] If it is assumed that unrelated individuals have no property, the 46 million nonfarm families had tangible assets of approximately $62,000 per family. Excluding the financial assets of the farms with sales of $20,000 or more, assets per farm averaged $237,000 in 1970. For all farms the average value of tangible assets was $98,000 in the same year.

### Conclusion: Distribution of Costs and Gross Benefits

Most of the costs of the three major farm programs are imposed through the federal tax system. But not all. Some are imposed through higher product prices. The higher prices have been unimportant for cotton and feed grains, but costs of wheat products to consumers have been increased by a $0.75 per bushel charge for the marketing certificate for all wheat used for food purposes, as well as by export subsidies. In 1970 these two factors probably increased the price of wheat by $0.95 per bushel.

The income elasticity of demand for wheat is either zero or negative. Thus the cost of the higher wheat price is proportional to population numbers and falls as heavily, in absolute amount, on low-income consumers as on high-income consumers. The total cost imposed on consumers in 1970 due to the marketing certificate and the higher prices due to the export subsidy was approximately $495 million. Families with incomes below the national median thus paid half of the total or about $250 million.

While data on the distribution of wheat payments are not available by net farm income or family income, we do know that about 67 percent of the payments in 1970 went to 19 percent of the participants in the wheat program and that the average payment for this group was $3,175,[28] or not far from the poverty income level for a family of three. Most of the costs imposed upon consumers by the marketing certificate and higher market prices of wheat results in a transfer of income from consumers who have incomes that are lower than the incomes of those who receive the direct payments financed by the marketing certificates.

Very approximate calculations indicate that the direct payments in the cotton, wheat and feed grain programs have been distributed among farm families by income level in about the same way as

## Table 8
DISTRIBUTION OF NUMBER OF FARMS, NET INCOME FROM FARMING, GOVERNMENT PAYMENTS AND TOTAL FARM ASSETS BY VALUE OF SALES CLASSES, AND FARM ASSETS PER FARM, 1970

| Value of Sales ($ in thousands) | Farms | Distribution of Government payments | Distribution of Farm assets [a] | Distribution of Real estate assets [b] | Total Farm Assets [a] Per Farm ($ in thousands) | Real Estate [b] Per Farm ($ in thousands) |
|---|---|---|---|---|---|---|
| Under $2.5 | 38.3% | 7.1% | 14.4% | 13.7% | $ 40.1 | $ 25.6 |
| 2.5-4.9 | 14.1 | 6.6 | 7.5 | 6.5 | 54.7 | 33.1 |
| 5.0-9.9 | 13.6 | 10.0 | 11.3 | 9.9 | 88.0 | 51.7 |
| 10.0-19.9 | 13.7 | 18.7 | 20.3 | 19.9 | 158.0 | 104.2 |
| 20.0-39.9 | 12.3 | 24.3 | 20.3 | 20.7 | 178.8 | 122.6 |
| Over 40.0 | 8.2 | 35.3 | 26.5 | 29.2 | 341.9 | 253.6 |

[a] Total farm assets, including assets owned by landlords. Includes financial assets. Distribution of assets less debts approximately the same as for total assets. The percentage distribution, in same order: 15.0, 7.5, 10.8, 20.3, 20.2 and 26.0. For all farms, debts equaled 19 percent of total assets.

[b] Value of land and buildings, including those owned by landlords.

**Sources:** *Farm Income Situation*, July 1972, pp. 68-73, and USDA, Economic Research Service, *The Balance Sheet of the Farming Sector, 1970*, Agriculture Information Bulletin No. 350, January 1971, p. 25.

When total income of the farm operator families is considered, there is a steady decline in the percentage of income derived from government payments from the second largest sales group to the smallest sales group. Farm operators in the smallest sales group derived only 2 percent of their family income from government payments. The two highest sales groups received 12.7 percent and 15.7 percent.

It cannot be said that the government payments make the distribution of net farm income more unequal than it would be in the absence of the program. But this is faint praise for a program that gives almost three-fifths of its benefits to families with average incomes that are nearly 50 percent above the national average.

It is quite clear that a very large fraction of the payments under the farm programs goes to families with incomes that are relatively high by any standard. Conversely, only a small fraction of the payments goes to families with incomes that are substantially below the national average. Admittedly the farm program is not the only federal subsidy program that has this effect; too many subsidy programs benefit primarily those who are already well off and largely neglect low-income groups. But the conclusion that farm programs are no worse in their income distribution effects than many other government programs is hardly an argument for the continuation of these programs in their present form.

## Government Payments and Farm Assets

As has been noted several times, nearly all of the net benefits from direct payments result in increased returns to farm land. Table 8 compares the distribution of direct government payments and the distributions of total farm assets and value of real estate by value of sales classes for 1970. The figures for both total assets and value of real estate include the parts owned by landlords and by farm operators. As noted above, approximately 40 percent of the value of farm land is owned by landlords, some of whom are farm operators.

Farms with sales of $40,000 or more have 26.5 percent of total assets and 29 percent of the value of land. This group of farms received 35 percent of government payments. Their average total assets were $341,000 and their net assets (total assets minus debts) were $273,000. The two highest value sales groups that received almost 60 percent of government payments had average total assets of $249,000 and net assets of $200,000.

three-fifths (59.3 percent) of payments were paid to the 21.5 percent of farm operators that had sales of $20,000 or more. The average income of families operating these farms was $16,913 from farm sources and $19,552 from all sources.

Table 7 presents data for 1970 and 1971 on average family income from farming, from all sources and from government payments, as well as the ratio of government payments to the two measures of income. If only farm income is considered, government payments are the highest percentage of such income for the farms with sales of $10,000 to $19,999 in 1971. In 1970 government payments represented a larger fraction of farm income for the sales group of $20,000 to $39,999. Table 7 indicates that when only net farm income is considered the payments do not depart far from being proportional to income. Farms with sales in excess of $40,000 received government payments averaging $4,289 in 1971 compared to payments of $499 for farms with sales of $2,500 to $4,999.

### Table 7
RELATIONSHIP OF GOVERNMENT PAYMENTS TO FARM INCOME AND TOTAL INCOME OF FARM OPERATOR FAMILIES, 1970 AND 1971

| Year and Sales Classes ($ in thousands) | Farm Income | Total Income | Government Payments | Government Payments as % of | |
|---|---|---|---|---|---|
| | ......(dollars per farm)...... | | | Farm income | Total income |
| **1970** | | | | | |
| $40.0 plus | 29,104 | 35,245 | 5,137 | 17.6 | 14.6 |
| 20.0–39.9 | 10,473 | 14,102 | 2,961 | 28.3 | 21.0 |
| 10.0–19.9 | 6,475 | 9,970 | 1,740 | 26.9 | 17.5 |
| 5.0–9.9 | 3,634 | 8,606 | 927 | 25.5 | 10.8 |
| 2.5–4.9 | 2,128 | 7,583 | 596 | 28.0 | 7.9 |
| Under 2.5 | 1,077 | 9,054 | 235 | 21.8 | 2.6 |
| All | 5,757 | 11,678 | 1,271 | 22.1 | 10.9 |
| **1971** | | | | | |
| $40.0 plus | 27,289 | 33,736 | 4,289 | 15.7 | 12.7 |
| 20.0–39.9 | 9,721 | 13,546 | 2,140 | 22.0 | 15.8 |
| 10.0–19.9 | 6,026 | 9,702 | 1,452 | 24.1 | 15.0 |
| 5.0–9.9 | 3,397 | 8,618 | 771 | 22.7 | 8.9 |
| 2.5–4.9 | 1,993 | 7,448 | 499 | 25.0 | 6.7 |
| Under 2.5 | 1,039 | 9,518 | 195 | 18.8 | 2.0 |
| All | 5,581 | 11,811 | 1,093 | 19.6 | 9.3 |

**Source:** U.S. Department of Agriculture, *Farm Income Situation*, July 1972, pp. 72-73.

Table 5

SOURCES OF INCOME OF FARM OPERATOR FAMILIES BY VALUE OF SALES CLASSES, AVERAGES PER FARM, 1960 AND 1971

| Year and Sales Classes | Farm Income | Off-farm Income | Total | Distribution of Farms by Sales Class (percent) |
|---|---|---|---|---|
| | ....... (dollars per farm) ....... | | | |
| *1960* | | | | |
| $40,000 plus | 18,955 | 2,177 | 21,132 | 2.9 |
| 20.0–39.9 | 8,652 | 1,678 | 10,330 | 5.7 |
| 10.0–19.9 | 5,368 | 1,258 | 6,626 | 12.5 |
| 5.0–9.9 | 3,305 | 1,573 | 4,878 | 16.7 |
| 2.5–4.9 | 1,961 | 1,849 | 3,810 | 15.6 |
| Under 2.5 | 850 | 2,731 | 3,581 | 46.6 |
| All | 2,962 | 2,140 | 5,102 | 100.0 |
| *1970* | | | | |
| $40,000 plus | 27,289 | 6,447 | 33,736 | 8.8 |
| 20.0–39.9 | 9,721 | 3,825 | 13,546 | 12.7 |
| 10.0–19.9 | 6,026 | 3,676 | 9,702 | 13.6 |
| 5.0–9.9 | 3,397 | 5,221 | 8,618 | 13.4 |
| 2.5–4.9 | 1,993 | 5,743 | 7,448 | 14.2 |
| Under 2.5 | 1,039 | 8,479 | 9,518 | 37.3 |
| All | 5,581 | 6,230 | 11,811 | 100.0 |

Source: U.S. Department of Agriculture, *Farm Income Situation*, July 1972, pp. 68 and 72.

Table 6

DISTRIBUTION OF PAYMENTS OF AGRICULTURAL STABILIZATION AND CONSERVATION PROGRAMS, 1970 AND 1971

| Size of Payments | Percent of Producers | | Percent of Total Payments | |
|---|---|---|---|---|
| | 1970 | 1971 | 1970 | 1971 |
| Under $500 | 47.20 | 53.44 | 6.40 | 8.01 |
| Under $1,000 | 67.33 | 70.85 | 16.11 | 17.52 |
| Under $2,000 | 82.80 | 84.92 | 30.61 | 32.74 |
| Under $5,000 | 94.37 | 95.30 | 54.54 | 56.97 |
| Under $25,000 | 99.59 | 99.61 | 86.85 | 87.56 |
| Over $25,000 | 0.41 | 0.39 | 13.15 | 12.44 |

Source: U.S. Department of Agriculture, *Agricultural Statistics, 1971* and *1972*.

gram 4 percent of the farms received 32 percent of the payments and 11.1 percent received 54 percent.

Turning to the distribution of government payments by the value of farm sales, 8.8 percent of the farms with sales of $40,000 or more received 34.5 percent of direct government payments in 1971. Nearly

## Table 4
REAL INCOME OF FARM OPERATORS, TOTAL AND BY SOURCE AND NUMBER OF FARM OPERATORS, 1960 AND 1971[a]

|  | Sources of Income | | | Farm Operator Families ($ in millions) |
|---|---|---|---|---|
|  | Farm | Off-farm | Total[a] |  |
|  | ($ in billions) | | | |
| 1960 | 13.04 | 9.42 | 22.46 | 3.962 |
| 1971 | 13.49 | 15.06 | 28.55 | 2.876 |
| Change, 1960 to 1971 | | | | |
| Absolute | 0.45 | 5.64 | 6.09 | −1.086 |
| Relative | 3% | 59% | 27% | −28% |

[a] Income in dollars of 1967 purchasing power. Farm income is realized net income of farm operators.
**Source:** U.S. Department of Agriculture, *Farm Income Situation*, July 1972, pp. 46, 47 and 72.

The importance of off-farm income varies among the various farm operator groups. As shown in Table 5, the percentage of total income derived from off-farm sources declines as the size of the farm operation increases.[25] However, even for farms with sales in excess of $40,000 (averaging $132,000), almost a fifth of total net income was derived from off-farm sources. For the smaller farms, off-farm income is much more important, increasing to 89 percent for farms with sales of less than $2,500 and 77 percent for the $2,500 to $4,999 sales group.

How are government payments distributed among farm operators? The distribution is considered in three different ways: (1) by size of payment, (2) by value of sales classes, and (3) by states. A comparison can be made with farm income for the last two, but this is not possible for the first.

Table 6 gives the distribution, by the size of payment per producer, of direct payments under all farm programs that make such payments. Separate data are not available for the three major commodity programs. The distribution should not be much different than that given in Table 6, since the payments under the cotton, wheat and feed grain programs have constituted from 80 to 85 percent of all direct payments to farmers. Data are available on the distribution of payments by the size of base or allotment for 1970.[26] Payments under the cotton program were the most unequally distributed: only 2.6 percent of the farms received 38 percent of total payments. Under the feed grain program 10.8 percent of the farms received 42.4 percent of the payments, while under the wheat pro-

Population Survey significantly underestimates the incomes of individual entrepreneurs, including farm operators. In 1971 there were 273,000 farm wage workers who worked more than 250 days during the year.[21] These were nonmigratory workers who worked an average of 317 days at farm work; their annual cash wages were $3,788 and their daily wage was slightly under $12.00. In 1966 the value of wages in kind (housing, meals) was about a third of the cash wages for regular hired workers. If the same relationship held in 1971, annual wages would have been about $5,000.

In considering the impact of the farm programs upon the distribution of income, it must be noted that a very low-income group associated with agriculture—the hired farm worker—receives nil benefits. However, the discussion in this section refers only to farm operator families—families who are responsible for the operation of a farm even though the farm may not be the major source of income. In 1971 there were 2,876,000 such families. Their average family income, as estimated by the U.S. Department of Agriculture, was $11,811.[22]

Before reviewing the distribution of government payments among farm operators, there are some characteristics of the income of farm operator families that are worthy of note. Between 1960 and 1971 per-capita real income from all sources of persons living on farms increased by 97 percent. This compares with an increase of approximately 43 percent in per-capita income for the United States.[23] The increase in the real income per farm operator family was slightly less than the increase in per-capita real income of persons living on farms, namely, 75 percent. This difference was due to two factors—a decline in the average size of farm operator families and a reduction in the relative importance of hired farm workers in the total farm population between 1960 and 1971.

The sources of the increase in real farm family income are indicated in Table 4 (in 1967 dollars).[24] The total real income of the farm operator population increased by 27 percent; the number of farm families declined by 28 percent. These two changes account for the 75 percent increase in the real income of farm operator families between 1960 and 1971. If the farm population had not declined, income per family would have increased by only 27 percent. Almost all of the increase (92 percent) would have been due to increased off-farm income. In 1971 farm operator families received more than half of their income (52 percent) from off-farm sources compared to 41 percent in 1960. This tabulation makes it clear that farm programs directly affect only part—in 1971 less than half—of the income received by farm operator families.

from previous benefit payments. Further, a new entrant into farming, unless he has inherited farm land, transmits a large fraction of future anticipated benefits from the program to the former owner of the land. Thus after a period of time, many of the then owners of farm land earn little or no additional income as a result of the continuation of the programs.

## Benefits to Farm Families

**Ownership of Farm Land.** Since a very large fraction, if not all, of the net benefits from commodity programs go to land, the percentage of farm real estate that is owned by farm operators is of some interest. Only fragmentary information is available on the value of land owned by individuals farming that land. For 1969 the U.S. Department of Agriculture estimated the value of land owned by nonfarm landlords at $73.1 billion or 36 percent of the total value of all farm land.[19] But this is an underestimate of the value of land rented by farm operators since some farm operators rent land to other farm operators. In 1964 farm operators rented 9.4 percent of their land to others for operation. If it is assumed that the real estate that farm operators rent to other farmers is 75 percent as valuable per acre as the average, the value of farm real estate operated by the owners of that land would equal 60 percent of the total. In other words, perhaps as much as 40 percent of the net benefits accruing to land goes to landowners who do not farm the land they own.

Despite the absence of opinion survey data, the author believes that those who vote the money for farm programs believe that most of the benefits go to farm people living on family farms. If the analysis presented here is even approximately correct, at least a third of the net benefits go to individuals or corporations who do not engage in farming but only own farm land. Another small fraction goes to farm operators, not for their activities as farmers, but as landlords.

**How Benefits Are Distributed.** In the previous section it was argued that the incomes of farm wage workers have been increased little, if at all, by the farm programs. Families that depend upon farm wage work as their main source of income are among the poorest in the United States. In 1970 families whose head was a farm laborer or foreman had a mean income of $5,608 compared to a national average of $11,108.[20] Only families whose head was a private household worker had a lower income.

The same survey indicated that the mean income of farm operator families was $7,543, but it is generally agreed that the Current

land to the annual average income of farm operators plus the rent paid to nonfarm landlords. For 1960 through 1972 the annual average income of farm operators and rent paid to nonfarm landlords was $18.2 billion measured in 1972 dollars. The annual gain in the value of farm real estate, again in 1972 dollars, was $5.6 billion. Thus the total income to farm operators and nonfarm landlords during the period was $23.8 billion a year, of which the annual increase in land values, after adjustment for change in the cost of living in farm areas, represented 23 percent.

Not all of the increase in real farm land values should be attributed to the farm programs. Some undoubtedly is due to the increase in the productivity of farm land resulting from new knowledge and production methods and the relative decline in fertilizer prices. In some parts of the country the demand for land for nonfarm purposes has increased farm land values. Some argue that the economies of farm consolidation have been responsible for a part of the increase in land values. One third of the $68.5 billion or 90 percent increase in the value of farm real estate from 1950 to 1963, Tweeten and Nelson estimate, was due to the capitalization of benefits of farm programs. Because of changes in farm programs—less emphasis on higher market prices and a doubling of direct payments—it is uncertain what share of the increase in land values since 1963 should be attributed to them. If the share has continued to be a third, the land values as of the beginning of 1972 that could be attributed to the capitalization of farm program benefits would be about $51 billion or 22 percent of the total value of land.

On a rather different basis, the author has estimated elsewhere that elimination of all forms of protection to U.S. agriculture would result in a reduction in land values of $30 to $50 billion.[18] These are very large figures. In discussing future farm policy, these possible losses should not be ignored. However, some perspective may be gained by noting that farm land values in the United States increased by almost exactly $50 billion between 1969 and 1973. More than half of that increase occurred during 1971 and 1972. Part of the recent increase in land values was due to inflation, but the 9 percent increase in 1972 and the 7 percent in 1971 must also represent some optimism about the future profitability of farming.

It is something of a puzzle that there has not been more political concern about the capitalization of a large fraction of farm program benefits into land values. For one thing the fact of capitalization becomes an excuse or a rationalization for continuing the farm programs whether or not any other basis exists. Benefit payments become necessary to prevent the destruction of asset values resulting

Willard Cochrane, who was closely associated with U.S. farm programs from 1961 to 1964, has concluded that an increase in farm incomes resulting from increased levels of price support would quickly be capitalized into increased land values.[15] Luther Tweeten states:

> Land price is an important variable in public policy. Long-term fluctuations in farm income tend to be absorbed by land values. Raising the level of farm income by government programs of the type used from 1955 to 1969 tends to result in capitalization of program benefits into land.... While land prices on the larger, well-organized farms tend to adjust to farming income, leaving a parity return on resources, it does not necessarily follow that any level of farm income is equally satisfactory to farmers. A reduction in farm income can wipe out equities, raise mortgage foreclosures, and cause other financial hardships, while the market adjusts the land price down to a lower equilibrium level consistent with less farm income.[16]

Earl Heady and Leo Mayer make the same point:

> The second major improvement [in U.S. farm programs] ... should be modifications to prevent the capitalization of program benefits into real estate values.... After the resources change hands through the market, the gains of the program are cancelled and the function of public expenditure is mainly to maintain asset values so that the new owner does not suffer a capital loss.[17]

**Land Values and Agricultural Income.** Further evidence that a large fraction of the benefits of farm programs have been capitalized into the value of farm land is shown by the relationships between total net agricultural income and farm land value. Net agricultural income is defined as the sum of net operator income, rent to nonfarm landlords and farm wages. In the period between the two world wars, net agricultural income varied from 15 to 18 percent of the value of farm land. In 1960 it was 11.7 percent of that value, in 1971 only 9.3 percent. Thus the claim of farm real estate on net agricultural income has risen significantly during the past two decades of farm programs.

As noted earlier, the increase in land value has been a large component of the total return on farm land. From 1959 through 1965 the estimated current annual return on farm land averaged 5.7 percent while the annual capital gain was 4.7 percent. Another relevant comparison is the ratio of the annual increase in the value of farm

It is worthy of note that the return per farm of constant total area, but with a reduction in tobacco area of about a third, increased by 500 percent in dollars of constant purchasing power over the same period of time.[11]

The tobacco program has probably had more effect on the return to land than any other farm program in the United States. Hedrick's estimates of the decline in return to land used to produce tobacco in 1960 if the program were abolished are both instructive and discouraging. For both states he estimated that abandoning the program would reduce rent per unit of tobacco land in 1960 by 85 percent.[12] Without the program the return to land used in producing tobacco would be only 15 percent of what it was with the program in effect. The effect on market values of land is obvious. The prospective major reduction in land values is an important political reason for continuing the tobacco program.

Estimates of the value of allotments or bases for peanuts, cotton, corn, and rice have been made by Seagraves. None of them reaches the extreme found for tobacco, but none is so small as to be ignored, either. He found the market value of an acre of peanut allotment in North Carolina in the late 1950s to be about $669 and of an acre of cotton allotment $463. Virginia data indicated the value of an acre of peanut allotment to be $565 for the period 1956-1960. These are capitalized values—that is, the increase in land value associated with the ownership of an allotment acre.[13]

In recent years peanut allotments have been transferable. In 1970, when the average farm price of peanuts was 12.8 cents per pound, the annual rent paid per pound of peanuts for a peanut allotment was 2.5 cents or approximately 20 percent of the farm price of peanuts. The annual rental value of the allotment was $50 per acre and its capitalized value was $300. This is a national average. For North Carolina where the peanut yield is substantially above the national average the capitalized value of an acre of allotment in 1970 was about $750. In Virginia the capitalized value was approximately $610 per acre. In Texas, where peanut yields are much lower, the capitalized value was $280.[14]

In some states rice allotments can be transferred from farmer to farmer. Studies of such transfers indicate a capitalized value of $400 per acre in California and $240 in Texas. Estimates of the annual value of an acre of corn allotment in the early 1960s ranged from $10 to $20 per acre.

The conclusion that almost all of the long-run income gains from support prices above equilibrium levels goes to higher returns to land is supported by a considerable number of able economists.

Hedrick's results confirm the conclusion that in the long run all or virtually all of the income gains went to the landlord who owned the land and the tobacco allotment. He made estimates of the hourly return to labor for the cropper and his family members and compared them to average wages in manufacturing in the United States and to wages of various occupational groups in the two states. In 1922-27, which was a period of full employment, the Virginia cropper return was 32 percent of the national average wage in manufacturing; in 1952-62, it was 34 percent. The North Carolina percentages for the same years were 42 and 42. In other words, the increase in hourly returns to croppers was exactly the same as the increase in average wages in manufacturing.

In addition, recognizing that the national manufacturing wage probably was not available to Virginia and North Carolina farm workers, Hedrick included comparisons of occupational groups with education and skills more similar to those of cropper labor. Actually there are difficulties with the Virginia data because a significant fraction of employed workers in Virginia are federal employees. Since the trends in the earning ratios are the same, reference is made here only to the more comparable data for North Carolina. The first year for which a comparison is available is 1940 and the last year 1960. While the tobacco program was in effect before 1940, James A. Seagraves's estimates indicate that the annual return to an acre of tobacco allotment was rather modest in that year, namely, $30 compared to $600 in 1960.[9] Thus the comparison of relative earnings in 1940 and 1960 seems appropriate to reflect any effect the tobacco program may have had on the long-run earnings of labor used in producing tobacco.

The tabulation indicates the following changes in the ratio of earnings of cropper labor to earnings of other occupational groups (male workers) between 1940 and 1960: [10]

|  | 1940 | 1960 |
|---|---|---|
| Craftsmen, foremen, kindred | 0.51 | 0.50 |
| Operatives and kindred workers | 0.66 | 0.63 |
| Service workers | 0.92 | 0.78 |
| Laborers, except farm and mine | 1.02 | 1.05 |

In only one of the four comparisons was there a significant decrease in the relative earnings of cropper labor. Hedrick concluded: "it was found that neither tenure inflexibilities nor labor immobilities have permitted the control program to influence earnings of the human factor over the long run...." The real returns to the human factor increased by 145 percent or at an annual rate of 2.6 percent.

$0.58 per pound. Note that what was being paid for was the allotment, not the actual land. The farmer who rented the allotment had to provide the land. The market price for cropland suitable for the production of tobacco in 1963 was in the general range of $250-275 per acre; thus the *annual* rental value of an acre of tobacco allotment was equal to or greater than the market price of the land on which the tobacco was grown if that land did not have a tobacco allotment. Studies made in 1966 and 1967 found that the rents paid for tobacco allotments in North Carolina, the major tobacco producing state, were about $0.19 per pound compared to an average selling price for tobacco of $0.64. Eastern North Carolina land ranged from $450 to $580 per acre. These estimates were very close to an estimate derived by subtracting labor costs, other variable costs and land rent (exclusive of the rent of the allotment) from total revenue from a hectare of tobacco.

Regression analyses of the sales value of farms as affected by the size of the tobacco allotments indicate that a hectare of tobacco allotment had a capitalized or market value of $1,600 to $2,800 per acre in the late 1950s and early 1960s. This should be compared to the estimated market value of land without acreage allotments of about $250-275 per acre.[7]

The studies of tobacco program effects on returns to land that have been summarized above do not speak directly to the effects of the program on the return to farm labor. They show only that the return to land with an allotment and the market value of the allotment are very large relative to the value of the land actually used to produce tobacco. An important study has been made by J. L. Hedrick of the effects of the tobacco program on the return to farm labor in the states of North Carolina and Virginia.[8] He estimates that the effect of the tobacco program was to increase the price received by farmers in 1960 by approximately 20 percent.

A significant fraction of Virginia and North Carolina tobacco is produced under a cropper arrangement where the cropper receives a given fraction of the value of output (50 percent), pays half of current operating expenses such as seed, fertilizer and insecticides, and provides all of the labor. Over the period in which the tobacco program has been in effect, the share paid by the cropper to the landlord has not changed. On the surface it would appear that the owner of the land (and the allotment) and the cropper would share equally in the income gains from the higher prices received because of the tobacco program. In the very short run equal sharing would occur. But not in the longer run, according to the analysis presented above.

prices. It can be concluded that the magnitude of product price increases that have been achieved by supply management in recent years—4 or 5 percent at a maximum—has resulted in a one time increase in the return to farm labor equal to less than the labor return effect of one year's adjustment of labor supply through out-migration. As far as the return to labor is concerned, this seems a very tiny return for an annual governmental expenditure of more than $3 billion.

## Farm Programs and Land Values

It is possible to provide empirical tests of the general conclusions that supply management programs have significantly increased the return to land and have had little or no effect on the return to farm labor.

**Effects of Allotments.** Estimates have been made of the value of acreage allotments for several crops, including tobacco, peanuts, cotton, corn and rice. While some of these crops are not within the scope of this study, the programs are sufficiently similar so that the effects on land returns have been of similar nature, though varying in magnitude.

The tobacco program has been in continuous operation for three decades. It has been a supply management program operating by either acreage allotments or poundage quotas or some combination of the two. There have been no direct payments such as those made under the cotton, wheat and feed grain programs. From 1967 through 1972 there was an export subsidy that averaged about 7 or 8 percent of the farm price of tobacco.

Various methods have been used to estimate the value of an acre of tobacco allotment, either in terms of its annual rental or its capitalized value. They include linear programming, residual returns to land derived from estimates of production costs, regression analyses of actual farm sales prices as related to the size of the tobacco allotment and interviews of knowledgeable persons. At a time subsequent to most of the studies involved, a change in the tobacco program provided a market test of at least some of the estimates. Since 1963 the program has permitted farmers to transfer their allotments to another farmer living in the same county and, obviously, the transfer has been at a price.

One study found that in two counties producing flue-cured tobacco the annual rent for a tobacco allotment in 1963 was in excess of $300 per acre, or about $0.16 per pound of tobacco produced. The average price received by farmers for tobacco was about

uct prices. The various adjustments, actual or potential, are illustrated in Figure 1.

Assuming the demand conditions are as specified in Figure 1, this figure indicates approximately what the return to land would be if product prices increase by 10 percent and the elasticity of supply of land is zero. For no change in the quantity supplied, the resource price increases by 11.9 percent. This is more than three times the projected increase in the wage rate or return to labor for the same increase in demand.

John Floyd has made estimates of the differential effects on the returns to labor and to land of different methods of achieving a 10 percent increase in output prices.[5] Two are of interest here. One method assumed an increase in product prices with no controls over output or inputs and thus no concern about what happens to the excess supply. The other assumed limiting the amount of land enough to reduce farm output sufficiently to increase product price by 10 percent. The latter approach is followed by the supply management programs that we are considering.

His results show that for the same structure of agriculture, as measured by the ease of substitution between land and other inputs and the elasticities of supply of land and labor, a 10 percent increase in product prices achieved by acreage limitation will result in a smaller increase in the return to labor than if the 10 percent product price increase is achieved without controls on outputs or inputs. The reason for the smaller increase in return to labor is that farm output is reduced by the acreage limitation and there is less land to be used per unit of labor. Under a range of reasonable assumptions about the elasticities of product demand, of substitution and of labor supply, the increase in the return to labor achieved by acreage reduction is about a third to a half of the increase in return to labor that would result from a product price increase of the same size but achieved without acreage limitations.

In fact, if the long-run price elasticity of demand for farm products is near unity, it is highly probable that acreage limitations will have *no* effect upon the return to labor. And there are some not wholly unreasonable assumptions under which the imposition of acreage controls will reduce the demand and thus the wage of labor.

It can be concluded that at best acreage controls and higher farm prices have increased the return to farm labor to a very small degree. And it should be noted that any increase in the return to labor achieved by acreage controls and higher output prices is a once and for all increase.[6] A further increase in returns to labor would require a further reduction in acreage and still higher product

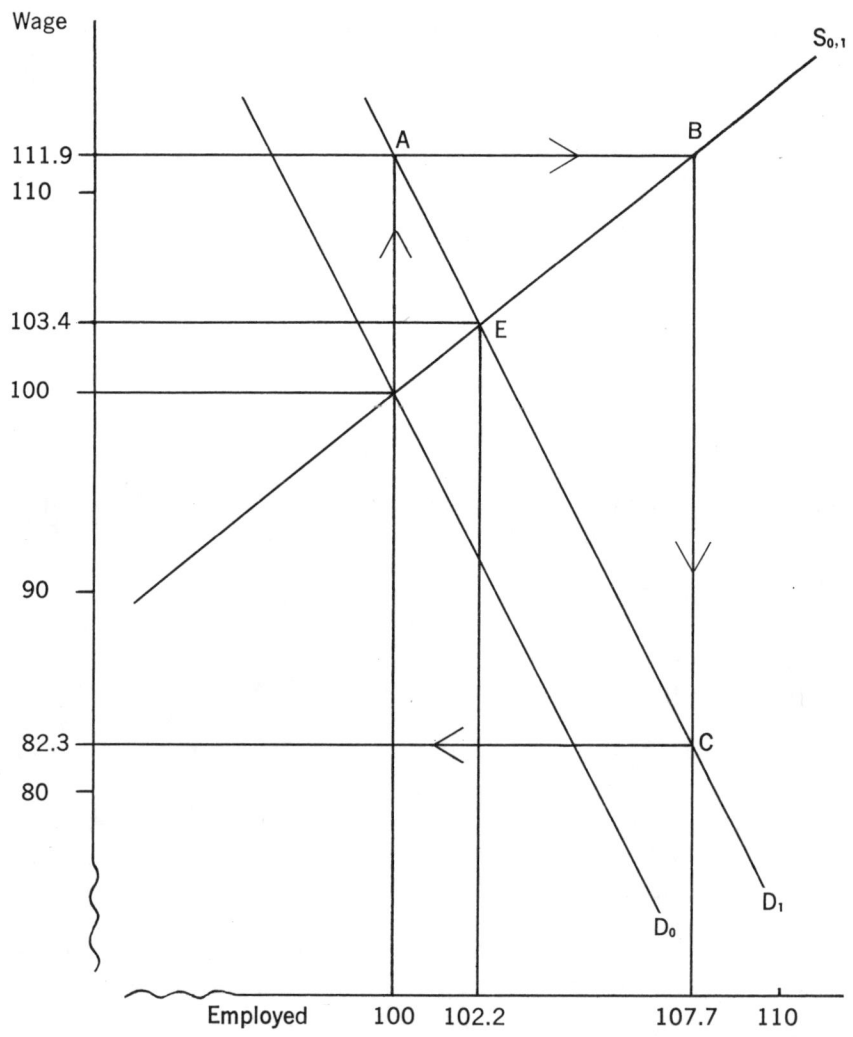

**Figure 1**

EFFECTS OF INCREASED FARM PRICES ON FARM WAGE RATES AND EMPLOYMENT

**Key:**
A—Demand equilibrium, if supply of labor is held constant
B—Supply equilibrium, if wage rate is 111.9
C—Demand equilibrium, if quantity of labor is 107.7
E—Equilibrium of supply and demand with $D_1$ and $S_{0,1}$
$D_0$—Demand curve for labor before output price increase
$D_1$—Demand curve for labor after output price increase of 10 percent
$S_{0,1}$—Supply curve of labor in both periods

labor with respect to the wage rate. Taken together this information permits one to estimate the change in the return to farm labor *if the supply of labor were held constant.* For the purposes of this illustration, the elasticity of demand for labor with respect to the wage rate is −0.26 and the elasticity of demand for labor with respect to real farm prices is 0.31. The latter elasticity tells us that if real farm prices increased by 10 percent and that if the wage rate remained constant the amount of labor demanded would increase by 3.1 percent. If the quantity of labor available is held constant, the price of labor must rise. The increase in the wage rate due to the 10 percent increase in real farm prices and a fixed supply of labor would be the product of 3.1 percent and the reciprocal of 0.26, the elasticity of demand for labor with respect to its price.[3] The amount of labor available, under the assumptions made, is 3.1 percent less than demanded at a constant price of labor. Because of the very low price elasticity of demand for labor in the short run, the wage rate must increase significantly to remove the excess demand. The increase in the price of labor would be 11.9 percent, as indicated in Figure 1.

But the substantial increase in the price of labor is due to holding the quantity of labor constant. The same analysis indicates that the short-run elasticity of the supply of labor with respect to the price of labor is 0.65. Thus if the increase in the return to labor remained at 11.9 percent, the quantity of labor supplied would increase by 7.7 percent (the product of 11.9 and 0.65). But this would be an impossible situation. An increase in the quantity of labor of this magnitude would not be acceptable to employers (even if the employer and worker were the same individual) without a substantial decline in the return to or price of labor. In fact, 7.7 percent more labor would be used subsequent to the 10 percent increase in output price only after the 11.9 percent increase in wage rate had been eliminated and a further decline in the wage rate of 17.7 percent had occurred. The 7.7 percent increase in labor supplied would result in an increase in the quantity of labor of 4.6 percent over and above the amount that would be employed at the wage rate *before* the increase in output prices. The 4.6 percent increase in quantity supplied, given the price elasticity of demand for labor, would reduce the price of labor by 17.7 percent (4.4 times the reciprocal of 0.26 or times 3.846). Obviously the increase in the quantity of labor supplied would not occur either. After adjustments in both demand and supply for labor, assuming no shift in the supply schedule due to a change in nonfarm income, the wage rate would increase by 3.4 percent and the quantity of labor employed by 2.21 percent.[4] This is the short-run outcome of a 10 percent increase in farm prod-

## Supply of Labor to Agriculture

The most systematic study of the supply of farm labor in the United States is by Edward W. Tyrchniewicz and G. Edward Schuh of Purdue University. In their study they derived estimates of the demand and supply functions for three categories of farm labor, hired workers, unpaid family workers and farm operators. The authors attach no significance to the results for operator labor, because the trend variable tended to explain almost all of the change in operator labor. However, the results for hired and unpaid family workers meet all of the usual statistical and economic criteria and are worthy of attention.

The study indicated that the supply of hired and unpaid family workers increased with higher farm wage rates and declined with an increase in nonfarm income adjusted for unemployment. Both the short-run and long-run elasticities of farm labor with respect to nonfarm income were negative and greater than unity. The short-run elasticities of supply were −1.42 for hired labor and −1.47 for unpaid family workers. The long-run elasticities were −3.38 for hired labor and −3.26 for unpaid family workers. Thus, holding farm wage rates constant, an increase in nonfarm income per worker of 10 percent would reduce the supply of farm workers by more than 30 percent. Of course, as the number of farm workers was reduced, the farm wage rate (or earnings of unpaid family workers) would increase. This would act to reduce, but not eliminate, the decline in the number of farm workers.

An increase in farm wage rates increases the supply of labor to agriculture. This elasticity was approximately 1.5 in the long run. Thus a 10 percent increase in farm wage rates would increase the quantity of hired and unpaid family labor by about 15 percent. The analysis indicates that if both farm wage rates and nonfarm earnings increased by 10 percent, the number of these two categories of workers in agriculture would decline by about 17 percent. This difference is presumably due to the difference in the real incomes that can be derived from farm and nonfarm employment. If farm wage rates and nonfarm earnings were identical, one would expect the elasticities of supply with respect to farm wage rates on the one hand and nonfarm earnings on the other hand to be the same. But the anticipated earnings are not now the same since there has been a net transfer of labor out of agriculture.

The analysis also provides estimates of the effect of real farm prices on the quantity of farm labor demanded with the farm wage rate unchanged and of the elasticity of quantity demanded for farm

## Returns to Land and Labor

Net farm incomes have been increased by the major commodity programs. While it is true that the increase in incomes has been much less than the gross transfer, it has been significant. The question is how the increase has been distributed among the major resources used in agriculture. In referring to the effects of the transfers on the distribution of net income, we are concerned with only those resources that participate in net income, principally labor, land and capital.

If all of the increase in farm incomes were derived from higher prices, the division of the increase among the resources would be largely determined by the elasticities of supply of each of the resources. This is not to say that the elasticities of demand for the resources would have no effect upon the distribution of the increased income. However, since the price elasticities of demand for the major resources are more nearly equal than are their elasticities of supply, the major distributional effects will be due to the elasticities of supply.[1]

It is well established that an increase in demand for the resources used in an industry yields a greater increase in the returns to a given resource the less elastic its supply.[2] The extreme cases are zero and infinite elasticities of supply. In the latter case an increase in demand has no effect on the return to a resource; its only effect will be on the amount of the resource employed. If the elasticity of supply is zero, an increase in demand for that resource has no effect on employment and its only effect will be a higher price. If just two resources are used and one has a price elasticity of supply of zero and the other of infinity, the resource with a zero elasticity of supply will receive a higher average price or return. Total payments to the other resource will increase, but no owner of that resource whether previously or newly employed will receive a higher wage or rent.

The price elasticity of supply is higher for labor than it is for land. Over a number of years it is probably substantially higher. While it is incorrect to argue that the supply elasticity of farm land is zero, since farm land can be used for other purposes such as forestry, recreation, roads, airports and urban areas, that elasticity is clearly very low. Even though there have been substantial changes in land rents and prices over time, the total amount of land in farms has changed little. The amount of cropland varies little even over fairly long periods of time.

CHAPTER V

# DISTRIBUTION OF FARM PROGRAM BENEFITS

There are two principal interests in the distribution of benefits from any program that transfers income. One is the effect of the transfers upon the distribution of income among the major factors of production. The other is the effect of the transfers upon personal or family distribution of income. Both types of distribution effects are considered in this chapter.

Two caveats are pertinent. The first is that the discussion of the distribution of benefits among farm families emphasizes the distribution of gross benefits—the distribution of the transfer payments and, in one instance, the distribution of gross income resulting from higher prices. It cannot be inferred from these data that net incomes were increased by the amounts indicated. Chapter IV showed that the net income increases were much smaller than the amount of the direct payments made to farmers. And there is no strong basis for assuming that the distribution of net benefits was proportional to the distribution of gross benefits, though there is probably a fairly high correlation between the two distributions.

The second caveat is that, while it is hoped that the analysis of the distribution of benefits is objective, my own biases or value judgments are that the social significance or value of income transfers that go primarily to land are less than those that go primarily to labor; also, transfers that go to relatively high-income families are less valuable than those that go to relatively low-income families. In other words, if the general public is asked to transfer income to agriculture, it is reasonable to expect that the transfers will benefit most those who have the least.

The rough analysis indicates that net farm income has been increased by an amount ranging from $1.0 billion to $2.0 billion in recent years as a result of the cotton, wheat and feed grain programs. This increase in net farm income has been achieved at a total cost to consumers and taxpayers ranging from $3 billion to $4 billion, with most of the cost being borne by taxpayers since market prices have been increased relatively little.

It is not possible from the above to say definitely how much of direct payments is retained by farm operators as net farm income. In U.S. Department of Agriculture farm income calculations, it is estimated that approximately $350 million is paid to nonfarm landlords. A larger, but unknown, amount is paid to landlords who are also farm operators and is counted as a part of net farm income.

Even if only a quarter of the amount estimated by Secretary Hardin as over and above the payment required to offset foregone earnings on diverted land has gone for the cost of increasing yields or retaining land in production of a particularly intensive use because of the payments, the increase in net income from the payments would be approximately $0.5 billion for 1968. Because payments have been somewhat larger under the Agricultural Act of 1970 and a smaller fraction has been required to induce participation, the recent increase in net farm income attributable to payments might be at most $1.5 billion. Any conclusion on this point is largely conjectural, but it is quite clear that a major fraction of the payments do not represent an addition to net income. Thus the elimination of the payments would have a much smaller effect on net farm income than the amount of the payments.

## Conclusion

The annual effect of direct payments on farm income has been estimated to range from $0.5 billion in 1968 to perhaps as much as $1.5 billion in 1971-73. Partly because of changes in program features provided in the Agricultural Act of 1970 and partly because of stronger demand conditions, a smaller fraction of the payments made in 1971 and later years has gone for supply management and compensation for income opportunities foregone.

The effect of supply management on net farm incomes has clearly been very small in recent years. If it is assumed that the restrictions on land used and the direct payments have had no effect upon yield, farm output has been reduced by about 2 to 2.6 percent, depending upon whether indirect effects upon livestock output are taken into account. The value of the decreased output ranges from $750 million to $1.05 billion. If the price elasticity of demand for farm output is approximately unity, the maximum increase in net farm income may have been $400 to $500 million. The increase in net income results from a reduction of expenses for the same level of gross income.

If the effect of the supply management programs on acreage seeded has been of the size indicated—20 million acres out of total probable seeded cropland of 325 million acres—it would not have taken much yield effect to offset a large fraction of the output reduction due to the acreage reduction. Studies of supply response have indicated that the response of yields to product price has been greater than the response of acreage. One estimate for the United States is that the yield response elasticity to product price for all crops has been 0.15 in the short run and 1.50 in the long run; the acreage response elasticity in the same study was 0.04 in the short run and 0.10 in the long run.[28] If these relative elasticities are reasonable approximations, and studies for other countries indicate that they are,[29] it may be that U.S. supply management programs attempt to control the wrong input variables.

These response elasticities do not provide a basis for estimating the effect of payments on yields. Uncertainties about the determination of projected yields and expectations about the permanence of the programs or some of their particular features also influence the behavior of farmers. But even if one assumes that the payments of $0.50 per bushel under the wheat program had an effect on yields equivalent to an increase in price of $0.10 per bushel, the long-run impact would have been to increase wheat yields by about 10 percent or about two to three bushels per acre. One may speculate that wheat output may have been increased by 100 million to 150 million as a result of the effect of the payments on yield. If the reduction in acreage due to the acreage restrictions has been as much as 7 million, the output reduction has been on the order of 200 million bushels.

The size of the payments has been much smaller for feed grains. A five-year period has been used to determine projected yields (in contrast to three years for wheat). It is reasonable to assume that the payments had some effect on feed grain yields, but it has almost certainly been smaller than for wheat.

Cotton yields have also been affected by high payment rates, but the major element in dissipating the transfer payment has probably been that some cotton is now produced in order to earn the payments. As a recent U.S. Department of Agriculture study indicates:

> Thus, the annual income to allotments, and indirectly to land, is about a third of the direct benefits. This implies that much of the benefits—two-thirds of the direct payments and all of the indirect benefits—are available to other factors of production. Cost of production estimates show that many cotton producers are apparently relying on program benefits to cover variable production costs.[30]

As shown earlier, the programs have probably idled about 20 million acres of farm land that would otherwise have been utilized. Part of the payments made through the programs has been required to compensate farmers for giving up the productive use of that land. As seen by the individual farmer, the payments required to induce participation do not represent additional income. For farmers as a whole, whatever reduction in output was achieved has an effect on gross and net farm income. However, the importance of the output reduction actually achieved has been considered above. The two amounts—the increase in farm income resulting from reduced output and higher prices and the payments actually required to pay for income foregone—should not be added.

In 1969 Secretary of Agriculture Clifford Hardin testified that the following percentages of the total payments made in 1968 were required to compensate for the supply management component of the farm programs: cotton, 35 percent; wheat, 51 percent; and feed grains, 89 percent. The total of the payments in that year was $2.9 billion.[26] Based on the payments made in each of the three programs, Secretary Hardin's estimates indicated that $2.2 billion of the direct payments made did not represent additional income. Looked at the other way, the remainder—$0.7 billion—was the upper limit of the increase in net income.

The conclusion that $0.7 billion was the upper limit of additional net income emphasizes that some part of the transfer payment over and above the costs of participating in the programs may have gone to something other than net income. The existence of the additional payments had some effect on the behavior of farmers and influenced their costs. Such effects were clearly unintended, but they were no less real because of it.

Payments are distributed to farmers according to two criteria: acreage determined by the allotment assigned to each farm and projected yield. Projected yield is based on the average yield for a recent three-to-five year period. If the projected yield for each farm reflects to a reasonable degree that farm's actual yield, future payments to be received depend upon yields in a given year. In recent years a participant in the wheat program has received from $1.50 to $1.75 per bushel as payment for more than a third of his wheat output. Averaged over the participant's total output, this amounts to $0.50 or more per bushel. The average market price has been in the general range of $1.25 to $1.35 per bushel. Thus it is reasonable that farmers take into account future payments when making decisions concerning the application of inputs that are expected to influence yield.[27]

The decline in price for all farm output is 6.4 percent and the calculated price elasticity of demand for all farm output is −.41.

All of us who make such projections realize that events may soon overtake us. Actual output of grains for the three years 1969-71 averaged only a million metric tons less than the projected level for 1970 under a free market, and the output of soybeans exceeded the projected level by 1.6 million metric tons. Yet after adjusting for the change in the price level between 1967 and 1969-71, cash receipts from crops exceeded the projected free market level by $1.0 billion and cash receipts from livestock products exceeded the projected level by $4.0 billion. It seems apparent that demand shifted more than assumed in the projection; it may also have been true that the price elasticity of demand was greater than assumed. Whatever the reason, it appears that a crop output of about 5 percent greater than was projected was readily absorbed by the market and that an additional increase of the same magnitude could have been absorbed without a loss in gross income even if the price elasticity of demand were as low as −0.5.

In recent years the income effects of supply management have been small. Supply management has not reduced the output of cotton, so no effect can be attributed to this major program. The effect of supply management on the output of other major crops, particularly wheat, feed grains and soybeans, appears to have been on the order of $700 million to $900 million annually, as a maximum. This estimate assumes that the programs had no effect on crop yields, a point that is discussed below. Assuming that the reduction in output has been of the size indicated, it amounts to approximately 2 percent of total farm output. The effect of such an increase in output on farm prices and farm income depends upon the price elasticity of demand. If the elasticity is approximately unity, gross farm income has not been increased at all and net farm income has been increased by at most half the fixed price value of the increase in output.

## Program Payments and Farm Income

The average level of direct payments for the three major commodity programs was $3.1 billion in 1969-71 and nearly $4.0 billion in 1972. These payments have increased net farm incomes. Unfortunately we do not know how much of the payment has been retained by farm operators and farm workers and how much has been "lost" through increased expenses or income foregone to meet program requirements.

farm output, which reflects the low elasticities in the domestic market, is estimated to be $-1.1$. The intermediate-run elasticity for a period of three years is approximately $-0.5$.

If the price elasticity of demand for U.S. farm output is approximately unity, and this conclusion seems reasonable, reducing U.S. farm output would have no long-run effect upon gross farm income and very little effect upon net farm income. Since with reduced output there is some reduction in farm expenses, the net returns to farm land, labor and capital would be increased somewhat. For small changes in the level of farm output—say 5 percent or less—the increase in net returns would be only about 5 percent *if* all costs of production other than land, labor and capital constituted half of the total value of output and such costs varied proportionately with output.

As indicated above, both my estimate of the output reduction due to supply management for recent years and that of Mayer, Heady and Madsen are about 2 percent. It is surprising that so small an increase in farm output would result in the large decline in gross farm income projected by Mayer, Heady and Madsen. Comparing gross farm income for a continuation of existing programs and for a free market, they project a decline in cash receipts from crops of $1.45 billion plus a decline of $1.0 billion from livestock products. The latter decline is largely offset by a decline in cash expenses—primarily due to lower cost feed—of $0.8 billion. The decline in cash receipts from crops and livestock, after removing most of the duplication, amounts to $1.65 billion. This is more than twice the value of the increased output of wheat, feed grains, cotton and soybeans.

The domestic price elasticity of demand for the output of cotton, wheat, feed grains and soybeans in the Iowa State study is approximately $-0.27$. A 5.3 percent increase in the output of this group of products was associated with an average price decline of 19.4 percent. The calculated result is consistent with the authors' statement that they used a price elasticity of demand for feed grains of $-0.25$.[25]

The value of farm sales to the domestic economy and for export can be approximated from the projection for 1970 under a continuation of the farm programs of the late 1960s. This value is approximately $40 billion. A crop output increase valued at $744 million might be increased by another $300 million to account for additional value added by livestock. This implies that the expansion in total farm output in the free market situation compared to the continuation of the farm programs would increase farm output by 2.6 percent.

income and the large amount of marketing and processing services associated with U.S. farm products, the price elasticity of demand at the farm level for all farm products appears to be of the order of $-0.1$ to $-0.2$. Thus if only the domestic market were involved, a 3 or 4 percent reduction in output would result in a very substantial increase in gross farm income. However, U.S. farm programs can no longer operate with the assumption that only the domestic market is involved. This may have been a reasonable assumption during the 1930s, but it is no longer the case today. Even before the large increase in exports in 1972 and 1973, exports represented the outlet for about 15 percent of total farm production. Estimates for recent years are that 18 to 24 percent of the harvested cropland has been used to produce products for export, either directly or indirectly through livestock products. The importance of exports as an outlet for cropland is of interest because influencing the use of land has been the tool of supply management.

When the United States reduces the output of a product that it exports there are two effects: (1) a reduction in consumption in the importing country due to the higher price and (2) an expansion of production in the importing country and all exporting countries that produce the same product. While the U.S. is a major exporter of feed grains (40 to 50 percent of world trade), wheat (about a third) and cotton (20 to 25 percent), its share of total production in the industrial non-Communist countries is about the same as its share of world trade for the feed grains and wheat. The U.S. share of world cotton production is also about the same as its share of world exports.

If there were free trade in farm products—or moderate tariff duties—it would be relatively easy to estimate the price elasticity of demand for our farm exports. Enough is known about price elasticities of demand and supply to make a rough approximation under those circumstances. However, there are significant barriers to trade in farm products that prevent a decline in export prices from being reflected in the prices in importing countries. The variable levies imposed by the European Economic Community (EEC) represent such a trade restriction.

Luther Tweeten has analyzed the price elasticity of demand for U.S. farm exports.[24] On the assumption of no significant barriers to trade, he estimates a long-run elasticity of approximately $-16$ for the level of U.S. exports of 1963-65. After adjusting for noncommercial sales and some trade restrictions (principally the EEC variable levies), he estimates a long-run price elasticity of demand for exports of $-6.4$. The weighted long-run elasticity of demand for total

results obtained by Mayer, Heady and Madsen.[22] They estimated farm prices, production and income under alternative farm programs, including a return to the free market and a continuation of the cotton, wheat and feed grain programs of the late 1960s. The estimated diversion for 1970 under continued programs was 53.5 million acres, not far from the average for 1962-68 and probably equivalent to 58 million acres diverted under the Agricultural Act of 1970. Because part of the acreage expansion estimated under a shift from present programs to the free market situation includes that to be used for soybeans, the comparative output levels for the two situations have been calculated including soybeans.

The farm prices projected under a continuation of the cotton-wheat-feed grain programs in 1970 were used to weight the output of cotton, wheat, feed grains and soybeans under the two policy alternatives. The estimated value of the output of this group of commodities with continued commodity programs was $13,966 million; the value for the free market situation was $14,706 million. Since the same prices were used in valuing output, the difference is a measure of the estimated output expansion that would result if all diverted land were permitted to return to cultivation. The increase in output would have a value of $741 million, near my lowest estimate above.

The increase in acreage harvested of the above group of crops due to the elimination of diversion was projected by Mayer, Heady and Madsen to be 15 million acres. The crops under consideration account for two thirds of total harvested area. Nearly two thirds of the remaining harvested cropland is devoted to hay, which is not likely to be much affected by the elimination of diversion since the acreage of hay appears to have been little affected by the programs.[23]

## Income Effects of Supply Management

The objective of a supply management program is to increase farm income. If the direct payments associated with the major programs are considered separately, supply management increases farm income by increasing the margin between receipts and expenses. Supply management reduces output, thus increasing the market prices received for farm products. Whether the increase in prices increases gross income from the sales of farm products depends upon the price elasticity of demand. A major assumption of all supply management programs is that the price elasticity of demand is less than unity. As a consequence, a smaller output sells for a larger amount.

The elasticity of demand for farm products in the domestic market is certainly less than unity. Given the high level of per-capita

grain plantings by 5 million acres. The estimate for wheat was in terms of harvested area—an increase of 7.7 million acres. If this is translated into seeded area, assuming average weather, it would imply an increase in planted area of approximately 9 million acres. The sum of the three increases is 21 million acres.

If the estimate of what farmers will do in 1973 turns out to be approximately correct, farmers' behavior will be quite consistent with the estimate that acreage diversion reduced cropland used for crops by about 20 million acres, assuming the real farm prices of recent years. Obviously if farm prices stay near the 1972-73 levels, the cropland area will increase. Over a period of several years the increase in cropland could be substantial, but it would be due to higher farm prices and not to the elimination of the diversion or set-aside programs.

### Output Effects of Supply Management

How much has total farm output been reduced by acreage diversion? Tweeten and Quance have estimated the amount of output that would have been produced if *all* diverted land were returned to production and if the average productivity of that land were 80 percent of that of average land used.[21] For the seven years 1962 through 1968, they figured the annual value of output not produced because of the diversions at $2.5 billion. The average acreage diverted was 55 million acres. As indicated above, the available evidence suggests that the elimination of the diversion programs would not result in anything like 55 million diverted acres being returned to current crop production. My estimate is that 20 million acres would be returned. Thus, instead of the crop value not produced due to the programs being $2.5 billion annually, it is more on the order of $700 million to $900 million.

The difference between these two estimates is clearly important in terms of the price and income effects of eliminating the diversion programs. Based on the value of farm output (the amount available for sale to the rest of the economy, including consumption as food on farms) of $40 billion in 1969, the Tweeten-Quance estimate indicates that farm output would increase by 6 percent if the diversion programs were eliminated. An increase of this magnitude would have a significant impact on farm prices and incomes. However, if the added output from the return of the diverted acres were $700 million to $900 million, farm output would increase by only 2 percent.

The general order of magnitude of the increase in output value of $700 to $900 million, with constant prices, is consistent with the

necessary to divert 1 million acres to reduce cropland harvested by 430,000 acres. If the effectiveness of diversion were the same in the 26 states in which the sum of cropland harvested and acreage diverted declined, the reduction in cropland harvested due to diversion would have been 10.7 million acres. The sum of the effects attributed to diversion for the two groups of states combined would be approximately 25 million acres. But this estimate is clearly on the high side since the effectiveness of the diversion in the states in which cropland declined must be less than in the states in which total cropland was stable. Thus this rather rough analysis gives a result that is consistent with the estimate that diversion of 60 million acres has resulted in a decline in crops harvested of no more than a third of that amount.

Obviously the three different efforts to derive an estimate of the effectiveness of land diversion in influencing acreage seeded or harvested do not represent independent analyses. The underlying data are basically the same. Yet it is reassuring that the last two approaches yield similar results, namely that 60 million acres of diversion or set-aside reduces the land devoted to the major crops by about 20 million acres. The first and more limited approach indicates a somewhat greater effectiveness of the programs in affected actual acreage, but there is reason to believe that the actual effect was smaller than indicated.

With the changes that have been made in the farm programs for 1973 there will be a reasonably good test of the above analysis. The test, which will be farmers' actual behavior in planting crops, will be flawed somewhat by four considerations: (1) program changes were not made in time to influence the seeding of winter wheat; (2) while there are no diversion requirements or potentialities in the wheat and cotton programs, farmers can earn payments by diversion under the feed grain program; (3) the feed grain program includes provisions that subsidize the expansion of soybean acreage; and (4) farmers will be making their planting decisions in the spring of 1973 on the basis of price expectations that are much more favorable than those of recent years or those likely to prevail in the long run. The first two considerations will limit the increase in planted area between 1972 and 1973; the last two will operate to increase the planted area over what it would have been with more "normal" price expectations.

As the above was being written, Secretary of Agriculture Earl L. Butz predicted the probable seeding plans of U.S. farmers for 1973 for wheat, soybeans, and feed grains.[20] He estimated that soybean plantings would increase by 7 million acres and total feed

A recent analysis of the change in cropland harvested by states between 1951 and 1969 reaches conclusions consistent with this estimate.[17] For each state the change in cropland harvested and acreage diverted in 1969 was calculated.[18] There was no limitation on planting in 1951, while 58 million acres were diverted in 1969. Thus if diversion had been fully effective—an acre of reduction in cropland harvested for each acre of diversion—cropland harvested in each state would have declined by the amount of the diversion, except for random factors such as the influence of weather and ignoring long-run trends in the amount of cropland.

There were 26 states in which the decline in cropland harvested from 1951 to 1969 exceeded the acreage diverted. In these states cropland harvested declined by 36.4 million acres and total diversion was 24.9 million acres. Thus, in effect, 11.4 million acres of cropland disappeared—or, more accurately, was converted to some other use than growing a crop or earning payments in a government program. There were 22 states in which the decline in cropland harvested was less than the acreage diverted. In these states cropland harvested declined by 14.1 million while 32.7 million acres were diverted in 1969. Thus in these 22 states cropland harvested plus acreage diverted increased 18.2 million between 1951 and 1969. The first group of 26 states had 44 percent of total cropland harvested in 1951 and only 39 percent in 1969. In spite of the much greater reduction in cropland harvested in the 26-state group than in the 22-state group (25 percent versus 7 percent), the first group had approximately the same percentage of national diversion in 1969 as it did of cropland harvested in 1969. The much greater reduction in cropland harvested in the one group of states than in the other cannot be explained by differences in the amount of diversion.

One further comparison is of interest. Between 1954 and 1964 the group of 26 states reduced total cropland (including cropland used for pasture, soil improvement crops and idle, as well as cropland harvested and fallow) by 21 million acres.[19] Total cropland in the remaining states was constant. While the time periods are not the same as used above, the changes in cropland for the states in which the reduction in cropland harvested was greater than the acreage diverted suggests that a substantial fraction of the diverted acreage would not return to cultivation if the diversion programs were discontinued.

A firm conclusion cannot be drawn from these comparisons as to the part of the reduction in cropland harvested between 1954 and 1969 that was due to acreage diversion. In the 22 states in which the sum of cropland harvested and acreage diverted increased, it was cropland harvested of 28 million acres—which is the figure for the increase in cropland neither harvested nor pastured. This is thought to be a maximum because there is some presumption that some amount of cropland existed in 1964 for the sole purpose of earning income under one farm program or another.

Another approach based on historical comparisons is to contrast recent levels of cropland harvested with those that prevailed in the early 1950s when input and output price relationships were such that real total farm operator income was greater than in 1970-72 with the same weighted quantity of total inputs. In 1951-53 cropland harvested averaged 339 million acres and crop failure 12 million acres. In 1970 and 1972 cropland harvested averaged 284 million acres and crop failure 7 million acres.[15] If it is assumed that all of the decline in the amount of crop failure has been due to improved cultural practices, the 1951-53 cropland harvested area might have been 344 million acres under today's farming conditions. If a direct comparison were made between the adjusted 1951-53 cropland harvested and the 1970 and 1972 average of 284 million acres, the decrease in cropland harvested would be 60 million acres. But this should be reduced by about 8 million acres for the increase in summer fallow, reducing the maximum decrease to perhaps 52 million acres.

The above comparisons ignore the decline in total cropland over the past two decades. From 1954 to 1967 total cropland declined by 29 million acres.[16] Assuming that there has been no further decline in total cropland since 1967, the 43 to 48 million acre decline in cropland used for crops between 1954 and two recent years, 1970 and 1972, can be said to consist of two major components: (1) the decline in total cropland and (2) the impact of diversion or set-aside programs on the use of cropland for crops. The decline in total cropland, assuming the percentage of total cropland used for crops was the same in 1954, 1970 and 1972 (82 percent), would account for 24 million acres of the total decline in cropland for crops. This leaves approximately 19 to 24 million acres to be explained by other factors, including diversion or set-aside. In the absence of diversion or set-aside payments, some cropland used for crops would probably be used for cropland pasture, since one effect of the payments appears to have been to have reduced cropland pasture, perhaps by as much as 5 million acres. The 1970 and 1972 diversion was approximately 60 million acres. If real farm prices stayed at approximately the level of those two years, the amount of cropland that would come back into cultivation in the absence of diversion requirements would probably be no more than 20 million acres.

## Table 3
### UTILIZATION OF CROPLAND, UNITED STATES, 1954–1969
*(million acres)*

| Cropland Use | 1954 | 1959 | 1964 | 1969 |
|---|---|---|---|---|
| Crops [a] | 380 | 358 | 335 | 334 |
| Harvested | (339) | (317) | (292) | (290) |
| Failure | (13) | (10) | (6) | (7) |
| Summer fallow | (28) | (31) | (37) | (37) |
| Idle or in cover crops | 19 | 33 | 52 | 51 |
| Pasture [b] | 66 | 66 | 57 | 88 [c] |
| Total | 465 | 457 | 444 | 475 [c] |

[a] Cropland harvested, crop failure and summer fallow.
[b] Cropland used only for pasture.
[c] Due to different methods of census enumeration, the data on cropland pasture and total cropland for 1969 are not comparable to the data for earlier years.
**Sources:** U.S. Department of Agriculture, *Agricultural Statistics, 1972*, p. 506, and U.S. Department of Agriculture, Economic Research Service, *Changes in Farm Production and Efficiency: A Summary Report, 1972*, Statistical Bulletin No. 233, p. 7.

1954 and 1964, but it should be noted that crop failure—which is largely a weather-induced variable—also declined by 7 million acres. Cropland idle or used for soil improvement crops increased by 33 million acres while the cropland used for pasture declined by 9 million acres. Some of the decline in cropland used for pasture may have occurred because idling that land or classifying it as a soil improvement crop may have been the most economical method of meeting diversion or set-aside requirements.

One of the striking aspects of Table 3 is the decline shown in total cropland. Since total cropland was 18 million acres larger in 1949 than 1954, the decline started before 1954. While some of the farm programs that began in the late 1950s, especially the Conservation Reserve, may have speeded up the transfer of cropland to other uses, it is unlikely that farm programs have had much long-run effect on the downward trend in cropland. If they have had an effect, it has probably been to moderate the downward movement somewhat because of the substantial payments that could be derived. This is not to argue that farm output has been increased by the slowing of the decline in cropland but simply that more land is now classified as cropland than would probably have been the case in the absence of diversion payments.

The above analysis is consistent with the view that the diversion of 55.5 million acres in 1964 resulted in a maximum reduction in

**Historical Comparisons.** The most recent period in which there was no limitation on land used for the major farm crops was 1951-53. During those years the average planted area for wheat and feed grains was 227 million acres. In 1970, when acreage diverted under the wheat and feed grain programs was 53 million acres, the planted area was 59 million less than in 1951-53; in 1972 when the area diverted was 58 million acres, the planted area was 49 million acres less than in 1951-53.[11] These comparisons seem to imply that there was nearly a one-to-one inverse relationship between acreage diverted and the acreage planted.

In my opinion, this implication is seriously in error. It ignores the fact that some major fraction of the diverted land is land that would not be used for crops or other productive purposes in a given future year.[12] Prior to the existence of farm commodity programs farmers left some cropland idle each year. In 1929, for example, there were 54 million acres of cropland that was not harvested or pastured; in 1944 when farm prices were very favorable, 50 million acres of cropland were neither harvested nor pastured.[13] In these two years cropland neither harvested nor pastured was about 12 to 13 percent of total cropland. In 1949, when real farm prices had declined significantly from the war and postwar peaks, 64 million acres of cropland were not used. In 1954 when there were very mild restraints on the use of cropland, 61 million acres were in this category.

In 1964 total acreage diversion under all farm programs was 55.5 million acres. The amount of cropland not harvested or pastured was 89 million acres, or only 28 million acres more than in 1954. Of the increase in cropland not harvested or pastured between 1954 and 1964, 9 million acres or nearly a third was accounted for by the increase in cultivated summer fallow. This is a cultural practice adopted in relatively dry areas as a means of conserving moisture to increase yields and to reduce the variability of yields. While it requires leaving land idle one year, the reduction in costs and the increased yield has made it an increasingly profitable practice. Part of the increase has been associated with the greater use of fertilizer on wheat. But even if some of the increase in fallow has been due to government programs (the wheat program permits fallow land to be counted as set-aside land), the output effect of acreage diversion in the form of summer fallow is quite modest.[14]

Table 3 provides estimates of the uses of cropland for various years from 1954 to 1969. Because of differences in the method used to take the 1969 Census of Agriculture, the data for 1969, especially for cropland used only for pasture, are not fully comparable with other years. The harvested area declined by 47 million acres between

diversion and how much was due to farmer response to the same set of supply and demand conditions. The data presented in Table 1 do show a relationship between the amount of diversion and the acreage seeded or harvested. There is considerable variation from year to year in the nature of this relationship. Table 2 provides comparisons between year-to-year changes in diversion and acreage seeded or harvested.

Because of the interrelatedness of crop production, Tables 1 and 2 include total diversion as well as diversion under the wheat and feed grain programs. In addition, a separate program called the Conservation Reserve, which was phased out in 1969, involved 14.0 million acres of diversion in 1965. The change in the farm programs that became effective in 1971 may have reduced the effectiveness of diversion in influencing the area devoted to the major grains. However, even in the period from 1966 through 1970, an increase in diversion in the wheat and feed grain programs was associated with a change of about half to three fourths as large in the seeded area. But these were changes at the margin, which tell us little or nothing about the effect of the first 20 million acres of diversion upon planted area.

There are other approaches that can help in understanding the effect of diverting land upon planted or harvested area. One is to compare recent experience with an earlier period when there was no program limitations on the crop plans of farmers.

## Table 2

ANNUAL CHANGES IN ACREAGE DIVERTED AND WHEAT AND FEED GRAIN SEEDED AND HARVESTED ACREAGES, 1965–1972
*(million acres)*

| Years Compared | Change in Diversion | | Change in | |
| --- | --- | --- | --- | --- |
| | Total | Wheat and feed grains | Seeded area [a] | Harvested area [b] |
| 1965–66 | 5.9 | 1.0 | − 2.2 | 1.8 |
| 1966–67 | −22.5 | −22.7 | 17.0 | 12.4 |
| 1967–68 | 9.0 | 12.1 | − 3.9 | − 9.2 |
| 1968–69 | 8.2 | 17.8 | − 9.2 | −10.0 |
| 1969–70 | − 0.9 | 2.9 | − 1.4 | − 7.7 |
| 1970–71 | −19.9 | −20.8 | 14.3 | 10.5 |
| 1971–72 | 24.5 | 24.7 | − 5.4 | −12.3 |

[a] Seeded area of wheat, corn, oats, barley and grain sorghum for all purposes.
[b] Area harvested for grain; excludes harvested area for silage and forage; same crops indicated for seeded area.
Source: U.S. Department of Agriculture, *Agricultural Statistics, 1972,* pp. 637, 2, 35, 44, 51, 52 and 65.

opinion, no doubt that in most if not all years for the past decade the wheat and feed grain programs have reduced acreage planted. But the amount of output reduction achieved is very difficult to determine.

One set of figures is often cited to indicate that a significant reduction in output has been achieved. These are the data on the amount of farm land diverted under the various programs. For all programs that involve diverting land to nonproductive uses, the acreage diverted between 1969 and 1972 has ranged from a low of 37 million acres in 1971 to a high of 62 million in 1972.[10] Under the feed grain and wheat programs alone diversion ranged from 32 million acres in 1971 to 57 million acres in 1972.

But since the U.S. Department of Agriculture changes the features of the wheat and feed grain programs on the basis of anticipated supply and demand conditions, it is very difficult to know how much of the change in acreage seeded or harvested was due to

Table 1

LAND DIVERSION AND ACREAGE SEEDED TO WHEAT AND FEED GRAINS, 1956–1972

*(million acres)*

| Year | Diversion | | Acreage Seeded [a] | | | Total Acreage Harvested [b] |
|---|---|---|---|---|---|---|
| | Total | Wheat and feed grains | Wheat | Feed grains | Total | |
| 1956 | 13.6 | — | 60.6 | 158.1 | 218.7 | 180.4 |
| 1957 | 27.8 | — | 49.8 | 158.2 | 208.0 | 184.3 |
| 1958 | 27.1 | — | 56.0 | 148.0 | 204.0 | 187.8 |
| 1959 | 22.5 | — | 56.7 | 154.1 | 210.8 | 191.6 |
| 1960 | 28.7 | — | 54.9 | 147.9 | 202.8 | 188.6 |
| 1961 | 53.7 | 25.2 | 55.7 | 128.1 | 183.8 | 164.7 |
| 1962 | 64.7 | 38.9 | 49.3 | 124.0 | 173.3 | 154.3 |
| 1963 | 56.1 | 31.7 | 53.4 | 127.8 | 181.2 | 159.7 |
| 1964 | 55.5 | 37.5 | 55.7 | 119.3 | 175.0 | 157.0 |
| 1965 | 57.4 | 42.0 | 57.4 | 116.3 | 173.7 | 154.8 |
| 1966 | 63.3 | 43.0 | 54.4 | 117.1 | 171.5 | 156.6 |
| 1967 | 40.8 | 20.3 | 67.8 | 120.7 | 188.5 | 169.0 |
| 1968 | 49.8 | 32.4 | 62.5 | 116.8 | 179.3 | 161.1 |
| 1969 | 58.0 | 50.2 | 54.3 | 115.8 | 170.1 | 151.1 |
| 1970 | 57.1 | 53.1 | 49.6 | 119.1 | 168.7 | 143.4 |
| 1971 | 37.2 | 32.3 | 54.6 | 128.4 | 183.0 | 153.9 |
| 1972 | 61.7 | 57.0 | 55.4 | 122.2 | 177.6 | 141.6 |

[a] Seeded area of wheat, corn, oats, barley and grain sorghums for all purposes.
[b] Area harvested for grain only.
**Source:** U.S. Department of Agriculture, *Agricultural Statistics, 1972*, pp. 637, 2, 35, 44, 51, 52 and 65.

## Acreage Effects of Supply Management

**Cotton.** For the past four years and again for 1973 the cotton program has not reduced cotton production. If it has had any effect, it has been to increase the amount of production. In 1969 and 1970 participation in the cotton program required no diversion of land.[7] In 1971 and 1972 approximately 2 million acres had to be devoted to soil conserving uses, but the amount of diversion was so small as to be without effect. In fact, the acreage of cotton planted in 1971 and 1972 increased over 1970—by 350,000 and 1,900,000 acres respectively. The increase after 1970 was primarily a response to higher market prices.

The Agricultural Act of 1970 sets no limit on the maximum acreage of cotton on any farm. Farmers who produce cotton are assigned a farm base allotment. The purpose of this allotment is not to restrict the amount of cotton planted, but to serve as the basis for the allocation of payments. However, unless the farmer plants 90 percent of his base, his future farm base allotment is reduced. Since farmers can sell or lease their allotments, the 90 percent planting requirement probably has only a limited positive effect on output. The size of the payments (approximately 15 cents per pound in 1971) may have induced farmers to continue in cotton production when they would not have done so in response to the market price.

A study published in *Cotton Situation,* a U.S. Department of Agriculture publication, indicates that, except for 1966-67, the acreage restraint features of the cotton program have had no effect on either cotton acreage or cotton yields.[8] Acreage diversion did have a major impact in those two years. In all other years from 1950 through 1969, however, the acreage and yield response of cotton producers was well explained by the anticipated market prices for cotton and for competing crops. When the cotton program was significantly modified in the 1964 to 1966 period by reducing the price support loan level from approximately 32 cents per pound in 1963 to 20 cents per pound in 1967, cotton acreage moved to a lower level even though payments were made on virtually the entire output.

It is quite clear that the elimination of the cotton program would not result in an increase in cotton production. It could well result in a reduction in output. Because farmers have not had to divert any significant amount of land (none in two out of the last four years), eliminating the program would have no significant effect on the production of any other farm crop.[9]

**Wheat and Feed Grains.** The determination of the output reduction for wheat and the feed grains is much more difficult. There is, in my

## How Supply Management Operates

Supply management in the cotton, wheat and feed grain programs has functioned by influencing the amount of land devoted to a particular crop or group of crops. Since 1970 the influence on land used for crops has been through inducing farmers to remove part of their land from current use. Under the Agricultural Act of 1970 there has generally been no limit to the amount of land that can be devoted to one of the major crops under consideration. If a farmer meets the set-aside standards and certain minimum additional requirements, he is free to use the rest of his cropland for any purpose that he desires. Prior to 1971 a wheat farmer was required to abide by an allotment assigned to each farm though, even then, he could gain additional land by planting wheat in place of feed grains if he had a feed grain base. Prior to 1971 feed grain producers also had a base, but the major factor in their planting decisions seems to have been the reward for additional voluntary diversion.

The reduction in output by influencing acreage planted is a complex process. The land withdrawn from cultivation may not be of the same quality as the land actually cultivated. Some land may be listed as diverted or set-aside acreage that the farmer had no intention of planting. Clearly this has been true of cultivated summer fallow, which is a cultural practice used in relatively dry areas as a means of conserving moisture. Once a farmer has made the decision to divert or set aside part of his cropland, he may farm the remaining land more intensively than would otherwise have been the case. He has more labor and equipment to devote to each unit of the smaller area.

In addition, the rules that generally prevailed for establishing the payment rates for diverted acreage related such payments to average yields for the immediate past period of three to five years. Thus farmers had an incentive to increase yields in order to receive higher payments in future years.[6] These considerations mean that one cannot estimate the output effect of diversion by multiplying the acreage diverted or set aside by average output per acre.

The effects of the programs on actual yields are highly conjectural. However, even if one excludes the question of land quality, there is no doubt that the yield effects have been positive. What is uncertain is how large these effects have been. Let us assume, as a first approximation, that there have been no yield effects and then later indicate what impact rather modest changes in yields would have had upon the reduction in output that can be attributed to supply management.

incomes—the difference between gross receipts and expenses—will increase. Increasing farm prices will raise net farm income if there is no requirement that the market be cleared at those prices over the period of time involved. But if the market must be cleared, which means that the amount supplied must equal the amount demanded, increasing prices may fail to increase net farm income.

Most persons in any way associated with agricultural policy would be amazed if told that increasing farm prices, even when markets must be cleared, could have any effect other than increasing net farm income. The reason for this is the acceptance as a fact that the price elasticity of demand for farm output is very low. The evidence is overwhelming that domestic demand is quite price-inelastic, but the demand for wheat, feed grains and cotton is not solely a domestic demand. As indicated in a later chapter, the total elasticity of demand for U.S. farm output may be quite large in the long run. If this is true, it means that the proper approaches to farm policy do not include the artificial raising of prices.

In recent years very little emphasis has been put upon increasing the prices of cotton and the feed grains as a means of increasing farm incomes. Cotton prices in the domestic market have reflected export prices, and cotton output has been affected little if at all by the cotton program since 1968. Feed grain prices have also been at approximately export prices, with only occasional and minor use of export subsidies to raise domestic prices above export prices. A somewhat different policy has been followed in the case of wheat, where for the past five years export subsidies have been used to maintain exports while raising domestic prices about 15 percent above export levels.

For the past several years direct payments have been much the most important means of increasing the incomes of wheat, cotton and feed grain producers. For 1969-71 the annual average payment level was $3.1 billion. It was not true, however, that net farm income increased by that amount. Farmers did incur costs as a result of diverting or setting aside land. Some farmers may have produced crops, especially cotton, at a loss in terms of the market price but found production profitable because of the payments. Since the output of wheat and feed grains was restricted, part of the payments was required to compensate for income that was foregone. There has been no estimate made, to the author's knowledge, of the amount of the payments that was retained as net income. However, the increase in net farm income derived from the payments, including increased returns to landlords, was probably of the order of $1.5 billion from 1969 through 1971.[5]

elimination of all or most programs. Unlike the studies referred to above, program comparisons were made for the same date and both short- and long-term adjustments were provided for the return to a free market. The earlier studies provided for little or no resource adjustment during the transition to a free market.[3]

Projections were made for 1970. Projected net farm income was $15.6 billion assuming continuation of the major commodity programs of the late 1960s, and $11.3 billion assuming a free market situation after long-term adjustment.[4] Thus, the projected decline in net farm operator income resulting from the change was $4.3 billion or 27 percent. Under the free market assumption with short-run adjustment, the decline in net farm income was estimated at $5.7 billion or 37 percent, or approximately the same as in the earlier studies referred to above. A decrease in government payments of $2.9 billion represented the major source of the income decline. The decrease in net cash receipts, after reflecting the effect of decreases in feed prices on the costs of purchased feed, was estimated at $1.65 billion. Because output was assumed to increase, some additional operating expenses were projected. But the two decreases in government payments and in net cash receipts were only slightly larger than the decline in net farm operator income.

If these projections are reasonable indications of what would happen to the level of farm incomes with the elimination or substantial modification of the major commodity programs, there would clearly be very serious adjustment problems facing American agriculture. But the outcome of any projection effort follows from the assumptions made. If these assumptions fail to reflect the conditions that will prevail for the appropriate time period, the projections will turn out to have been in error. Conditions do change, new information is accumulated and it is always easier to look back than it is to look ahead. Thus in arguing, as this essay does, that the projections reviewed above give a far too pessimistic picture of the effects of reducing or eliminating direct payments and acreage limitations, no implicit or explicit criticism of the projections is intended. They were done by competent scholars and on the basis of assumptions that seemed reasonable to them at the time.

### Increasing Farm Income

The major commodity programs have attempted to affect the level of farm incomes in two ways, by increasing prices received by farmers and by direct payments. Simply increasing prices received by farmers or making payments does not automatically ensure that net farm

CHAPTER IV

# MAJOR COMMODITY PROGRAMS AND FARM INCOME

A key reason for the continued existence of the cotton, feed grain and wheat programs has been the belief that their elimination would cause a major decline in net farm income. Over the past decade projections have been made indicating that if farm prices were determined by supply and demand in a free market, net farm operator income would decline substantially, perhaps by 40 percent or more. Some of these projections assumed the elimination of more than the three programs considered here. Except in the case of dairy products, cotton, wheat and feed grains, elimination of governmental farm programs would have little effect upon total net farm income.

A 1959 study done by the U.S. Department of Agriculture, with the advice of an advisory committee of the land grant colleges, projected farm output, farm prices and net farm income for 1965 on the assumptions that (1) all production controls (except those on tobacco) were ended and (2) price supports were maintained at "levels that would permit an orderly reduction, over a 7- to 10-year period, in the current excessive stocks of storable commodities." [1] The projected decline in net farm income was 39 percent, from $11.5 billion in 1955-57 to $7 billion in 1965. Farm output was assumed to be 20 percent greater in 1965 than during the base period.

A like study, undertaken for the Joint Economic Committee of the U.S. Congress, reached approximately the same result, namely, a net income decline of 36 percent between 1959 and 1965.[2] Net realized farm income for 1965 was put at $7.2 billion. Other studies made in the same period came to similar conclusions.

More recently, studies made at the Iowa State Center for Agricultural and Economic Adjustment have set forth output, price and income projections based on a variety of assumptions, including the

benefits have been smaller than the costs imposed upon taxpayers and consumers. The fact that net income benefits are smaller than gross benefits or costs should come as no surprise. When a transfer is made through higher market prices, producers respond to the higher price by employing additional resources. Thus some part of the transfer goes to resources other than those that provide net income to farmers. When a transfer is made through a direct payment, with requirements imposed upon the recipient, some part of the transfer will also be lost. If the requirement is that a resource (land) must be idled, the farmer will lose the alternative income that he would have earned from that resource. Or if the requirement is that a farmer must produce a minimum amount of a product in order to receive payments currently or in the future, he may continue to produce at a level that would be justified only because of the expected payments. In other words, in the absence of the payments, he would produce less of the product because the market price does not cover his costs. But given the payments, he continues to produce because the payments are equal to or greater than the loss suffered from production and sale at the market price.

The next largest group of farms, those with sales of $10,000 to $19,999, had actual returns that ranged from 74 to 98 percent of the parity returns for 1964 and 1966. This group of farms accounted for 15 percent of cash receipts, 18 percent of net farm income and 22 percent of government payments. Farms with sales below $10,000 had actual incomes below any of the parity standards.

Similar calculations have not been made by the U.S. Department of Agriculture for later years. Net farm income was high in 1966, so that more recent comparisons of actual to parity incomes might show a somewhat less favorable picture than did 1966. Yet it is striking that this most complete set of comparisons has not been kept up to date. Obviously the desire to know whether farm incomes are at "a satisfactory level" is not a very strong one.

## Other Criteria for Evaluation

The rather general consideration of the effectiveness of the three commodity programs in achieving five rather vaguely stated objectives is not adequate to justify the imposition of annual costs upon consumers and taxpayers of approximately $3.5 billion. Even if one accepts the view that the programs have raised the average level of farm incomes, as one must, there are additional important criteria that should be considered. How much has farm income been increased? What types of farm income—returns to labor or capital or land—have been increased the most? Have relatively low-income farm people gained from the programs to any significant degree? Have those who have benefited had incomes that are higher than the majority of those who incurred the costs? Is supply management by government programs required to provide levels of incomes for resources engaged in agriculture equivalent to what similar resources would earn in the rest of the economy? These are only some of the questions whose answers are pertinent to a fuller evaluation of the cotton, wheat and feed grain programs.

Chapters IV and V attempt to answer the questions posed above. Chapter IV considers the evidence relating to the effect of the three major commodity programs on the level of total farm income. Chapter V discusses the distribution of the benefits, including the direct payments, among farm families and the major factors of production and briefly considers how the costs of the farm programs have been distributed by income levels.

It is concluded in Chapter IV that the net income benefits of the programs have been significantly smaller than the gross benefits that have been distributed. This also means that the net income

farms and for part-time and part-retirement farms as well. Off-farm income was not included; an effort was made to exclude all resources used to earn off-farm income.[5]

The study included an estimate of the returns that farm resources could earn if these resources were employed outside of agriculture. The alternative return for farm labor was based on what the farm working force, after adjusting for the education, age and sex distribution of that labor force, would have received in nonfarm employment. Since these characteristics of the farm working force varied by economic class of farm, the parity returns for labor varied by class of farm. The actual base for the comparison with nonfarm employment was the average hourly wage rate for manufacturing employees. In 1966, the last year for which the calculations were made, this hourly rate was $2.71. For the largest of the group of farms, the alternative earnings were estimated to be $2.86 per hour; for the smallest of the commercial farms, $2.39. The average for all farms was $2.35 per hour or 86 percent of the average for manufacturing.

The determination of the alternative return to capital invested in agriculture was estimated in four different ways. One was to assume that a farmer sold all of his assets, invested the proceeds in farm land and rented the land to another farmer. A second was to assume that all farm assets were sold and the proceeds were invested in a portfolio of common stocks included in Standard & Poor's 500-stock average. Two rates of return were calculated for each of these alternatives—one included only current returns (rent and dividends) and the other included current returns plus the average annual rate of capital gains for the previous ten-year period. On a current yield basis for 1966, the return from renting land was 5.6 percent compared to 3.4 percent dividend yield. However, if capital gains were included, the return from investment in farm land was 11.8 percent compared to an 11.0 percent return from investment in common stocks.

With parity returns estimated as described, it was determined that the actual farming income of farms with sales of $20,000 and more in 1966 exceeded the parity return by all four standards (ranging from 7 percent to 67 percent above). In 1964, actual income was 3 percent below parity for one standard and from 1 to 58 percent above for the other three. In 1959, actual income was below the parity standard for three out of the four comparisons (ranging from 39 percent below to 29 percent above). Farms with $20,000 or more of sales accounted for 69 percent of cash farm receipts, 57 percent of net farm income and 49 percent of government payments in 1966.

supply and market price of wheat, feed grains and cotton, the major effect of the three programs upon consumer prices has been due to the wheat marketing certificate. If livestock and product prices are high, as they have been and are for manufactured dairy products, it is not because of high feed prices. Other programs not under discussion in this essay have increased consumer costs, including the programs covering sugar, peanuts, and rice.

From the above assessment it might be concluded that the farm programs could be considered reasonably successful. A closer look at several of the programs' objectives indicates, however, that the assessment has not been a very rigorous one. Let us look more closely at the first objective: to raise the average level of farm incomes to a more satisfactory level. What is a more satisfactory level? Would we know when such a level had been reached and the programs could be eliminated or reduced? The objective assumes that farm incomes have been and are too low. But what is the basis for that assumption?

Congress has defined three different measures of parity income for the farm population. The first two defined parity of income in terms of the relationship between the per-capita incomes of the farm and nonfarm population during 1910-14. One of the measures referred to the total income of the farm population and the other to the per-capita net income from farming operations for farm families and per-capita net income of the nonfarm population. By one of these measures the farm population has achieved income parity in all years since 1940 and by the other in all but three years since 1941.[4]

A third measure of parity income was included in 1948 legislation. It defined parity of income as "that gross income from agriculture which will provide the farm operator and his family with a standard of living equivalent to those afforded persons dependent on other gainful occupations." This concept has never been measured and without further guidelines is probably not measurable. Very few farm people depend entirely upon agriculture for their income and it is not clear what is meant by the concept of standard of living.

In the Agricultural Act of 1965 the secretary of agriculture was asked to make a study "of the parity income position of farmers, including the development of criteria for measuring parity income of commercial family farmers. . . ." The concept of parity income that was used was the annual return that a farmer could get by using his labor and capital in other employments. Because of the emphasis in the request upon parity income of commercial family farmers, parity income comparisons were made for four size groups of commercial

The politics of agriculture are clearly the politics of the attainable. Idealism has had a very small role in this very pragmatic setting. Whenever it has appeared that there is a groundswell of opposition to the commodity programs, adjustments have been made in the form of lower product prices, as during the early 1960s, or by making supply management efforts more economical and effective.

Whatever criticism one may make about the wisdom of holding a substantial fraction of farm land out of production each year, U.S. farm programs do not appear to have adversely affected farm efficiency in utilizing the available resources. It may be that the rationing of land has induced more rapid adoption of newer and low-cost inputs, such as new seed varieties, fertilizers, insecticides, herbicides and new types of cultural practices. Because land has been made scarce and the gains from higher yields substantial, farmers may have reacted more promptly to new opportunities than they would have otherwise. In any case, during the period of the programs, farmers have made rapid adjustments to changing conditions. These adjustments, combined with the efficient markets for farm inputs and farm products, have produced a situation in which the United States enjoys a substantial comparative advantage over the rest of the world in the production of several farm products. The United States is a low-cost producer of feed grains, soybeans, wheat, poultry and tobacco and is competitive with other producers of cotton, pork and grain-fed beef.

When it became obvious in the early 1960s that export markets were expanding, there was a significant change in price support policy to give the private market a much greater role in export trade. During the 1950s farm price support levels were substantially above world market levels for wheat, cotton and the feed grains. Exports could be made only by the payment of export subsidies or by sales from the stocks of the Commodity Credit Corporation. The lowering of price support levels to or slightly below export prices permitted the private market to ration supplies between domestic and world markets. This change in policy, which is an indication of the pragmatic nature of farm policy making, was coincidental with a substantial expansion of exports in commercial markets and was undoubtedly partly responsible for some of the growth in exports.

One can hardly claim complete success in achieving the final objective—which is the provision of an adequate and stable supply of food and fiber at reasonable prices. The wheat marketing certificate has increased the cost of wheat to food processors by approximately 50 percent. However, apart from the probably rather small long-run effect of the acreage diversion programs upon the

for the success of supply management programs designed to increase product prices.

To be fair, an evaluation of a program or set of programs should consider the success of those programs in achieving their stated objectives. This is true even if one does not accept one or more of the objectives as appropriate ends for a governmental policy. Thus, this evaluation first considers the success of U.S. commodity programs in achieving their explicit or implicit objectives. It then considers the appropriateness of those objectives and examines other objectives or considerations that deserve weight in the determination of commodity programs.

## Objectives and Performance

Legislation in the United States is more often than not quite ambiguous about the objectives that are to be achieved. But in the case of the farm commodity programs it is not too difficult to identify the following as the most important objectives:

1. Raise the average level of farm incomes to a more satisfactory level.
2. Achieve a reasonable degree of stability in farm prices and incomes.
3. Manage the supply of key farm products so that the first two objectives can be achieved without imposing unacceptably high costs upon taxpayers and consumers.
4. Improve the capability of American agriculture to compete in international markets while protecting it carefully but not completely from imports of competitive products.
5. Provide an adequate and stable supply of food and fiber for U.S. consumers at reasonable prices.

These objectives have been achieved to a substantial degree. In years of high production or diminished demand, farm prices and incomes have been higher than they would have been without the farm programs. Farm prices have been more stable, both because price supports have prevented substantial declines when crops were big and because stored surpluses have been marketed to keep prices down when crops were short or demand was greater than anticipated.

Up to the present time the management of the supply of farm products has been carried out at a politically acceptable level of costs. At least the programs have been maintained. When it appeared that costs were getting too high, program changes were made.

CHAPTER III

# EVALUATION OF FARM PROGRAMS

Any governmental program that involves substantial expenditures by taxpayers and consumers should be periodically evaluated. Rigorous evaluation is particularly appropriate when conditions have changed as much as have those in U.S. agriculture over the past decade.

The family farm is still the dominant form in U.S. agriculture. It has become larger in terms of total output and land area and much more dependent upon goods and services purchased from the rest of the economy. Total farm employment, including that of farm operators, members of their families and hired farm workers, has declined from 12 percent of national employment in 1950 to less than 5 percent today.[1]

Since the basic framework of U.S. farm programs was established in the 1930s, two other changes of major significance have occurred. One is the very substantial growth in nonfarm incomes earned by farm families, not only by small operators but also by farms with annual sales of $10,000 and above. Even the largest farms—those whose sales exceed $40,000 and which receive nearly 60 percent of all cash farm receipts—obtain a fifth of their total net income from off-farm sources.[2]

The second major change is the substantial increase in the importance of exports as a source of demand for U.S. farm products. In the 1930s exports accounted for only 10 percent of farm cash receipts, whereas they now account for 15 percent or more. For major products that utilize 70 percent of total U.S. cropland [3]— soybeans, wheat, cotton, tobacco, feed grains—exports in substantial volume are essential to maintain the present scale of agriculture. The increased importance of exports has a significant implication

as in fact they have, to unanticipated levels. To be successful, government programs must anticipate and facilitate changes that are under way rather than assume that agriculture is sluggish and slow to adapt. Whenever there is a contest between farmers and bureaucrats, it is highly probable that farmers will win.

mately 20 percent. However, the increase in productivity of farm workers was so substantial that real farm wage rates increased by 3 percent annually and the net income of farm operators from farming increased by approximately 2.5 percent each year.[12] Over the same period, real weekly earnings for all nonfarm workers increased by slightly less than 2 percent annually.

Thus agriculture not only must adjust but it does adjust—and at rates that are seldom equaled by other sectors of the economy. In the face of declining real prices, U.S. agriculture has somewhat improved its relative income position over the past two decades. To do so, it has had to reduce its work force by more than half in large part through migration.

### Conclusion

Clearly farming is not what it used to be. Mechanical power has been substituted for animal power. The largely self-contained farm is a thing of the past. Current inputs purchased from the rest of the economy now account for half of the total inputs used in agriculture. When the depreciation of farm machines and equipment is added, agriculture depends upon the rest of the economy for three-fifths of its inputs.[13] Farming has become a highly sophisticated production process, depending upon fertilizers, tractors, electric motors, hydraulic devices, air conditioning, pesticides, herbicides, vitamins, antibiotics, synthetic proteins and computers. The management of such enterprises requires flexibility and intelligence and a great deal of knowledge of prices and production alternatives.

An indication of the rapidity of change that has occurred in the structure of U.S. agriculture can be found in the increased importance of purchased inputs. An analysis of the relative importance of all farm inputs for 1957-59, the latest available, reveals a major change from the previous decade. In 1947-49 farm labor and real estate accounted for 59.2 percent of all inputs used in agriculture. By 1957-59 these two categories accounted for only 37.8 percent. Fertilizer and lime increased from 3.3 percent of all inputs to 8.6 percent and power and machinery from 16.0 to 26.5 percent. Purchased inputs as a whole increased from 40.8 percent of all inputs in 1947-49 to 62.2 percent in 1957-59.[14] Between 1957-59 and 1971 the quantity of purchased inputs used in agriculture increased further by 33 percent, while nonpurchased inputs declined by 19 percent.[15]

Agriculture is a highly dynamic industry that has adjusted to change and will continue to do so. Governmental policies that ignore this fact will be thwarted and distorted and their costs can rise,

the number of farm workers. And this is the way the adjustment process has worked. For the past two decades, U.S. farm employment has decreased 4 percent annually.

It might be thought that if there were rapid improvements in technology and efficiency in farming—an increase in output per unit of all inputs—this might minimize the needed reduction in the amount of labor. Such changes in technology do increase the productivity of labor. If there were no effect on farm prices, the results would be favorable to the return to farm labor. But if there were no reduction in the quantity of inputs used in farming, output would increase and prices received would decline by more than the increase in output because of the relatively low price elasticity of demand. Thus, rapid technical change increases the required outflow of farm labor.

The above line of reasoning can be put another way. Agriculture is continuously adjusting to a moving target—namely, rising real wages in the rest of the economy. Wages in the rest of the economy represent the alternative available to those who work in agriculture. Returns to labor in farming can increase only as the marginal physical product of labor—that is, the additional output of farm products due to adding or subtracting one worker—rises and/or as the real price of farm products increases. The combined effects of these two possibilities must be of the same order of magnitude as the annual increase in real wages in the rest of the economy.

Because of the slow growth in demand for farm products and because of the dynamic nature of agriculture, especially its ability to increase output at least as fast as demand, real farm prices have not increased over the long run. If anything, real farm prices have fallen slightly throughout the twentieth century. Thus the entire increase in the real return to farm labor has come from an increase in the marginal physical product of farm labor—through increasing the productivity of farm workers. While some of the increase in productivity has been due to changing technology and improved efficiency, most has come from changing the quantity of other resources combined with each farm worker.

Since 1950 the total quantity of inputs used in agriculture has remained constant, according to the official index of the U.S. Department of Agriculture.[11] The amount of labor used on farms declined by 56 percent while all inputs other than labor increased by a minimum of 35 percent. Thus in the early 1970s the amount of all other inputs per farm worker was three times greater than in 1950. Prices received by farmers did not increase as much as prices paid by farmers. The relative price of farm products declined by approxi-

incomes increase by 10 percent consumers purchase only 2 percent more farm products per-capita at the same relative price.

The income elasticity of demand for all goods and services when an economy is at full employment is unity. This means that if the income elasticity of demand for farm products is only 0.2, the income elasticity for all other goods and services is somewhat greater than 1.0. Thus the growth in demand for farm products would be somewhat less than one fifth that of all other goods and services as a result of per-capita income growth.

The growth in demand for a product is a function of population as well as income trends. When there is population growth this softens the difference in demand growth rates due to income change. For example, if population grows by 1 percent annually and per-capita income by 2.5 percent, the demand for farm products increases about 1.5 percent while the demand for all other products increases somewhat more than 3.5 percent. In these circumstances, the demand for farm goods increases only 16 percent over a period of a decade while the demand for nonfarm goods increases by 41 percent.

The slower growth in demand for farm products than for other goods and services requires continuous resource adjustments in agriculture. As indicated above, agriculture clearly has the capacity to increase output through the use of additional inputs and by increasing resource productivity. But with the slow growth of demand, the full utilization of this capacity is not possible with the continued use of the same amount of land and labor unless farm people are willing to accept continuously declining real income. If farm output increased at the same rate as nonfarm output, the farm output would find a market only at lower prices since supply would increase faster than demand. This would mean lower returns to farmer-owned resources—labor and land.

Farmers can share in the benefits of economic growth over the long run only if farm output rises at the same rate as demand. This requires a continuous outflow of labor from agriculture. In effect, all of the adjustment must occur through the transfer of labor since the vast majority of farm land has little alternative use outside of agriculture. If real farm prices remain unchanged (supply increases at the same rate as demand), the net productivity of farm labor must increase at the same rate as the real increase in per-capita income in the economy if farmers are to share fully in income growth. For the net productivity of labor to increase at this rate, there must be an increase in the quantity of other resources used with labor. Since the growth in demand is so slow, the main way in which more resources per farm worker can be used is through a reduction in

2 percent annually. Thus the annual rate of increase in farm output per worker has been approximately 6 percent.

In order to compare the rise in average output per worker in agriculture and in the rest of the economy, changes in average gross domestic product (value added) per worker are more meaningful. Using this criterion and measuring product in constant prices, the annual increase in labor productivity in agriculture has been 5.4 percent and only 2.9 percent in the rest of the economy.[7]

This comparison does not mean that agriculture has been more efficient than other sectors of the economy. It shows, rather, that agriculture has made a rapid adjustment to changing conditions during the period. Other inputs have been substituted for labor and many new methods of production have been adopted. Some of the substitutions that have occurred include a quadrupling of fertilizer use, a doubling of tractor horsepower used on farms, completion of the shift to hybrid corn, and the introduction of hybrid grain sorghums (which were soon planted on virtually the entire acreage).[8]

**Land.** Because the primary supply management tool of the commodity programs has been to influence the amount of land devoted to particular farm crops, changes that have occurred in land productivity or yield are of considerable interest. Since 1950 the wheat yield has almost doubled, the corn yield more than doubled and the grain sorghum yield increased by 150 percent. Cotton yields nearly doubled between 1950 and 1963 but then, as the price of cotton was reduced and some insect and disease problems occurred, yields declined to 60 percent above the 1950 level.[9] An important factor in the increased yields has been the four-fold increase in fertilizer. But many other factors were involved—improved seeds, new cultural practices, greater density of plant populations, new and improved herbicides and insecticides, and greater timeliness of operations due to more and improved machines and tractors.

## Agriculture Must Change [10]

If farm people are to share in the fruits of economic growth, they have no choice but to change in response to rapidly evolving conditions. Agriculture is a declining industry in the sense that, as real per-capita incomes increase, consumers spend a declining fraction of their income on food and other farm products. In other words, the income elasticity of demand for farm products is less than unity. For example, if the income elasticity of demand for farm products (at the farm, not at retail) is 0.20, this means that when per-capita

though not in numbers of farm workers. Family farms are smaller than all farms, but the percentage increase in size has been the same for both.

## Part-time Farming

The division of agriculture between larger farms and family farms masks major changes that occurred within the family farm group. One of the most important on family farms has been the substantial increase in part-time farming and the rising importance of nonfarm income. In 1971 the 1.5 million farms with sales of $5,000 or less had average net income from farming (including government payments) of $1,304. Their income from off-farm sources averaged $7,723 or more than five times their income from farming.[5] This group accounted for more than half of all farms.

In addition it may be noted that in 1971 farms with sales of $5,000 to $9,999 had $3,397 of net income from farming and $5,221 from off-farm sources on the average. By contrast, farms with sales from $10,000 to $19,999 (averaging $15,600), obtained more than a third of their total net income from off-farm sources that year.

In 1930 less than one in six farms were part-time farms. By 1971 almost two out of three farm families received more than half of their income from off-farm sources. The increase in the importance of off-farm income has meant that by 1971 off-farm income of farm families exceeded net income from agriculture. This is for all farms, not just family farms. Since 1950 there has been a remarkable increase in the contribution of off-farm income to the incomes of farm families. Such income accounted for a third of farm family income in 1950, about two-fifths in 1960 and slightly more than half in 1970.[6]

The sources of the off-farm income have considerable relevance to the effectiveness of commodity programs in increasing the incomes of farm families. Data for 1964 show that 60 percent of such income that year came from wages and salaries and 11 percent from a nonfarm business or profession. Thus the majority of the off-farm income came from work activity. If farm prices were increased significantly by farm programs, the output response could be affected in an important way by a shift of labor from nonfarm to farm activities by persons already living on farms. Similarly when farm prices fall, farm workers may shift more of their work effort into nonfarm activities.

## Increasing Productivity

**Labor.** For the past two decades farm employment has declined at an annual compound rate of 4 percent while farm output has grown by

The objective of maintaining the family farm as the dominant form of organization in American agriculture has been largely achieved. This does not mean that all U.S. farms are family farms. It does mean that, for the period of time for which data on the importance of family farms are available, their fraction of total farm sales has been substantially greater than half. There has been no down trend in that proportion.

As is so often true with respect to social and economic objectives, there is no simple or generally accepted definition of a family farm. A definition that is both reasonable and measurable is that a family farm is one on which the operator and the members of his family supply at least half of the total labor. On the assumption that each farm has a full-time operator and that family members provide half as much work as the operator, family farms have been defined to include all those farms on which hired workers provide less than 1.5 man-years of work. This is, of course, a very low level of hired employment, especially if comparisons are made with nonfarm enterprises.

Using this definition, it has been estimated that larger than family farms accounted for 30 percent of all farm sales in 1929 and 33 percent in 1949.[1] Using a slightly modified definition and statistical approach, 37 percent of all sales in 1949 were made by larger than family farms; the same approach indicated that the relative importance of such farms was about the same—38 percent—in 1969.[2] Thus over a period of four decades there has been little change in the relative importance of those farms that employ more than 1.5 years of hired labor.

A larger than family farm should not be confused with a corporate farm. Most farms are operated as individual proprietorships, not as corporate enterprises. A recent study found that in 1967 all corporations engaged in farming activities accounted for only 8 percent of all farm sales.[3] And many of these corporations were apparently family corporations, organized for tax advantages or for easier intergenerational transfer of the farm.

The number of family farms, as well as the number of all farms, has declined over time. Roughly speaking, the total number of farms has declined from 6 million during the 1930s to less than 3 million today, and family farms have continued to account for approximately 95 percent of all farms throughout this period. The average size of all farms has increased from about 160 acres in 1930 to 388 acres in 1971, while cropland per farm has increased somewhat less in percentage terms—from 84 to 151 acres.[4] Family farms, too, have become substantially larger in total sales and land area,

CHAPTER II

# U.S. AGRICULTURE: STRUCTURE AND CHANGE

A major argument of this essay is that the changes in U.S. agriculture over the past four decades have been very great and that the farm programs have not fully reflected those changes. This is not to say that farm programs have not been modified or have failed entirely to respond to new conditions. But the basic philosophy and purposes of the programs have evolved much less than the underlying circumstances.

Only some of the major shifts in agriculture can be highlighted in a few pages. Hopefully the reader will realize from this brief survey of change in farming over the past four decades that agriculture is a dynamic, evolving sector of our economy. It has adjusted rapidly to changing circumstances and has the capacity for further adjustment.

### The Family Farm

One of the continuing and important threads in U.S. farm policy has been the maintenance of the family farm. This objective influenced land policy from the beginning of the republic. It has been important in the development of farm credit policy. Both the land grant colleges and the agricultural extension service have been strongly influenced by the desire to provide the individual and relatively small farm with the latest available information on profitable production practices and management techniques. It was recognized that the family farm would be at a disadvantage in competition with large farms since it could not undertake research and would have difficulty in learning the latest developments without substantial assistance.

1973), almost 100 percent of the payments are income transfers. In the wheat program, probably half of the 1971 and 1972 payments were for supply management. In the feed grain program, the 1970 act has substantially increased the importance of income transfers compared to the situation in 1968. Perhaps as much as half of the payments made in 1972 constituted income transfers.[6]

And, in fact, no significant set-aside has been imposed upon the participants in the cotton program in the administration of the 1970 act.[4] It is something of an anomaly that a program designed to limit ouput requires a farmer to plant 90 percent of his allotment (or base) in order to retain that allotment. Similar, though less restrictive, requirements for a minimum productive effort are imposed under the wheat and feed grain programs.

The feed grain program permits a reduction or even elimination of payments if set-aside requirements are less than 20 percent of the feed grain base. However, if the announced program requires a set-aside of 20 percent or greater, the secretary must make a preliminary payment of $0.32 per bushel. This payment cannot be later reduced regardless of how high the market price of corn may go. The stated objective with respect to the level of payments on corn is the difference between the farm price during the first five months of the marketing year and $1.35 or 70 percent of parity, whichever is higher. Yet, because of the preliminary payments, the payments are made even if the market price for the entire crop exceeds the price objective.

The legislation specifies minimum payment levels that must be provided under the wheat and cotton programs and, somewhat less specifically, for the feed grain programs. The secretary may offer additional payments for voluntary diversion if he feels that the amount of diversion required for participation in the program would result in too large a total supply. This feature of the 1970 act has been used twice—once in the 1972 feed grain and once in the 1972 wheat program. Similar features of the 1965 act were used on several occasions for feed grains and wheat.

It is quite clear from the provisions governing payments that these payments have two different purposes—to pay for supply management and to make a direct income transfer to participating farmers. The part of the payment that goes for supply management is to offset the income foregone on the acreage that farmers withhold from production. The income transfer is the part of the payment that is not required to induce the acreage adjustments called for by the program. Secretary of Agriculture Clifford Hardin estimated in 1969 that half of the 1968 payments in the wheat program, 65 percent of those in the cotton program and 11 percent in the feed grain program represented income transfers.[5]

The Agricultural Act of 1970 has apparently increased the importance of income transfers in the total payments. In the cotton program, where there is no limit on the amount of cotton that can be produced and only minimal diversion requirements (none in

program was having a larger restraining impact than had been anticipated.[2]

In the program announced in December 1972, feed grain producers were required to set aside 30 percent of their feed grain base in order to receive maximum payments; in the January revision, only a 25 percent set-aside was required for full compliance and full payments. In the December program, a new feature was introduced which permitted a lower level of payments if the participant set aside 15 percent of the base; in January such partial participation was possible if there was no set-aside and feed grain acreage was no greater than in 1972.

Some of the complexity of the farm commodity programs is illustrated by the change which permitted payments for simply holding feed grain acreage at the 1972 level. This change apparently was designed to increase the acreage of soybeans, a commodity not directly included in any of the commodity programs. However, the payments for diversion have influenced the soybean acreage since, generally, the payments that could be earned by set-aside have been greater than the rent that could be earned from soybean production.[3] With soybean prices at the end of January almost double their 1969-72 average, some action seemed required to free land for soybean production.

## Payments as Income Transfers

The Agricultural Act of 1970 provides the secretary of agriculture with considerable discretion, as shown by the program changes for 1973. However, there are several significant inflexibilities built into the legislation, especially with respect to the amount of payments that must be made. Under the wheat program the secretary "shall provide for the issuance of wheat marketing certificates" equal to the difference between the parity price of wheat and the average farm price of wheat during the first five months of the marketing year for the crop, or from July through November. This payment must be made even if there are no set-aside requirements for wheat, and there are none for 1973. The wheat marketing certificates are paid on only that part of output that is used domestically as food—about a third of production in recent years. On that part of the output, the value of the marketing certificate was about $1.65 in 1971. This may be compared to the average price received by farmers of $1.31.

The cotton program also provides for payments even when no supply limitation or acreage set-aside requirements are imposed.

How have the changes in the programs been determined? The legislation does not specify how the secretary of agriculture should react to a given situation. No secretary has ever spelled out the criteria that he uses—at least not in any detail. Yet the main factors that trigger changes in the program features are fairly clear. Two are of major importance—the trend in farm prices and changes in the stocks of the particular commodities.

In 1967 feed grain prices were lower than in 1966, so the 1968 program was designed to increase the acreage diversion on feed grain farms. In 1966 the farm price of wheat was substantially higher than in 1965, so no diversion was required for participation in the wheat program in 1967. Generally speaking, changes in stock levels give the same signals as do price changes since a fall in price is associated with an increase in stocks and a rise in price with a decrease in stocks. At the beginning of the 1967 wheat marketing year, the national wheat carry-over was only half of what it had been two years before. Two years later stocks increased to a level that was double the beginning 1967 level. And for 1969 acreage diversion was again required of participating wheat producers.

In effect, the secretary of agriculture attempts to predict demand for the coming crop year. He then determines what the probable supply, including carry-over stocks, would be if the commodity program remained unchanged. If he believes that continuation of the same commodity program would result in a supply greater than the market would absorb at the price support level, the program is modified to increase the amount of land set aside and reduce the amount devoted to one or more crops. If he believes that extending this year's program into the following year would bring forth a supply smaller than the amount that would be demanded at a price somewhat above the price support level, the program is modified to allow more land to be devoted to the particular crop or group of crops.

The provisions of a program may be changed during the crop planning period if conditions change significantly between the time a program is announced and the time production decisions are finally made. The feed grain program for the 1973 crop announced on December 11, 1972 was revised on January 31, 1973. The new information that probably resulted in changing the program to permit larger plantings included: (1) a more rapid disappearance (use) of wheat, soybeans, grain sorghums and corn than had been expected, (2) the continuing rise in the market price of soybeans, and (3) a report on prospective plantings in 1973 indicating that the December

not put an absolute and fixed floor under market prices. Farmers who participate in the programs have the opportunity of obtaining nonrecourse loans. To do so, they must provide acceptable storage of the commodity pledged for the loan on their own farms or put the product in an approved storage facility. When the loan comes due, the farmer generally has three alternatives: (1) to deliver the grain to the Commodity Credit Corporation in complete fulfillment of the loan, both principal and interest, (2) to renew the loan for another year, or (3) to repay the loan, with interest, and retain the product for use or sale. The first alternative is chosen only when the market price is below the loan rate plus the accumulated interest. The second or third alternative is chosen whenever the market price is above the loan rate and accumulated interest. Thus when the market price is on the "weak" side, farmers deliver grain or cotton to the Commodity Credit Corporation (CCC). It is in this way that the CCC accumulates its stocks of farm products.

Farmers frequently take price support loans when market prices are substantially above the loan rate, because such loans are a convenient and relatively low-cost means of obtaining credit. Thus farmers who have no intention of delivering their grain or cotton to the CCC obtain price support loans as a matter of good business practice. It is argued, and correctly so, that the existence of price support loans minimizes the decline in prices in the months immediately following harvest.

## Supply Management

The working of the supply management part of the wheat and feed grain programs can be readily illustrated. Supply management operates through changes in the requirements for participation in programs and by changing the rates of payment for participation. For example, in 1971, following the low corn yield in 1970 due to blight, a farmer who participated in the feed grain program could earn the available payments by setting aside 20 percent of his feed grain base acreage. He could not obtain additional payments by a larger set-aside. In 1972, following the large 1971 feed grain crop because of increased acreage and good yields, a farmer had to set aside 25 percent of his base. He could earn additional payments by a further set-aside, up to 15 percent. As a result, the number of acres set aside under the feed grain program in 1972 was almost exactly twice the 18.6 million acres set aside in 1971. The change in acreage of feed grains harvested was much smaller than the change in set-aside area, however, a point to be considered later.

CHAPTER I

# MAJOR FEATURES OF U.S. COMMODITY PROGRAMS

American farm programs for cotton, wheat and the feed grains are full of complexities (some of which are presented in Appendix A for readers who have only the most general knowledge of how the programs operate). Despite these complexities, each of the programs has four major features in common. Differences in program details are primarily means of relating one or the other of these features to the circumstances of the particular crop. The major features are:

1. Price supports in the form of nonrecourse loans are provided on specified commodities for farmers who participate in the programs.
2. Participation in the programs may require that farmers divert or set aside part of their usual cropland and such land is generally not available for productive purposes during all or part of the year.[1]
3. Payments are made to farmers who participate in the programs.
4. Participation in each of the programs is voluntary.

These are the major features of the programs under the Agricultural Act of 1970. An occasional reference will be made in this study to the programs as they existed during the last half of the 1960s and to some exceptions made since 1971 even in the major features described.

**Price Supports**

Since 1965 price support levels have been established which permit U. S. supplies to move freely in both the domestic and international markets most of the time. The price support technique used does

7

received nearly full compensation for the values that have been created by the programs.

Current supply management and price support programs should not be changed on the assumption that a new era of prosperity for American agriculture has arrived. Rather they should be changed because they have been exceedingly costly to taxpayers and consumers and of little benefit to farmers, except those who own farm land. Farm labor has received no benefit. The degree of supply management achieved in recent years has been very small. Most of the direct payments have gone for loss of foregone income, for maintaining production in order to continue to receive payments, and into higher land values. There is now cause for concern that farm land values have gotten too high; policy makers should consider whether they wish to be responsible for making them even higher.

Further, farm programs should be changed because the inconsistencies between U.S. farm programs and a liberal trade policy must be eliminated if export opportunities are to be increased. Finally, they should be changed because change is in the long-run interests of farmers. Not to do so will continue to penalize the young farm family entering agriculture as a result of hard work rather than through inheritance.

In sum, a new approach is needed because outmoded programs have imposed higher and higher costs and provided fewer and fewer benefits.

the current opportunity to increase exports of farm products will be seriously and adversely affected by the continuation of existing domestic and trade policies in the major industrial nations. If the negotiations are to be successful, the United States must recognize that several of its farm programs require significant modification to reduce the protection that we provide some parts of our agriculture. We cannot have it both ways. Other countries will not reduce their barriers if we refuse to modify our own.

The United States is a low-cost producer of several major farm products, especially soybeans, the feed grains, wheat, poultry and tobacco. It may also be in a position to export substantial quantities of high-quality fed beef. With free trade, it is probable that U.S. farm exports would increase by $4 billion to $6 billion over what they would be if existing farm and trade policies were continued. Imports of farm products would increase, but the combined effects on the demand for both labor and land would be to increase both. In the case of land the increase would be substantial.

If we are to maximize our opportunities to export and to achieve efficient and full use of our farm resources, farm policy should become more fully market-oriented. The long-run policy should include farm price supports at levels somewhat below those expected to prevail under normal demand conditions and with average weather conditions. Price supports at this level would provide some degree of price stability and security, while permitting the market to function without undue interference. There should also be provision for standby acreage diversion or set-aside. Climatic conditions can result in a substantial surge in output for two or three consecutive years and market conditions can be depressed, either by domestic or international circumstances. While supply management has not had much effect on farm output in recent years, there is evidence that it could achieve a significant impact on output for a year or two. Payments made for such standby set-asides should be no higher than required to induce farmers to voluntarily limit crop acreages to the degree deemed necessary. It is unlikely that such standby provisions would be required very often, but they should be available when needed.

Transition payments should be provided to minimize the adverse effects upon asset values that would result from immediate termination of the large payments that have been made in recent years. Transition payments to those who have allotments or bases for cotton, wheat and feed grains would be less costly to taxpayers than continuation of the present programs for three to five years. By that time the present owners of allotments or bases would have

$2 billion. Most of the net benefit has been capitalized into the value of farm land. Little has been left for payment to human resources.

Moreover, most of the benefits of farm programs have gone to farm families who have incomes larger than the national average family income. Almost none has gone to low-income farm families, whether farm operators or hired farm workers.

In recent years the reduction in farm output that can be attributed to supply management has not exceeded 2.0 to 2.6 percent of total farm output. As the nation is now learning, most of the 55 to 60 million acres of land that farmers have diverted or set aside in recent years was land that would not have been planted or seeded to crops. A large fraction consisted of cultivated summer fallow; some of the rest was land of poor quality that would have been left idle or used for pasture.

It is probable that, with farm prices at 1969-72 levels, no more than 20 million acres of the land that has been idled by the three main commodity programs would return to annual cultivation. This land, when combined with other resources, would produce an output of $700 to $900 million or about 2 percent of the value of total farm output. For wheat and feed grains, the two farm products most directly affected, the increase in production would not exceed 5 percent. If the demand for soybeans continues strong, the increase in wheat and feed grains could be substantially less than 5 percent.

A major assumption of the supporters of supply management has been that fairly small year-to-year changes in production result in much larger and opposite changes in farm prices and incomes. The substantial increase in exports of farm products and the significant change in the type of farm output means that this assumption now lacks any significant validity. Over the years farm production has been shifting to more livestock products, especially beef. A second major assumption has been that agriculture has the capacity to increase output faster than demand grows and that the government must intervene to prevent continuous overabundant production. It is now clear that the surplus capacity of agriculture has been very small in recent years, much smaller than generally assumed. In spite of certain features of governmental programs, farmers have adjusted quite fully to the basic underlying economic conditions.

The importance of exports to American agriculture is now much greater than it was when the basic features of our farm programs were institutionalized in the 1930s. It is essential to the economic well-being of American agriculture that the forthcoming round of trade negotiations succeed in reducing barriers to trade in farm products. Unless these negotiations are successful to some degree,

Average farm operator family income from farming reached an all-time high in 1972. That year, adjusting for changes in purchasing power, it was more than five times the 1932 level. Further, farm families now receive almost as much income from nonfarm sources as they do from farming whereas, in the late 1930s, their nonfarm income was only half as large as their farm income.

The comparison of farm incomes in 1972 and 1932 should not be taken too seriously. It is made here only to emphasize that the emergency conditions of the Great Depression no longer prevail.

The rationale that may have fully justified the farm programs of four decades ago is hardly convincing for today's condition. It is of interest therefore that today's rationale, although different from the one used in the Great Depression, is marshalled to support almost the same set of farm programs. This does not prove that the new rationale is wrong, but it does raise questions that merit consideration.

This essay focuses on the operation and effects of three farm crop programs—wheat, cotton and the feed grains. Approximately 62 percent of all U.S. cropland is planted in these three crops. During 1971 and 1972, the first two years of the operation of the Agricultural Act of 1970, payments to farmers participating in the three programs averaged $3.3 billion a year. The last chapter examines the dairy price support program. Dairy production is important and a strikingly different approach has been followed for dairy products. Several farm programs, specifically those for sugar, peanuts, rice and tobacco, will not be dealt with here except incidentally.

## Summary of Findings

The major farm commodity programs for cotton, wheat and feed grains impose substantially greater costs upon taxpayers and consumers than the benefits realized by farm families.

In recent years commodity programs have attempted to increase farm incomes by supply management and by direct payments. Supply management was designed to reduce supplies and increase market prices, and direct payments were to compensate farmers for idling part of their land.

A large fraction of the total or gross income transfer to agriculture has gone to replace income foregone, to induce production that would not have been undertaken in the absence of the payments, and has been paid to landlords who own approximately two-fifths of all farm land. With a total cost to consumers and taxpayers for the three programs of $3 billion to $4 billion in recent years, it is estimated that farm operators have retained a maximum of $1 billion to

# INTRODUCTION AND SUMMARY

During this quarter century there have been two opportunities for a major change in agricultural policy in the United States. The first was after the end of World War II. That opportunity was lost. There is now a second opportunity. It is important to both farmers and nonfarmers that the second opportunity not be lost. An equally propitious time for change with little or no loss to farmers and with substantial gain to nonfarmers may not come for many years.

### Focus of the Study

The Agricultural Adjustment Act of 1933 was designed to meet an emergency. There was great economic distress in farm areas, and farm foreclosures were commonplace. From 1929 to 1932, prices received by farmers declined 57 percent while prices paid fell only 32 percent. In constant dollars the net income of farm operators from farming fell by more than half. By any reasonable definition of the term, there was an emergency in rural areas in 1933.

Although there have been many changes in details, the major farm commodity programs of today—four decades later—are similar to those devised and implemented in 1933. The principal features of the 1933 act were acreage controls, payments to farmers agreeing to abide by the acreage limitations, and price supports. The basic philosophy has remained that government must intervene to adjust supply to maintain prices that are politically acceptable or, failing to achieve an increase in market prices, to make payments to producers of certain farm crops to bring returns to an acceptable level.

The economic circumstances of agriculture in 1973 are substantially different from those in the depths of the Great Depression.

| V | DISTRIBUTION OF FARM PROGRAM BENEFITS | 51 |
|---|---|---|
| | Returns to Land and Labor | 52 |
| | Supply of Labor to Agriculture | 53 |
| | Farm Programs and Land Values | 57 |
| | Benefits to Farm Families | 63 |
| | Government Payments and Farm Assets | 68 |
| | Conclusion: Distribution of Costs and Gross Benefits | 70 |
| VI | FARM PROGRAMS AND AGRICULTURAL TRADE | 73 |
| | Farm Programs and Trade Policy | 74 |
| | Free Trade Benefits for Agriculture | 75 |
| | Agricultural Resource Demands under Free Trade | 77 |
| | Preparations for Trade Negotiations | 80 |
| | Conclusion | 82 |
| VII | FARM PROGRAMS OF THE FUTURE | 83 |
| | Poor Farm Families | 85 |
| | The Basis for a New Approach | 86 |
| | Outlines of a New Commodity Program | 88 |
| | An Opportunity That Should Not Be Missed | 94 |
| | **APPENDIX A:** Major Provisions of Cotton, Wheat and Feed Grain Programs | 95 |
| | **APPENDIX B:** Distribution of Gross Benefits of All Farm Programs, by State | 103 |
| | **NOTES** | 107 |

# CONTENTS

**INTRODUCTION AND SUMMARY** .................... 1
    Focus of the Study ............................. 1
    Summary of Findings ......................... 2

**I MAJOR FEATURES OF U.S. COMMODITY PROGRAMS** ......................................... 7
    Price Supports ................................. 7
    Supply Management ........................... 8
    Payments as Income Transfers ................. 10

**II U.S. AGRICULTURE: STRUCTURE AND CHANGE** ...... 13
    The Family Farm ............................. 13
    Part-time Farming ........................... 15
    Increasing Productivity ......................... 15
    Agriculture Must Change ....................... 16
    Conclusion ................................... 19

**III EVALUATION OF FARM PROGRAMS** ................ 21
    Objectives and Performance ..................... 22
    Other Criteria for Evaluation ................... 26

**IV MAJOR COMMODITY PROGRAMS AND FARM INCOME** ......................................... 29
    Increasing Farm Income ....................... 30
    How Supply Management Operates .............. 32
    Acreage Effects of Supply Management .......... 33
    Output Effects of Supply Management ........... 41
    Income Effects of Supply Management ........... 42
    Program Payments and Farm Income ............. 45
    Conclusion ................................... 48

D. Gale Johnson is professor of economics at the University of Chicago.

ISBN 0-8447-3101-3

Evaluative Studies 7, May 1973

Library of Congress Catalog Card No. L.C. 73-81728

© 1973 by American Enterprise Institute for Public Policy Research, Washington, D. C. Permission to quote from or to reproduce materials in this publication is granted when due acknowledgment is made.

*Printed in the United States of America*

# FARM COMMODITY PROGRAMS
## An opportunity for change

### D. Gale Johnson

American Enterprise Institute for Public Policy Research
Washington, D. C.

# Evaluative Studies

This series of studies seeks to bring about greater understanding and promote continuing review of the activities and functions of the federal government. Each study focuses on a specific program, evaluating its cost and efficiency, the extent to which it achieves its objectives, and the major alternative means—public and private—for reaching those objectives. Yale Brozen, professor of economics at the University of Chicago and an adjunct scholar of the American Enterprise Institute for Public Policy Research, is the director of the program.

# FARM COMMODITY PROGRAMS